1001
Hadith

Contents

1001 Hadith

Any sane Muslim, and just a reasonable person, probably asks himself this question: «What is Islam? Who is he,
a Muslim - a real Muslim? What was our Prophet ﷺ, may
Allah bless him and grant him peace? You can watch a lot
of shows, surf the Internet, listen to research, and even read
books. But every time we will be faced with someone else's
opinion, not our own. This opinion may be correct, or it may
be harmful. Allah Almighty says in the Holy Quran: «And
obey Allah and His Messenger and do not quarrel, otherwise
your strength will weaken and your power will go away. Be
patient, for Allah is with those who are patient! (Surah 8,
verse 46). Therefore, the issue of returning to the authentic
tradition of the Messenger of Allah and the Holy Quran is
very important for all Muslims, for Allah says: «O you who
believe! Obey Allah and obey the Messenger and those in authority among you. If you argue about something, then return
it to Allah and His Messenger, if you believe in Allah and
the Last Day. This is better and more beautiful in the end.»
(Surah 4, verse 59)

Islam is a religion that the Almighty made corresponding
to the desire for truth originally inherent in man - fitrah. Such
an establishment is necessary so that a person could reach
the heights of spiritual perfection. Many dreamed and kindly
envied the time when the companions of our Prophet ﷺ lived
their lives with him, watched him, prayed with him, saw him,
his manners, his decisions on all issues, and his attitude to the
environment, people. A frequently asked question today is
the following: «Oh, if I were next to the Prophet ﷺ and I had
the opportunity to ask about the problem that worries me!».
More far-sighted people would dream of asking a different
question: «Why are Muslims today in such a deplorable state,
who is to blame and what should we do?» Reasonable people
try to give their answers to these questions, often incorrect
ones. So what to do? Glory to Almighty Allah, today we have
the opportunity to be transported in a time machine 14 centuries ago, and not for a short period, but forever to become a
companion of our Prophet ﷺ. «The difference between past,

present, and future is just a persistent illusion,» said Albert Einstein. How is this possible?

We must thank the Lord for giving His Messenger many companions who carefully memorized the actions and sayings of the Prophet ﷺ, tried to make their way of life as much as possible repeat the purest sunnah - the example of our Prophet ﷺ. We must thank Almighty Allah that He allowed the scientists to meticulously record and analyze these messages of the Companions, so that you and I have this unique opportunity, having read and studied the path of the Messenger of Allah, to try as much as possible to follow the direct path of the Prophet ﷺ, find answers to questions that concern us, which the Prophet, as if foreseeing, answered in advance, so many centuries ago! The Almighty says in the Holy Quran: «Allah showed mercy to the believers when He raised among them a Messenger from among themselves; he recites to them His signs, purifies them and teaches them Scripture and wisdom, although they were previously in clear error »(Surah 3, verse 164). «And We sent you a mention so that you explain to people what was sent down to them - maybe they will think!» (Surah 16, verse 44)

The scrolls for Adam were for the leadership of a small group of people, while the scrolls for Idris were already needed for a small village. Nuh brought the law to the already established sedentary and urban civilization of that time. The divine law brought by the prophets has no contradictions among themselves. This Divine law is a single whole, complementing one another. An example of the perfection of religion from Adam to Muhammad, peace be upon them, is comparable to the example of the perfection of the science of mathematics from elementary school to higher mathematics at universities.

But while the prophets were alive, the laws of Allah remained unchanged, but after the death of the prophets, the distortion of the divine foundations begins. Those people who considered themselves followers of this or that prophet distorted those parts of the laws and prophetic foundations that were contrary to their interests. And this story was repeated by all the prophets. People skillfully removed passages from the texts, introduced innovations, and crossed the boundaries of what was permitted. «But some of them hide the truth, although they know» (Surah 2, verse 146). The wisdom of Allah Almighty is that the Sharia of the last Prophet, sent to all mankind, is preserved until the end of days. The striving for the truth that was originally inherent in people, which was mentioned at the beginning, does not change with time. However, the desire to satisfy their passions did not change with time and among the oppressors.

Allah wanted the Quran to be an argument for people until the Day of Judgment and therefore what is contrary to the oppressors and their minions, Allah does not explicitly say in the Quran, but it is given in the tradition of the Messenger ﷺ. For example: «And We made that vision that we showed you, only a temptation for people and a tree cursed in the Quran» (Surah 17, verse 60) - the tree is the Umayyad dynasty. If this were openly stated in the Quran itself, then surely Mu'awiyah and his son Yazid, as the leaders of this dynasty, would have distorted the Quranic revelation so that it would correspond to their interests and political predilections. As is known from the history of Islam, Yazid was the one who gave the order that for three days the inhabitants of Medina were allowed for the soldiers of his army: «Their women and property are halal for us!». It was then that the mosque of the Prophet in Medina was flooded with the blood of the companions of the Messenger of Allah (Tarikh ibn Kathir, volume 6, page 234). These are the soldiers of Yazid, reading namaz in Mecca in front of the Kaaba, then destroying it, saying at the same time: «Obedience to the Caliph and obedience to Allah came into conflict, and verily, obedience to the Caliph is higher than obedience to Allah!». From historical reliable sources, the authors of which were Ibn Kathir, as well as Jarir at Tabari, with my desk history book in 40 volumes and the same 40-volume explanation of the Quran - tafsir, it is known what the wicked Muawiyah and Yazid did with the descendants of the Prophet ﷺ. It is surprising that our bookstores still sell books by the followers of these criminals, and the biography of Muawiyah is cynically titled «The Fifth Righteous Caliph»! After reading the book that you have in your hands, you can see for yourself that the two phrases of the oppressors given above were on the lips of their mentors for the first time, their names are not a secret, you just need to read thoughtfully and carefully, because it's not just some kind of fiction, but answers to the most burning questions of mankind.

We believe in the Holy Quran. It is sent down by Allah. Not a single word in the Quran has been changed or distorted, subtracted, or added. The Quranic revelation implies, first of all, that all the words in the Quran are from Allah Almighty. So, for example, the Quran says: «We perform prayer when the sun declines to the darkness of the night» (Surah 17, verse 78). However, the fact that all Muslims perform morning prayers in two rak'ahs, Zuhr, Asr, and Isha in four, and Maghrib in three, is not indicated in the Quran. We learn all this from the Messenger of Allah: «And he does not speak out of passion. It is only a revelation that is sent down. He was taught by the mighty one, the possessor of might »(Surah 53, verse 4-5). Also, referring to His Messenger, Allah says: «And We sent you a mention so that you explain to people what was sent down to them» (Surah 16, verse 44). From these and other verses, we clearly understand that Allah sent down the Quran, and the explanation of the Quranic revelation lies with the Messenger of Allah. What the Messenger of Allah explained to us from the Almighty is the tradition of the Messenger ﷺ or the so-called sunnah.

Thus, using only the Quranic tradition of revelation, we will not be able to understand the meaning of the divine words. This is the need for an explanatory revelation, i.e. Sunnah of our Prophet ﷺ. Just as issues such as prayers, fasting, and Hajj are not elucidated in detail in Quranic revelation, there is a great need for clarifying revelation. This is one of the main differences between the law of the last prophet and the laws of the prophets before him. The laws brought by the prophets before Muhammad ﷺ were distorted by subsequent generations to suit the personal interests of certain groups of people, while the law brought by the last prophet contained certain wisdom of Allah, which was to ensure that this law remained undistorted until the Day of Judgment. That is why it is very important to study the Quran while looking for explanations of the Quranic revelations in the tradition of the Prophet ﷺ. After all, it was not for nothing that when the close people of the Messenger were asked about his temper, the answer was always the phrase: «His temper was the Quran.»

Sunnah is translated as consuetude, for example. The Sunnah consists of messages about the actions, sayings, and unspoken approval of the actions or words of other people by the Prophet ﷺ, as well as his qualities. In the Quran, surah al-Ahzab, verse 21, it is said: «The Messenger of Allah is a fine example for you», i.e. The Sunnah should serve as a model and guide both the Muslim community as a whole and each Muslim individually. Moreover, it is a direct command of Allah - obedience to the Prophet, expressed in following his example, is equated in the Quran, Woman Surah, verse 80, with submission to Allah Himself: «He who obeys the Messenger obeys Allah.»

The Sunnah serves as a reliable criterion for the believer, allowing him to separate all kinds of innovations that arose immediately after the death of the Prophet ﷺ. Therefore, close attention was paid to the issue of the reliability of reports about the Prophet. A special discipline of the study of hadith has developed. A hadith is a separate account of what Muhammad ﷺ said or did. The whole set of hadiths constitutes the sunnah. Each hadith consists of two parts: «isnad» - a list of people who transmitted this or that message to each other, and «matn» - the message itself or the informational part of the hadith. The quality of the isnad was seen as a guarantee of the authenticity of the hadith. So, it was important to establish the presence of a continuous chain of transmitters. Their full names, years of life, and biographies were found out to make sure that the transmitters could meet each other and evaluate their moral qualities, the ability to correctly reproduce what they heard, as well as many other subtleties.

The consequence of this was the compilation of huge handbooks with biographies of hadith transmitters and indications of the extent to which they are trustworthy. A special terminology was developed related to the assessment of the degree of authenticity of hadiths, and they were divided into three groups: reliable - «sahih», good - «hassan» and weak - «zaeef». Naturally, reliable hadiths enjoy the greatest authority, and the six collections listed below are recognized as the most authoritative collections of hadiths, which are known to everyone under the popular name «Kutub Sittah», i.e. six books. Al-Kutub al-Sitta (Arabic الكتب الستة -«Six Books») are the six major Sunni collections of hadith collected by Islamic theologians about 200 years after the death of the Prophet Muhammad. Another name is «As-Sihah al-Sitta», that is, «reliable six».

«Al Jami» Bukhari

«Sahih» Muslim

«Sunah» Tirmidhi

«Sunah» Abu Dawud

«Sunah» an Nasai

«Sunah» ibn Majah

Of course, there are also other collections of hadiths, such as «al Mustadrak» al-Hakim, «Musnad» Ahmad ibn Hanbal, and the collections of hadiths of Tabari, Bayhaki, and some others, less known. These collections, in contrast to the «Kutub Sittah», included not only hadiths of the sahih category but also two other categories, which does not make them less valuable. The 1001 Hadith collection, which I have compiled for you, consists of the hadiths from the above six «Kutub Sittah» collections. I would very much like this thousand hadiths to be for a respected reader the first stage of a long journey of studying hadiths from complete collections, as well as other important books, the most recommended from my list should be the aforementioned «History» of Tabari and his own Tafsir of the Quran. Naturally, every time you read a new book from those recommended by me, you should return to the Quran. And every time you will witness a miracle - the Quran will speak to you on a new, higher level!

Everyone should be aware that the Sunnah of the Prophet ﷺ outlined in repeatedly verified and trustworthy hadiths is a unique phenomenon in the history of all religions since people do not have such a huge amount of reliable information about any of the other prophets. Acquaintance with the hadiths requires a special approach because the sunnah is a direct guide to action in all their religious and worldly affairs, which means that there is not and cannot be anything that can be ignored.

The influence of the sunnah on the life of entire peoples is so long and deep that there is no need to prove that the psychology and logic of the behavior of a Muslim can only be understood by taking into account all the factors under the influence of which his personality was formed, and in this respect the paramount importance of the Quran and the sunnah is undeniable. The names that Muslims should give their children, the food they eat, and the clothes they wear, all of these are from the tradition of the Messenger ﷺ. Even songs, fairy tales, and adventures, such as «Kalila and Dimna», and «1001 Nights» are directly related to the traditions and problems of Muslims - Prince Ali will finally come and destroy the evil tyrant Abu Nazar (Nebuchadnezzar in Arabic - Bakht-an - Nazar)! Therefore, acquaintance with the Sunnah could contribute to the eradication of all kinds of speculation, superstition, and lies erected both on Islam and on its Prophet ﷺ, which would only benefit everyone. Unfortunately, in our ummah (i.e., the followers of the Prophet Muhammad), people who came to power after the Messenger of Allah destroyed and burned hadiths that contradicted their interests and intentions.

In the book «Musnad» by Ahmad and «Sunan» by Darimi and many other sources, it is stated that Abdullah ibn Amr ibn As cites a hadith that says: «The Quraysh said to me: «Do you cite everything that you hear from the Messenger of Allah? Indeed, the Messenger of Allah is the same person as we are, he speaks in anger and joy »(Vol. 2, p. 176 «Sunan» Abi Daud, «Mustadrak ala Sahihain» al-Hakim, Vol. 1, p. 106). It turns out that if we rely on this tradition, the Messenger of Allah, being in a good mood, says to Abu Dhar: «Heaven and earth did not know more truthful than Abu Dhar», or Ammar: «Ammar with the truth.» In another story, it is said that the Messenger of Allah, being angry with Hakim ibn Abi As, cursed him. From this tradition, it can be understood that the Quraysh, even during the lifetime of the Messenger of Allah, already forbade people to write down the hadith of the Prophet ﷺ. Abdullah ibn Amr ibn As says: «I conveyed the protests and the prohibition of the Quraysh to the Messenger of Allah, to which he told me: «Write everything you hear from me! I swear by Allah, nothing comes from me but the truth.»

It is very hard to accept the truth. The Messenger of Allah, being about to die, said: «Bring me paper and ink, I will write you something, after which you will never go astray.» (This hadith is in all six collections, but I give it in Bukhari's version only). Surprisingly, Umar ibn Khattab did not allow the request of the Prophet ﷺ to be fulfilled while saying the words that remained as an order not to write down hadith for more than 133 years, and only Abu Jafar Mansur gave the order for permission to write down the hadith of the Prophet of Islam. Umar said: «The book of Allah is enough for us!» After that, a dispute broke out between the companions, some wanted to fulfill the request of the Prophet, and others carried out the order of Umar. Umar saw that some of the companions wanted to bring what the Prophet had asked them to, and expressed his opinion: «Verily, the man (the Prophet) is delirious!» Some companions said: «Let's go, let's bring what the Prophet asked us,» then the Prophet ﷺ answered them all: «After all this?!», and then continued: «Get up and go away, it is not befitting in the presence of your Prophet to make disputes!».

Only during the reign of Ali and Umar ibn Abd al-Aziz, the recording of hadith was allowed for a very short time. Umar ibn Abd al-Aziz himself was poisoned by the Umayyads, and after his death, there was again a ban on recording hadith. That is why you can see for yourself that the collections of hadiths were compiled already 2-3 centuries after the Hijra, by looking at the dates of birth of the authors of these collections. As for me, a modern story called «The Da Vinci Code» about the predecessor of Muhammad - Jesus, peace be upon them both, immediately comes to mind. Then, too, people who knew the truth could not say it directly, but encoded their messages in pictures and icons - Jesus is not God, not the son of God, Jesus is the prophet of God. In the case of Islam, scientists also could not directly tell the truth, because the usurpers and oppressors were always on the leash of corrupt scientists who immediately reported the truth and destroyed the records along with their authors and collectors. Therefore, the hadiths must be read carefully, who conveyed which message, because, in the previous message or the next message a few pages later, you can find an addition that explains the hadith that is incomprehensible at first glance. So we have our «Bukhari code» and «Tirmidhi code» in our hands, which answers many questions.

Muslim in his Sahih cites a hadith from hudhayfah, in which we read: «Among my companions, there are 12 hypocrites. They will not enter Paradise until the camel enters the eye of the needle.» Ibn Hazm narrates a hadith, where he gives the names of five of the 12 hypocrites, while among the transmitters he names Walid ibn Jumaya, who, according to some scholars, was weak in the transmission of hadith. Although Ibn Hibban, Ahmad ibn Hanbal, Dhahabi, and many other scholars considered this person to be a reliable transmitter, giving such characteristics as «reliable», «truthful» and «righteous», I will not give their names to respect the absolute and undeniable authenticity. Just read the hadiths and you will name them.

Hadiths were recorded, despite the prohibitions, by many companions. You can see their names at the beginning of the hadith, from whom this particular hadith was narrated. For example, Abdullah ibn Masud, despite the threats, did not hand over his scroll with hadiths for burning, thanks to him we can now have an idea about many aspects.

The Messenger of Allah said: «O Ali! Write down everything I tell you.» Ali answered: «O Messenger of Allah, are you afraid that I will forget something?», to which the Messenger⁕ replied: «No, for I asked Allah that you do not forget anything, but write it down for your companions.» Ali said, «Who are my companions?» The Prophet pointed to the little sons of Ali - Hassan and Hussein and said: «They are the first of them.» Therefore, we must thank the Lord that He has preserved the offspring of the Prophet as the rope to which all sane Muslims must cling tightly. Now, perhaps, is the time to bring the so-called hadith «Sakalayn», which means two weights or two values. This hadith is the most famous and widespread, the authenticity of which no one doubts. The Messenger of Allah ﷺ said: «O people! I leave you two valuable things, if you keep them, you will never go astray. The Quran and my family Ahl al-Bayt. Look, be attentive to them after me.» The Messenger repeated these words very often, but the largest gathering of people in front of whom he recited this covenant was a place called Ghadir Khumm, immediately after returning from the farewell Hajj.

It is reported that Zadhan Abu Umar said: I heard 'Ali in Ar-Rahba when he called people and asked who was with the Messenger of Allah ﷺ on the day of Ghadir Khumm when he said what he said. Thirteen men stood up and testified that they heard the Messenger of Allah (ﷺ) say: «If I am the ruler of anyone, then Ali is also his ruler.» Musnad Ahmad №641, Sahih category, i.e. reliable. Narrated by Ziyad bin Abi Ziyad. «I heard Ali ibn Abu Talib conjure people and say: «I conjure you with Allah, did any Muslim hear the words of the Messenger of Allah ﷺ about what he said on the day of Ghadir Khumm? And the twelve men who were at Badr stood up and testified.» Musnad Ahmad №670

And here is a hadиth that took place before the event of Ghadir Khumm. It was narrated that 'Ali (رضي الله عنه) said: It was asked: «O Messenger of Allah ﷺ, who should be appointed responsible after you are gone? He said: «If you appoint Abu Bakr, you will find that he is trustworthy and not interested in worldly gains seeking the Hereafter. If you appoint 'Umar, you will find him strong and trustworthy and not afraid of blaming anyone for the sake of Allah. If you appoint Ali, which I don't think you will, you will find him leading the right path and led, he will lead you on the straight path.» Musnad Ahmad №859

If you look at the last period of the life of the Messenger of Allah, especially the period of illness, you can easily see that he was very worried about the future of his nation. Even during the period when the disease worsened, all his thoughts were only about instructing people on the true path and preserving the ideals of Islam and the Quran. The sacred hadith «Sakalain» is of great value and importance in this regard, and everyone who knows it is personally responsible to the Prophet ﷺ. The Messenger of Allah indicated the straight path for us so that after his death we would not go astray from the true path. He did not leave his Islamic nation without guidance and guidance. This hadith does not refer only to a specific period. On the contrary, the hadith indicates that following and obedience to the decrees of the Quran and the prophetic family is obligatory for all Muslims, regardless of the time and place of their residence.

The number of companions who transmitted this hadith exceeds 50, it is given in well-known and reliable collections, such as «Sahih» Muslim, «Sunan» Tirmidhi, «Sunan» Darimi, «Musnad» Ahmad ibn Hanbal, an Nasai, «Mustadrak ala Sahihayn» Hakim, a total of 190 collections of hadith. Here is one of the typical instructions: the Messenger of Allah gave us a sermon in which he said: «Indeed, the Lord calls me to Himself and I answered His call. You will meet me at the heavenly source Hauz, the size of which is equal to the distance between Busra and Sagnai. The bowls next to that source are equal to the number of stars in the sky. Be careful! I leave among you two valuable things. One of them is the Quran, the other is my family Ahl al-Bayt. They are like ropes that stretch from Allah to you. Hold on to them and never get lost! One end of this rope is with Allah, the other is with you.» So the verse of the Quran «Hold on to the rope of Allah, everyone, and do not be divided!», I hope, will sparkle for you in a completely new way. On this basis, the resolution of all problems and the unity of Muslims can be embodied only by obeying and following this testament of the Prophet and the Quran, just as during the life of the Messenger of Allah, the basis of the unity of Muslims was the Prophet himself. Therefore, all currents of Islam, madhhabs, sects need to wake up from sleep and turn to that unity, which is indicated in the Holy Quran.

Ahl al-Bayt is the Prophet ﷺ himself, Fatima, Ali, Hasan, Hussein, and their descendants. In a hadith from the wife of the Prophet ﷺ Umm Salama, it is said that when the verse about purification (Surah 33, verse 33) was sent down in her house, the Messenger, calling to Allah, said: «O Lord, they are my family!» In the continuation of the umm, Salamah says: «I asked the Messenger of Allah:« Am I not from your family? Lord, they are more worthy! Muslim in Sahih cites a hadith, when this verse was revealed, the Messenger of Allah called Ali, Fatima, Hasan, and Hussein and said: «O Allah! They are my family!» In the same collection of Muslims from Aisha, a hadith is given as follows: «Indeed, the Messenger of Allah in the morning before the prayer of Fajr, left the house, while he was wearing a black cloak. He went up to Hassan and covered him with a cloak, then covered Hussein with his cloak. Also, the Messenger of Allah covered Ali and Fatima with this cloak, after which the verse descended: «Verily, Allah wants to remove the filth only from you, the family of his house, and cleanse it with complete cleansing.»

In «Mustadrak ala sahihayn» Hakim cites hadith №4577 from Zayd ibn Arkama: «When the Messenger of Allah was returning from his farewell pilgrimage, in a place called Ghadir Khumm, he ordered everyone to stop. By order of the Prophet ﷺ, the place chosen by him was cleared. Then the Messenger of Allah turned to us with a sermon: «The Lord called me to Himself and I answered His call. Indeed, I leave among you two valuable things, one of which is more valuable than the other - the Quran and my family Ahl al-Bayt. Think about how you will treat them. They will never separate from each other until they join me in the spring of paradise. Indeed, Allah is my protector, and I am the protector of every believer. Then the Prophet ﷺ raised Ali's hand and said: «To whom I am the protector, Ali is the protector.»

But many people who took an oath of allegiance to the Prophet ﷺbetrayed him and began to kill members of his family one by one. It was narrated by Abdullah bin Nujayyi from his father that he traveled with Ali (رضي الله عنه) - he was the one who carried his ablution vessel. When he reached Ninawa on his way to Siffin, Ali (رضي الله عنه) exclaimed: Be patient, Abu Abdullah; Be patient, Abu Abdullah, on the banks of the Euphrates. I said what did he say? He said, «Once I went to the Prophet ﷺ and his eyes were full of tears.

I said: «O Prophet ﷺ of Allah, did someone upset you? Why are your eyes full of tears? He said, «No, but Jibril left me some time ago. He told me that al-Hussein would be killed on the banks of the Euphrates, and he said: «Do you want to smell his dust (the dust of the earth where he falls)?» I said yes. He reached out and took a handful of dust and gave it to me, and I couldn't help but cry.» Musnad Ahmad №648

The name of the real fifth righteous caliph is known to everyone - Imam Hasan ibn Ali, taking office, after he was sworn in by Muslim believers, said: «We are the party of Allah! The party of Allah is the winner. We are the family of the Prophet and the people closest to him. We are Ahl al-Bayt, whom Allah has cleansed from filth. We are one of the two valuable things the Prophet left behind. We are the second book of Allah, in which you will find the explanation of everything. Lies have no way for us!» However, we know from history that Muslims rushed to get knowledge from others. And it came to the point that in the field of Islamic law (fiqh), the majority were forced to resort to qiyas (free judgment) and istihsan (agreement), for the reason that scholars of faqihs could not find an answer to new questions that appeared over time, relying on exclusively to the Quran. Due to the ban on the transmission and distribution of the hadiths of the Prophet ﷺ, Umar ibn Abd al-Aziz, having come to power, saw that the sacred Sunnah of the Prophet was on the verge of extinction and decided to cancel the decree of Umar ibn Khattab. It is after this that scholars begin to record the surviving hadiths, using the small number of manuscripts that have survived after more than a hundred years of prohibition. A lot of hadiths were irretrievably lost, for those who knew the traditions of the Messenger of Allah by memory, by that time were no longer alive.

Umar said: «I heard that the Messenger of Allah said:» All family ties will be severed on the Day of Judgment, except for my family ties. «And I wanted to have family ties and kinship with the Messenger of Allah» (narrated by al-Hakim). From the point of view of the Arabic language, the word «sakl», the singular from the dual derivative «sakala-in», has the meaning of a high position and place. The word «sakl» puts the Quran above all divine books. Therefore, the word «sakalain» with the Quran and Ahl al-Bayt was used by the Messenger of Allah because following and observing their rights is a very difficult matter and not given to everyone. When Ibn Abbas was asked: «Why are they called the Prophet» sakalain «, he replied:» Since it is not easy to follow them. In another tradition, Ibn Abbas said: «for following them is very difficult and difficult.» Even during the lifetime of the Prophet, some people already showed their resistance and expressed doubts. It was narrated that 'Ali (رضي الله عنه) said: The Messenger of Allah (ﷺ) sent me to Yemen, and I said: «O Messenger of Allah, are you sending me to people who are older than me to judge between them?» He said: «Go, for Allah, Exalted is He, will strengthen your tongue and direct your heart.» Musnad Ahmad №666

I would like to express a wish to my brothers and sisters to reflect on the meaning of all the hadiths given in this book, the hadith «Saqalayn», which is like a light that indicates the true path that the Messenger of Allah himself set for us so that we do not fall into error and split, they did not break up into many groups and currents, but united under the shadow of a single ideology, they rushed to fulfill the Divine prescriptions. «If only one day remained for the existence of this world, the Lord would extend this day to send a man from my descendants, whose name is the same as my name, and the name of his father is the name of my father! He will fill the earth with justice and impartiality, as it was before him full of injustice and tyranny.» (Abu Daoud, Tirmizi) The Prophet also said: «Mahdi will be from my family, from among the descendants of Fatima» (Abu Daud, ibn Maja).

Whenever you allow yourself to think by inertia, in line with the opinions of other people, with an eye to circumstances, and so on, you are thinking about something that is not at all what you want. You follow not your own, but borrowed desires. Use your imagination and decide for yourself what you want to think about and what you want to do. It was narrated that Al-Harith ibn Abdullah al-A'war said: I said: «Amir al-Mu'minin will come, and I will ask him about what I heard tonight.» After «Isha» I came to him, and he recited the hadith of Ghadir Khumm. Then he said: «I heard the Messenger of Allah ﷺ say: «Jibril came to me and said:« O Muhammad, your ummah will betray you after you leave. Where is the solution, O Jibril? He said: «The Book of Allah, may He be exalted, by which Allah will destroy every tyrant.» Whoever clings to it will be saved, and whoever refuses it will be doomed.» He repeated this twice. «Verily, this (Quran) is the Word that separates (truth from falsehood and prescribes strict laws to mankind to eradicate evil). And this is not fun» [At-Tariq 86:13-14]. It does not wear out from repetition, and its wonders never end; it contains news of what was before you, a judgment of what is happening among you, and a prediction of what will happen after you leave. Musnad Ahmad №704

For a person, only the question remains: «What follows from this?» - and it follows that a person should strive for knowledge, and goodness, should avoid evil, because such is the will of God, and do not forget that for each of his actions and movements of the soul, he will be judged to the fullest extent, without any allowance for predestination, so, as if in any life situation, the choice of behavior depends on him, and only on him.

In order not to delay your acquaintance directly with the hadiths themselves, with this I conclude my introduction to this short collection of hadiths, which, of course, you should carefully read and make the basis for your life, turn your attention to the really important aspects and ask yourself: « Are we really among those who adhere to the path and example of our Prophet ﷺ? Can we be called Sunnis, i.e. those people who adhere to the pure sunnah? Oh dear, brother and sister! Think and be careful! Be impartial, for the truth is revealed before you. And do not deny the importance of following the true Sunnah of our beloved Prophet ﷺ.

«Al Jami» Bukhari

Imam Bukhari was born in Bukhara in 194 AH (810). Allah endowed him with the ability to memorize hadith when he was still a child. Here is what he writes in his books about himself: «The idea of the need to memorize hadith was inspired in me when I was just starting to study, and I was ten years old or less. Then I left school and began to study with one or another teacher. When I was sixteen years old, I already remembered the books of ibn al Mubarak and Waqia by heart and knew their sayings. Then, together with my brother and mother, I went to Mecca, where we settled for the sake of collecting hadith, and when I was eighteen years old, I began to classify information about the companions and followers, as well as their statements. Once, the ruler of Bukhara, Emir Khalid bin Ahmad az Zuhali, sent a man to Muhammad bin Ismail al Bukhari to tell him the following: «Bring me al-Jami», «Tarikh» and your other books so that I can hear what is written in them, from you». To this, al-Bukhari gave his messenger the following answer: «Verily, I do not humiliate knowledge and do not deliver it to the doors of people, and if you need any of this, then come yourself either to my mosque or to my house.» And the emir sent for al-Bukhari, wanting him to teach hadith only to his children and no one else was present at these meetings, but al-Bukhari refused this and said: «I cannot choose to listen to some and not allow others.» In the process of work, Imam al Bukhari wrote down six hundred thousand hadiths, not counting the two hundred thousand recorded by his teacher. Then he compiled a short collection of these hadiths in the book al-Jami, which is known to everyone today. It includes 7275 hadiths. Consequently, we know today only less than 1% of the hadiths he collected. More precisely, 0.9%! Already from this collection, many disciples made their collections, the most famous of which, perhaps, is the collection of Imam al-Zubaidi, containing 2134 hadiths.

1)   We were told by 'Ubeydullah ibn Musa, who said: We were informed by Hanzala ibn Abu Sufyan, from 'Ikrimah ibn Khalid from Ibn 'Umar, may Allah be pleased with them both, who said: said: «The Messenger of Allah ﷺ said:» Islam is based on five (pillars): testifying that there is no god worthy of worship except Allah and that Muhammad is the Messenger of Allah, performing prayer, paying zakat, performing hajj and fasting in Ramadan. №8

2)   We were told by 'Abdullah ibn Muhammad al-Ju'fiy, who said: We were told by Abu 'Aamir al-'Aqadiy, who said: We were told by Suleiman ibn Bilal from 'Abdullah ibn Dinar, from Abu Salih, from Abu Hurairah, may Allah be pleased with him, that the Prophet ﷺ said: «Faith (includes) more than sixty branches, and shame is (one of) the branches of faith.» №9

3)   It is reported that Abu Sa'eed al-Khudri, may Allah be pleased with him, said: «The Messenger of Allah ﷺ said: «Soon the time will come when the best property of a Muslim will be sheep, with which he will wander over the mountain peaks and those places where the rains fall, fleeing temptations with their religion.» №19

4)   It is reported that Sa'd ibn Abu Waqqas, may Allah be

pleased with him, said: «Once the Messenger of Allah ﷺ gave gifts to a group of people, among whom I was sitting. At the same time, the Messenger of Allah ﷺ did not give anything to one person who liked me the most of all of them, and I asked: «O Messenger of Allah, why did you treat such and such? By Allah, I believe that he is a believer!» He said: «Or a Muslim.» I was silent for a while, but I was haunted by what I knew about this person, and I again asked: «Why did you treat such and such like that? By Allah, I believe that he is a believer!» He said: «Or a Muslim.» But even after that, what I knew about this man continued to bother me, and I again asked the same question. In response, the Messenger of Allah ﷺ said the same thing and then added: «O Sa'd, indeed, (sometimes) I give something to a person, fearing that Allah will plunge his face into the fire, although I love another more than him». №27

5) It is reported that Ibn 'Abbas, may Allah be pleased with them both, said: «Once the Prophet ﷺ said: «Hell was shown to me, and it turned out that most of its inhabitants were women who showed ingratitude.» He was asked: «Did they not believe in Allah?» He replied: «They showed ingratitude towards their husbands and did not give thanks for the benefits (which were given to them). If you do good to some (of such women) for a long time, and then she sees something from you (such that she does not like it), she (necessarily) will say: «I have never seen anything good from you!» » №29

6) It is reported from the words of 'Abdullah ibn 'Amr ibn al-'As, may Allah be pleased with them both, that the Prophet ﷺ said: «The true hypocrite is the one who has four (properties), and who differs in any of them will be marked with one of the properties of hypocrisy until he gets rid of it. (Four such properties are distinguished by the one who) betrays when he is trusted, lies when he tells (about something), acts treacherously when he concludes an agreement, and commits law-

lessness when he is at enmity (with someone). №34

7) It is reported from the words of 'Umar ibn al-Khattab, may Allah be pleased with him, that (once) a Jew said to him: «O Commander of the Faithful! There is one verse in your Scripture that you are reading, (and I think that) if it were sent down to the Jews, then we would celebrate the day (of its sending down) as a holiday. ('Umar) asked: «And what is this verse?» He said: «Today I have perfected your religion for you, and have completed My mercy on you, and have approved Islam as your religion.» 'Umar said: «We know this day and the place where (this verse) was sent down to the Prophet ﷺ. It was Friday when he stood at Arafat. №45

8) It is reported that 'Ubada ibn as-Samit, may Allah be pleased with him, said: «(One day) the Messenger of Allah ﷺ went out (from the house) to tell (people) about the night of predestination, but at that time two Muslims entered into a squabble each with a friend, and then he said: «Indeed, I went out to tell you about (the time of the onset of) the night of predestination, but such and such began to quarrel with such and such, and (what I knew) disappeared. Perhaps this is better for you, (and now) wait for her on the seventh, ninth or fifth!» №49

9) It is reported that Ibn 'Abbas, may Allah be pleased with both of them, said: «When a delegation (of the tribe) 'Abd al-Qais arrived at the Prophet ﷺ, he asked: «Who are these people?» They replied: «Rabi'ah.» He said: «Welcome (to you, oh) people! You will not be put to shame and you will not regret it!» They said: «O Messenger of Allah, we can come to you only in the holy month, because we are separated from you by the infidels from the Mudar tribe, so give us a decisive command so that we pass it on to those who are left behind us and thanks to this we enter paradise!» And they asked him about drinks, and he ordered them (to do) four (things) and forbade them four (others). He told them to believe in Allah alone

and asked: «Do you know what faith in Allah alone is?» They replied: «Allah and His Messenger know (about it) better.» Then he said: «This is evidence that there is no god worthy of worship except Allah alone, Who has no partner, and that Muhammad is the Messenger of Allah, performing prayer, paying zakat, observing fasting in Ramadan and allocating you a fifth of the military booty.» And he forbade them four (things): khantam, dubby, nakyr and muzaf-fat (or: muqayyar), and then he said: «Remember this and pass it on to those who remained behind you.»

Note. «Dubba» - dishes made from dried pumpkin, which was used to make alcohol, «Khantam» - a special jug in which alcoholic drinks were transported, «Mukayyar» - (that which is smeared with resin), and «Nakyr» - the base of a palm tree, in which they made a hole and made alcohol. №53

10) It is narrated from the words of Abu Mas'ud, may Allah be pleased with him, that the Prophet ﷺ said: «If a person spends (funds) on his family, hoping only for the reward of Allah, it becomes sadaqah for him.» №55

11) It is reported that Abu Bakra, may Allah be pleased with him, said: «The Prophet ﷺ sat on his camel, which was held by a rein (or: halter) by one person, and then asked: «What day is this?» We didn't say anything be-cause we thought he would call it something else, but he said, «Isn't this the day of sacrifice?» We said yes. (Then) he asked: «What is this month?» We (again) remained silent, as we thought that he would call him something else, but he said: «Isn't this Dhul Hijjah?» We said yes. (Then) he said: «Indeed, the relationship between you should be such that your blood, your property and your honour are as sacred to you as this day of yours is sacred in this month of yours in this city of yours! Let the one who is present inform the absent one about this, but, verily, the present one can inform the one who learns this better than himself». №67

12) It is narrated from the words of Anas, may Allah be pleased with him, that the Prophet ﷺ said: «Facilitate, and do not create difficulties, please (people) with good news, and do not inspire disgust (to Islam)». №69

13) It is reported from the words of 'Ubaydullah ibn 'Abdullah that Ibn 'Abbas, may Allah be pleased with both of them, said: «When the (death) suffering of the Prophet ﷺ intensified, he said: «Bring me (accessories for) writing, and I will write for you that which will keep you on the right path.» However, 'Umar said: «The Prophet ﷺ is seriously ill, and we have the Book of Allah, and that is enough for us!» Then the opinions (of those present) were divided, a noise arose, and then the Prophet ﷺ said: «Leave me, you should not argue in my presence!» And Ibn 'Abbas came out saying: «Truly, this is the trouble that interferes between the Messenger of Allah ﷺ and what he writes». №114

14) It is reported that Umm Salamah, may Allah be pleased with her, said: «One night the Prophet ﷺ woke up and exclaimed: «Glory be to Allah! /Subhana-Llah!/ What disasters were sent down tonight and what treasures were opened! Wake up the inhabitants of the rooms, because it may turn out that dressed in this world will be naked in the other world!» №115

15) It is reported from the words of al-A'raj that Abu Hurairah, may Allah be pleased with him, said: «Verily, people say that Abu Hurairah (transmitted) many (hadith), but if it were not for two verses from the Book of Allah, then I would not narrate a single hadith. Then he recited (the following verses): «Verily, those who hide the clear signs and guidance sent down by Us after We have made it clear to the people in the Book, Allah will curse and curse those who curse, except for those who repented, corrected their deeds and became clarify the truth. I will accept their repentance, for I am the Receiver of repentance, the Merciful» (after which he said): «Indeed, our brothers from among the Muhajirs were busy with trade trans-

actions, and our brothers from among the Ansar were busy with matters related to their property, while Abu Hurairah contented only with what could satiate his stomach, relentlessly followed the Messenger of Allah ﷺ, being present where they were absent, and remembering what they did not remember». №118

16) It is reported that Abu Hurayrah (may Allah be pleased with him) said: «From (said) by the Messenger of Allah ﷺ, I memorized (what refers to) two types of knowledge. As for the first, I spread it (among people), as for the second, then if I spread it, (my) throat would be cut!» №120

17) It is reported from the words of Jarir (ibn 'Abdullah), may Allah be pleased with him, that during the farewell pilgrimage, the Prophet ﷺ ordered him: «Tell the people to be silent and listen!», After which he said: «Do not become unfaithful after me who cut off each other's heads!» №121

18) It is reported that 'Abdullah ibn 'Umar, may Allah be pleased with them both, said: «During the lifetime of the Messenger of Allah ﷺ, men and women performed ablution together». №193

19) It is reported from the words of 'Aisha that the Prophet ﷺsaid: «Any drink that intoxicates is forbidden / haram /». №242

20) It is reported that (once) people asked Sahl ibn Sa'd as-Sa'idi, may Allah be pleased with him: «How did they treat the wound of the Prophet ﷺ?» He replied: «Now there is no one left who would know about this better than me. 'Ali brought water in his shield, Fatima washed the blood from his face, and then (they) took a mat, burned it and applied (ash) to his wound». №243

21) It is reported that the wife of the Prophet ﷺ Maimun, may Allah be pleased with her, said: «(First) the Messenger of Allah ﷺ performed the same ablution as he performed before prayer, except for washing the feet, then he washed his genitals, washing away all the se-

cretions, then he poured water over himself, and then moved his feet and washed them. This was his big ablution after the desecration». №249

22) It is reported that 'Aisha, may Allah be pleased with her, said: «Usually I performed a full ablution with the Prophet ﷺ (and we took water) from the same vessel called «farak». №250

23) It is reported that Abu Hurayrah, may Allah be pleased with him, said: «(Once, when) the beginning of prayer was already announced and (in the mosque) the rows of standing (people) were aligned, the Messenger of Allah ﷺ came out to us. Having taken his place (in front), he remembered that he was in a state of defilement, and said to us: «(Stay) in your places,» after which he returned (to his home) and performed a big ablution, and then (again) went out to us (and we saw that) drops of water flowed from his head. He said: «Allah is great / Allahu Akbar /», and we prayed with him». №275

24) It is narrated from the words of Zainab bint Abu Salam that the mother of the faithful, Umm Salama, may Allah Almighty be pleased with her, said: «(Once) Umm Sulaym, the wife of Abu Talha, came to the Messenger of Allah ﷺ, the wife of Abu Talha, may Allah Almighty be pleased with both of them, and said: «O Messenger of Allah, indeed, Allah is not ashamed of the truth (so tell me) should a woman bathe if she sees in a dream that she has copulated with a man and she has a wet dream?» The Messenger of Allah ﷺ replied: «Yes, if (after waking up) she sees (her) allocation». №282

25) It is reported that 'Aisha, may Allah be pleased with her, said: «We left (Medina) for the sole purpose of performing Hajj, and in Sarif, my period began. Coming to me, the Messenger of Allah ﷺ (saw that) I was crying, and asked: «What is the matter with you? Have you started your period?» I answered yes. Then he said: «Indeed, this is ordained by Allah for the daugh-

ters of Adam. Do everything that a pilgrim does, but just do not go around the House (Kaaba)! »(' Aisha) said:« And the Messenger of Allah ﷺ sacrificed cows for his wives». №294

26) It is reported that Abu Sa'id al-Khudri, may Allah be pleased with him, said: «(Once) the Messenger of Allah ﷺ went to the place of prayer on the day of sacrifice (or: on the day of breaking the fast), and then, passing by (gathered) women, (stopped and) turned (to them with these words): «O women, give alms, for, truly, it was given to me to see that you are the majority of those who are in hell!» They asked: «Why, O Messenger Allah?» He replied: «Because you often curse (people) and show ingratitude towards your husbands. I have not seen anyone who lacks intelligence and (perfection in matters of) religion, who, like any of you, could deprive the mind of a prudent man to such an extent! «The women asked:» O Messenger of Allah, what is our imperfection in (deeds) of religion and lack of intelligence?» He said: «Is not the testimony of a woman (equal to) half the testimony of a man?» They said: «Yes.» He said: «This (indicates) the lack of her mind. Shouldn't (a woman) stop praying and fasting when her period starts?» They said, «Yes.» He said: «And this (indicates) her imperfection in (deeds of) religion.» №304

27) It is narrated from the words of Jabir ibn 'Abdullah, may Allah be pleased with him, that the Prophet ﷺ said: «I was given five (things) that were not given to any (of the prophets) before me: I was helped by fear (which captured the hearts of my enemies living from me) at a distance of a month's journey; (all) the earth was made for me a place of prayer and a means of purification, and therefore, wherever a person belonging to my community finds (time) prayer, he (may) pray (in this place); war booty, which was not allowed (to be taken) by anyone (of the prophets) before me, was allowed to me; I was granted the right of intercession, and (besides, earlier) each prophet went only to his

people, but I was sent to all people». №335

28) It is reported that the mother of the faithful 'Aisha, may Allah be pleased with her, said: «When Allah made prayer a duty, He made it a duty to pray from two rak'ats, regardless of whether it is performed where a person lives permanently, or in ways; subsequently, the prayer performed on the way was left unchanged, and the prayer performed at the permanent place of residence was increased». №350

29) It is reported from 'Abdullah ibn Shaddad from May-muna (that she) said: «The Prophet ﷺ used to pray on his mat/khumra/». №381

30) It is reported that Abu Maslama Sa'id ibn Yazid al-Az-di said: «(Once) I asked Anas ibn Malik, may Allah be pleased with him:» Did the Prophet ﷺ pray in his sandals? and he said yes». №386

31) It is reported that Hammam ibn al-Harith said: «I saw one day Jarir ibn 'Abdullah, may Allah be pleased with him, urinated, then performed ablution and wiped (with wet hands) his leather socks, and then got up and prayed. He was asked (about this) and he replied: «I saw that the Prophet ﷺ did the same.» (One of the transmitters of this hadith) Ibrahim (an-Naha'i) said: «It pleased (his comrades) since Jarir was one of those who accepted Islam late». №387

32) It is reported that Anas, may Allah be pleased with him, said: «When money was brought to the Prophet ﷺ from Bahrain, he ordered: «Pour it into the mosques,» and this was the largest amount ever sent to the Messenger of Allah ﷺ. Then the Messenger of Allah ﷺ went out to pray without even looking in the direction of the money, and when he finished praying, he approached (these riches), sat down next to him and began to distribute them to everyone, no matter who he saw. Then al-'Abbas approached him and said: «O Messenger of Allah, give (something) to me because I paid a ransom for myself and 'Akil!» The Messenger of Allah ﷺ said to him: «Take it», and he poured

(silver) into his clothes, tried to lift (the knot), but could not. Then he said: «O Messenger of Allah, tell someone to pick it up (and put it) on my back.» The Prophet ﷺ said: «No!» (Al-'Abbas) said: «Then give it to me yourself.» (The Prophet ﷺ) said: «No!» - after which (al-'Abbas) poured out (part of the money) and tried to raise (the rest, but could not). He (again) said: «O Messenger of Allah, have someone pick it up (and put it) on me (on my back).» (The Prophet ﷺ) said: «No!» (Al-'Abbas) said: «Then give it to me yourself.» (The Prophet ﷺ) said: «No!» - and (al-'Abbas had to) pour (another part of the silver), after which he picked up the bundle, put it on his shoulder and left, and the Messenger of Allah ﷺ marvelling at greed (al-'Abbas), followed him with his eyes until he was out of sight. As for the Messenger of Allah ﷺ himself, he did not get up until he had distributed everything to the last dirham». №421

33) It is reported that 'Ikrimah, may Allah have mercy on him, said: (One day) Ibn 'Abbas, may Allah be pleased with them both, ordered me and his son 'Ali: «Go to Abu Sa'id al-Khudri and listen to what he tells». We went (to him) and saw that he was fixing the wall. (Seeing us) he wrapped himself in his cloak, and then began his story, reaching the mention of the construction of a mosque, he said: «We all wore one unbaked brick, and 'Ammar (ibn Yasser) wore two. This was seen by the Prophet ﷺ, who began to shake off the dust from him with the words: «May Allah have mercy on 'Ammar, who will be destroyed by a group of oppressors! He will call them to heaven, and they will call him to hell!» - 'Ammar answered: «I resort to the protection of Allah from (similar) disasters!» №447

34) It is reported that Abu Salih as-Samman said: (Once) I saw how Abu Sa'id, may Allah be pleased with him, performed prayer on Friday, fenced off with something from people, and some youth from the Banu Abu Mu tribe 'Ait wanted to pass in front of him, but Abu Sa'id pushed him in the chest. This young man

looked (around) and, seeing no other possibility, again tried to pass in front of him, but Abu Sa'id pushed him even harder. Then he began to revile Abu Sa'id, and then came to Marwan and complained to him about how he had treated him. As for Abu Sa'id, he came to Marwan after him, and (Marwan) asked him: «What happened between you and your brother's son, O Abu Sa'id?» He replied: «I heard the Prophet ﷺ say: «If any of you begins to pray (turning his face) to that which will separate him from the people, and someone wants to pass in front of him (at this time), let (the one who prays) will push him away, and if he refuses (submit), let him fight him, for this is Shaitan!» №509

35) It is reported that Hudhayfah, may Allah be pleased with him, said: «(Once, when) we were sitting with 'Umar, may Allah be pleased with him, he asked: «Which of you remembers the words of the Messenger of Allah ﷺ about the test?» I said: «I (remembered everything exactly) as he said.» ('Umar) exclaimed: «Verily, you show (in this) courage!» - (after which) I repeated (the words of the Prophet ﷺ): «The temptation of a person, connected with his wife, money, children and neighbours, is redeemed by prayer, fasting, sadaqah, (inciting people to commit) what is approved (sharia) and withholding from what is blamed». ('Umar) said: «I do not mean this, but such a disaster/fitna / that will rage like a raging sea.» I said, «It will not harm you, O Commander of the Faithful, for verily you are separated from it by a locked door.» ('Umar) asked: «(This door) will be broken or opened?» I replied: «It will be broken.» ('Umar) said: «So (after that) it will never be closed!» (Huzhayfa said): «(I was) asked:« Did 'Umar know which door (in question)? I replied: «(He knew it as well) as that the night precedes the morning. As for (said by the Prophet ﷺ), I conveyed it to him without error. (Khudhaifa) was asked: «Who was this door?» He replied: «This door (appeared) 'Umar». №525

36) It is reported that 'Uthman ibn Abu Rawad, the broth-

er of 'Abdul-'Aziz said: I heard al-Zuhri say: «Once, when I went to see Anas ibn Malik in Damascus, may Allah be pleased with him, I found him crying. I asked him, «Why are you crying?» And he said: «I do not recognize anything of what I knew, except for this prayer, and this prayer is neglected!» №530

37) It is narrated from the words of Anas, may Allah be pleased with him, that the Prophet ﷺ said: «Adhere to moderation, making prostrations to the ground, and let (the praying one) not touch the ground with his elbows like a (lying) dog, and if he (wants) to spit, then let him does not spit in front of him or to the right, for, truly, (during prayer) he conducts a secret conversation with his Lord!» №532

38) It is reported from the words of Ibn 'Abbas, may Allah be pleased with both of them, that (sometimes) in Medina, the Prophet ﷺ performed prayers of seven and eight rak'ats (combining) the midday prayer with the afternoon and the sunset prayer with the evening. Ayub (as-Sakhtiyani) asked: «Perhaps it was during (heavy) rain?» (Jabir ibn Zayd, who narrated this hadith from Ibn 'Abbas) replied: «Perhaps». №543

39) It is reported that Anas, may Allah be pleased with him, said: «When the number of people increased, they began to discuss what they should do to find out when the prayer time had come. Some suggested kindling a fire or ringing a bell, and then Bilal was ordered to repeat the words of the adhan an even number of times, and the words of the iqama an odd number.». №606

40) Narrated Anas ibn Malik, may Allah be pleased with him, that the Messenger of Allah ﷺ said: «If supper is served, then start (dinner) before performing the sunset/maghrib/prayer, and take your time while eating». №672

41) It is reported that the wife of the Prophet ﷺ 'Aisha, may Allah be pleased with her, said: «During prayer, the Messenger of Allah ﷺ used to turn to Allah with a

prayer, saying:« O Allah, verily, I seek refuge in You from the torment of the grave, and I seek refuge to You from the temptation of the Antichrist, and I resort to You from the temptations of life and death! O Allah, verily, I seek refuge in You from (the burden of) sin and debt! «(Somehow) one person asked him, «Why do you so often ask for protection from debt?» (In response, the Messenger of Allah ﷺ) said: «Indeed, when a person burdened with debts speaks, he lies, and when he makes promises, he breaks them.». №832

42) It is reported that 'Aisha, may Allah be pleased with her, said: «(One day) the Messenger of Allah ﷺ came to me at a time when I had two girls singing a song about Bu'as, lay down on the bed and turned away. (And after some time, Abu Bakr entered my room and sharply asked me: «(How can) the flute of the shaitan (sound) from the Prophet ﷺ?!» Then the Messenger of Allah ﷺturned to him and said: «Leave them», when (Abu Bakr) got distracted, I made a sign to the girls and they left». №949

43) It is reported that Abu Sa'eed al-Khudri, may Allah be pleased with him, said: «On the day of breaking the fast and on the day of sacrifice, the Messenger of Allah ﷺ always went to the place of prayer and the first thing he started with was the prayer, after which he stood in front of the people sitting in rows to exhort them and give them his instructions and commands. If after that he wanted to send a military detachment somewhere, then he did it, and if he wanted to order something to be done, then he ordered, and then left. Abu Sa'id said: «People continued to adhere to this until (once) on the day of the sacrifice (or: breaking the fast) I went (to prayer) along with Marwan, who was (at that time) the ruler of Medina. When we arrived at the place of prayer, it turned out that there was a minbar installed by Kasir bin as-Salt, and Marwan suddenly wanted to climb on it before prayer. I pulled him by the clothes, but he released them (from my hands), got up (on the minbar) and said the khutba before prayer. I told him:

«By Allah, you have changed (the Sunnah)!» (In reply to me) he said: «O Abu Sa'id, what you know is already gone (into the past)!» Then I said: «By Allah, what I know is better than what I do not know!» (In his defence) Marwan said: «People would not sit down after prayer to listen to our (khutba), and therefore I said it before prayer». №956

44) It is narrated from the words of 'Aisha, may Allah be pleased with her, that once during her stay in Mina, Abu Bakr, may Allah be pleased with him, went to her when she had two girls playing the tambourine, as well as the Prophet ﷺ hiding behind his clothes. Abu Bakr spoke sharply to them, but the Prophet ﷺ opened his face and said: «Leave them, O Abu Bakr, because these are the days of the holiday, the days (stay) in Mina». №987

45) It is reported that Abu Hurayrah, may Allah be pleased with him, said: «The Prophet ﷺ said: «It is not permissible for a woman who believes in Allah and the Last Day to go on a trip that will take a day and night, without being accompanied by a close relative». №1088

46) It is reported from 'Amr ibn Rabi'a that his father said: «I saw the Prophet ﷺ praying, sitting astride his camel and heading in the direction where she turned». №1093

47) It is reported that 'Imran bin Husayn, may Allah be pleased with him, said: «I had haemorrhoids, and I asked the Prophet ﷺ about (how I should perform) prayer. He said: «Standing, but if you can't, pray sitting, and if you can't (do this, then pray to lie) on your side.» №1117

48) It was narrated from the words of Abu Hurayrah, may Allah be pleased with him, that the Messenger of Allah ﷺ said: «When any of you falls asleep, the devil ties three knots on the back of his head, striking each of them (and saying): «Your night will be long, sleep!» And if (a person) wakes up and remembers Allah, then one knot will be untied, if he performs ablution,

the (second) knot will be untied, and if he performs a prayer, it will be untied (and the third), and the person will wake up cheerful and content in the morning, otherwise, he gets up from sleep in a bad mood and be lethargic». №1142

49) It is reported that Jabir ibn 'Abdullah, may Allah be pleased with them both, said: «The Messenger of Allah ﷺ taught us how to ask for blessings in deeds, just as he taught us (this or that) surah of the Quran, and he told us: «When one of you wants to do something, let him perform an additional prayer of two rak'ats, and then say:« O Allah, truly, I ask You to help me with Your knowledge and strengthen me with Your power, and I ask You about Your great mercy, for, truly, You can, but I cannot, You know, but I do not know, and You know everything about the hidden! O Allah, if You know that this matter will be good for my religion, for my life and the outcome of my affairs, then predestinate it for me and make it easy for me, and then send down Your blessing on me in this; O Allah, if You know that this matter will become evil for my religion, for my life and the outcome of my affairs, then turn it away from me, and turn me away from it, and ordain good for me, wherever it is, and then bring me to satisfaction with him (or he said: for this life and the life to come)» The Prophet ﷺ added: «Then the person should name his need». №1162

50) It is reported that Umm al-'Ala, may Allah be pleased with her, a woman from among the Ansar, who gave the Prophet ﷺ an oath of allegiance to Islam, said: «The Muhajirs were distributed (among us) by lot, and we got 'Uthman bin Maz' un, whom we settled in our house, and (after a while) he fell ill and died. After he died, was washed and wrapped in his clothes, (to us) the Messenger of Allah ﷺ came, and I said: «May Allah have mercy on you, Abu-s-Saib, I testify that Allah has honoured you!» (Hearing these words) The Prophet ﷺ asked: «How do you know that Allah honoured him?» I said: «May my father be a ransom for

you, O Messenger of Allah, and to whom else will Allah honour?!» Then he said: «As for him, he has died, and by Allah, I wish him well, but I swear by Allah that I don't know what will be done even with me, although I am the Messenger of Allah!» Umm al-'Ala) said: «And by Allah, since then I have not spoken of anyone like that». №1243

51) It is reported that 'Ali, may Allah be pleased with him, said: «(Once) when we were attending a funeral in Baqi' al-Gharqad, the Prophet ﷺ approached us holding a small stick in his hand. He sat down, lowered his head and began to scatter the ground with this stick, while we sat around him, and (after a while) he said: «There is no one among you, just as there is not even a single living soul whose place is in heaven or hell already. it would not be determined, and it would also be determined whether she is unfortunate or happy. One person said: «O Messenger of Allah, should we not rely on what has already been predestined for us, and should we not give up deeds, because one of us who is among the happy will (anyway) comes to the deeds of happy, and who belongs to the number of the unfortunate (anyway) will come to the deeds of the unfortunate? (In response to this, the Prophet ﷺ) said: «As for the happy, it will be easier for them to do the deeds of the happy, and as for the unfortunate, it will be easier for them to do the deeds of the unfortunate,» after which he read (the following verses): «As for who gave, and was God-fearing, and recognized the best, then We will make it easy for him (the path) to the easiest». №1362

52) It is reported that Abu Hurairah, may Allah be pleased with him, said: - When the Messenger of Allah ﷺ died, Abu Bakr, may Allah be pleased with him, became (caliph), and some of the Arabs returned to disbelief, 'Umar, may Allah be pleased with him Allah asked: «How can you fight these people?! Indeed, the Messenger of Allah ﷺ said: «I was ordered to fight these people until they say:« There is no god worthy of wor-

ship except Allah, »and whoever says (these words, thereby) will protect his property and his life from me, unless (does not do anything for which it will be possible to deprive him of his property or life) by right, and then (only) Allah (will be able to demand) an account from him!» №1399

53) Abu Hurayrah (may Allah be pleased with him) reported that the Messenger of Allah ﷺ said: «A man said: «I must give alms!» - (after which) he went out (from the house) with his alms and (out of ignorance) put it in the hand of the thief. In the morning, people began to say: «Alms have been given to a thief!» Then (this man) said: «O Allah, praise be to You, I must give alms!» After that, he (again) went out (from the house) and put (alms) in the hand of the harlot, and in the morning people began to say: «This night, alms were given to the harlot!» Then (the man) said: «O Allah, praise be to You! (I gave alms) to a harlot, but I must give it (again)!» After that, he (again) went out (again) with his alms and (this time) gave them to a rich man, and in the morning people began to say: «Alms were given to a rich man!» (Hearing this) he said: «O Allah, praise be to You, (I gave alms to) a thief, a harlot and a rich man!» - and after that, someone came to him and said: «As for your alms to the thief, then perhaps thanks to this (in the future) he will refrain from stealing; As for the harlot, then perhaps she will renounce fornication, and as for the rich, then perhaps he will learn from this and begin to spend (in the way of Allah) what Allah has given him». №1421

54) Hakim bin Khizam, may Allah be pleased with him, reported that the Prophet ﷺ said: «The upper hand is better than the lower hand. Start with those whom you (must) support and the best charity is that which is given from wealth. To the one who himself seeks to refuse (requests), Allah will give the opportunity (not to ask others for anything), and Allah will save him (from the need for everything else)». №1427

55) It was narrated from the words of Abu Hurayrah, may

Allah be pleased with him, that the Messenger of Allah ﷺ said: «By the One in Whose hand is my soul, any of you should take a rope, chop wood (and bring it) on your back (to sell,) than to make requests to some person who can give him (something), or who can refuse. Prophet ﷺ said: «Indeed, for any of you to take a rope, bring a bundle of firewood on your back and sell it, thanks to which Allah will save him (from the need to ask), it is better than asking people who can give him (something), or they may refuse». №1470

56) It is reported that Abu Hurayrah, may Allah be pleased with him, said: «Dates were always brought to the Messenger of Allah ﷺ at harvest time. They were brought by one or the other (person), until next to (the Prophet ﷺ) a whole bunch (of fruits. One day) al-Hasan and al-Hussein, may Allah be pleased with both of them, began to play with these dates and someone of them he took one date, putting it in his mouth. Then the Messenger of Allah ﷺ looked at him, took (this date) from his mouth and said: «Do you not know that the members of the family of Muhammad do not eat (what is intended for) sadaqah?» №1485

57) It is reported that Marwan bin al-Hakam said: «I saw 'Uthman and 'Ali, may Allah be pleased with them both, (and was a witness that) 'Uthman forbade (people) to perform «hajj at-tamattu» and unite hajj with death. Seeing this, 'Ali said: «Here I am before You (performing) I will die and Hajj,» (and then) he said: «I will not deviate from the Sunnah of the Prophet ﷺ no matter what anyone says!» №1563

58) It is reported that 'Aisha, may Allah be pleased with her, said: «The Messenger of Allah ﷺ said to me:» If your tribesmen were not (so) close to disbelief, I would destroy the Kaaba and build it on the foundation of Ibrahim, peace be upon him, for verily, the Quraysh, in rebuilding the Kaaba, made it smaller, and I would also make a back door in it». №1585

59) It was narrated from the words of Usama bin Zayd,

may Allah be pleased with them both, that he asked (the Prophet ﷺ): «O Messenger of Allah, where will you stay? Is it not in your house in Mecca? (The Prophet ﷺ) said: «Did 'Aqil leave any buildings (or: houses)?» As for 'Aqil, he became the heir of Abu Talib along with Talib, while neither Ja'far nor 'Ali, may Allah be pleased with them both, inherited anything from him, since they were Muslims, and 'Aqil and Talib - were unfaithful. №1588

60) It is reported that Jabir bin Abdullah, may Allah be pleased with them both, said: «We used to eat the meat of the camels we sacrificed for no more than three (days during which we were in) Mina, and then the Prophet ﷺ gave us permission (to this), saying: «Eat and stock up,» and we ate (part of this meat) and took some with us». №1719

61) It is reported from the words of Anas, may Allah be pleased with him, that when the Prophet ﷺ saw some old man who was walking, supported by his two sons, he asked: «What is the matter with him?» (His sons) said: «He vowed to walk.» (The Prophet ﷺ) said: «Indeed, Allah does not need this person to subject himself to torment,» and ordered him to ride. №1865

62) It was narrated from the words of Abu Hurairah, may Allah be pleased with him, that the Messenger of Allah ﷺ said: «Indeed, faith will return to Madinah as a snake returns to its hole (in case of danger)». №1876

63) It is reported that Sa'd, may Allah be pleased with him, said: «I heard the Prophet ﷺ say: «Whoever does evil against the inhabitants of Medina, he will surely melt as salt dissolves in water». №1877

64) It is reported that Usama, may Allah be pleased with him, said: «(Once) the Prophet ﷺ climbed one of the towers of Medina, said:« Do you see what I see? Verily, I see that the places of confusion and disaster among your homes will be as (numerous) as the traces of drops (rain)!» №1878

65) It was narrated from the words of Abu Hurayrah, may Allah be pleased with him, that the Messenger of Allah ﷺ said: «If (a person) does not stop lying and acting on lies, Allah will not need him to refuse his food and drink». №1903

66) It is reported that 'Abdullah, may Allah be pleased with him, said: «(Once when) we were together with the Prophet ﷺ, he said:» Let the one who can (marry) get married, since this is most conducive to downcast eyes and protection of the genital organs; the one who cannot marry should fast, for fasting for him (will be like) bachelorhood». №1905

67) It is reported that 'Adi bin Hatim, may Allah be pleased with him, said: «When it was sent down (verse, which says):» ... eat and drink until the dawn allows you to distinguish the white thread from the black ...» (surah» al -Bakara», 187), I took black and white fetters and put them under my pillow, and at night I began to look at them, but I could not distinguish anything. In the morning I went to the Messenger of Allah ﷺ told him about everything, and he said (to me): «Indeed, this is the blackness of the night and the whiteness of the day». №1916

68) It is reported that Abu Sa'id, may Allah be pleased with him, said: «The Prophet ﷺ forbade fasting on the day of the holidays 'Eid al-Fitr and 'Eid al-Adha, as well as wrapping tightly in one garment and sitting, hugging his knees, throwing while on the body only one garment. №1991

69) He also forbade prayer after the morning prayer and the Asr prayer. №1992

70) It is reported that 'Aisha, may Allah be pleased with her, said: «During the time of Jahiliyyah, the Quraysh fasted on the day of 'Ashura, and the Messenger of Allah ﷺ also fasted on this day. When he arrived in Medina, he (did not stop) fasting that day and ordered others to observe this fast. When fasting in Ramadan was made obligatory, he stopped (fasting) on the day

of 'Ashura, and (since then) whoever wanted to, observed this fast, and who did not want, did not do it». №2003

71) It is reported that Anas, may Allah be pleased with him, said: «Once the Prophet ﷺ passed by a date fruit that had fallen from somewhere and said:« If I were not afraid that this might be (part of) alms/sadaqah/, I would have eaten it». Abu Hurayra (may Allah be pleased with him) also narrated that the Prophet ﷺ said: «I found a date fruit that was lying on my bed». №2055

72) It is reported from the words of 'Abbad ibn Tamim that his uncle said: «The Prophet ﷺ was told about the complaint of one person who feels something during prayer, should he interrupt the prayer (because of this)? He replied: «No, (let him not interrupt until) until he hears a sound or smells.» Az-Zuhri said: «There is no need to perform ablution unless you smell or hear a sounda». №2056

73) It is reported from the words of 'Aisha, may Allah be pleased with her, that (once) people said: «O Messenger of Allah, people bring us meat, but we do not know whether they pronounced the name of Allah over it or not.» (To this) The Messenger of Allah ﷺ said: «So say the name of Allah over it and eat it». №2057

74) It is reported that Jabir, may Allah be pleased with him, said: «(Once) when we were praying with the Prophet ﷺ, a caravan of camels arrived from Sham with food supplies. (Almost all the people) turned towards him (and left the mosque), and only twelve people remained with the Prophet ﷺ, and then it was sent down: «When they saw trade or fun, they dispersed, rushing to her» (surah «al- Jumu'a», verse 11)». №2058

75) It is reported that al-Bara bin Azeeb and Zayd bin Arkam, may Allah be pleased with them both, said: «During the life of the Messenger of Allah ﷺ we were merchants, and (once) we asked the Messenger of

Allah ﷺ about the exchange, (for what) he said: «If (money is transferred) from hand to hand, then there is nothing wrong with it, but postponing (calculation) is not good». №2061

76) It is reported that Anas bin Malik, may Allah be pleased with him, said: «I heard the Messenger of Allah ﷺ say: «Let the one who wants his inheritance to be increased and his life span extended, keep in touch with relatives». №2067

77) It is narrated from al-Miqdam, may Allah be pleased with him, that the Messenger of Allah ﷺ said: «No one has ever eaten anything better than the food (for which he earned) by the labour of his hands, and, verily, the Prophet of Allah, Dawood, peace be upon him, fed on what he earned with the labour of his hands». №2072

78) It is reported that 'Aun ibn Abu Juhaifah (may Allah be pleased with him) said: «I witnessed how my father, who bought a slave who knew how to bleed, (ordered to break his tools). I asked him about the reason for this and he said: «The Prophet ﷺ forbade taking money for a dog and blood, and he forbade women both to tattoo (others) and tattoo themselves, (and he forbade) how to make money from usurers, and engage in usury, and he cursed those who create images». №2086

79) It is reported that 'Ali, peace be upon him, said: «As a war booty, I got an old camel, and (in addition) the Prophet ﷺ gave me another old camel from the fifth part of the war booty (al-humus). And when I intended to marry Fatima, the daughter of the Messenger of Allah ﷺ, I arranged with a jeweller from the Banu Qaynuka tribe to go with me to bring «izhir» (fragrant reed), and then sell it to jewellers and use (the proceeds) for my wedding treats». №2089

80) It is reported that Anas ibn Malik, may Allah be pleased with him, said: «(At one time) a tailor invited the Messenger of Allah ﷺ to taste the food that he prepared.» Anas ibn Malik said: «And I went to this feast with the Messenger of Allah ﷺ. (The tailor) served the

Messenger of Allah ﷺ bread and soup, in which there were slices of pumpkin and pieces of dried meat, and I saw how the Prophet ﷺ took (slices) of this pumpkin from (his) side of the dish. (Anas) said: «And from that day on, I fell in love with a pumpkin(Edited)Restore original». №2092

81) It is reported that Jabir bin Abdullah, may Allah be pleased with both of them, said: «(Once, when) I, along with the Prophet ﷺ, took part in one of the military campaigns, my camel, exhausted, slowed down, and then the Prophet ﷺ drove up to me who said: «Jabir!» I answered: «Yes.» He asked, «What's wrong with you?» I replied, «My camel is walking slowly. He became exhausted, and therefore I fell behind. Then he dismounted, began to drive the camel with his stick with a bent end, and then said: «Sit down.» I sat down and (he walked so fast) that I had to restrain him so that he would not bypass the Messenger of Allah ﷺ. (Then the Prophet ﷺ) asked (me): «Are you married?» I answered yes. He asked: «On the girl or on the one who was already married?» I replied: «The one that was married.» He asked: «Why not a girl with whom you could play and who would play with you?» I said, «(The fact is) I have sisters and I wanted to marry a woman who would pick them up and comb them and look after them.» He said, «You're coming back, and when you get home (treat her) as gently as you can.» Then he asked: «Will you sell your camel?» I said: «Yes», and then the Prophet ﷺ bought it (from me) for an okiya (gold). And the Messenger of Allah ﷺ arrived before me, but I arrived in the morning, and we went to the mosque, at the door of which I met (the Prophet ﷺ). He asked: «Have you just arrived?» I answered yes. He said: «Then leave your camel, go inside and pray two rak'ats.» I entered and prayed, after which (the Prophet ﷺ) ordered Bilal to weigh me an okiya (gold), and Bilal weighed me even more, and I left. And then (the Prophet ﷺ) ordered: «Call Jabir to me.» I said (to myself): «Now he will return the camel to me,» and for me, there was nothing more hated (this

animal), but (the Prophet ﷺ) said: «Take your camel and (keep) its price for yourself». №2097

82) It is reported that Anas, may Allah be pleased with him, said: «(Once, when) the Prophet ﷺ was in the market, a man exclaimed: «O Abu-l-Qasim!» The Prophet ﷺ turned to him, but he said: «I only called such and such», and then the Prophet ﷺ said: «(You can) call (each other) by my name, but do not use when addressing (to each other) my kunya!». №2120

83) It is reported from Ibn 'Umar, may Allah be pleased with him and his father, that the Prophet ﷺ said: «(Once upon a time) three people set off on a journey, and rain overtook them. They took refuge in a cave, but (from the mountain) a huge stone fell (and tightly closed the exit from it). Then they said to each other: «Turn to Allah with a prayer through the best deed that you have done!» (After that) one of them said: «O Allah, I had elderly parents, and I went to pasture cattle, then I returned home, milked them and gave this milk to my parents, and then gave it to my children, close relatives and wife . But one day I lingered, and when I returned to them, they were already asleep, and did not want to wake them, and the children were crying at my feet (from hunger), and I waited for them until dawn came. O Allah, if you know that I did this, striving for Your Face, then slightly open this passage so that we can see the sky through it! And after that, the stone moved a little. Another said: «O Allah if you know that I loved one of my uncle's daughters as much as men can love women. She said, «You won't get what you want from me until you give me one hundred dinars.» Then I began to work until I collected this amount. When I sat down between her legs, she said: «Fear Allah and do not break this seal except by right!» Then I got up and left her. O Allah, if I did this, striving for Your Face, then deliver us from the situation in which we find ourselves! And after that, the stone moved two-thirds from its place. The third said: «O Allah, if you know that (once) I hired a worker for

a «farak» (measure) of millet and gave it to him, but he refused to take it. Then I took this millet and sowed it, and then I bought cows from its sale and hired a shepherd. Then the man came and said: «O servant of Allah! Give me my pay.» I told him, «Go to those cows and the shepherd, they belong to you.» He said, «Are you kidding me?» I said, «I'm not mocking you, they belong to you.» O Allah, if you know that I did this, striving for Your Face, then deliver us (from the situation in which we find ourselves)! – then the passage opened». №2215

84) It is narrated from the words of Abu Hurairah, may Allah be pleased with him, that the Prophet ﷺ said: «(When) Ibrahim, peace be upon him, moved with Sarah, he entered with her into (some) village (where he was) one of the kings (or: one of the tyrants). (He) was told: «(Here) Ibrahim came with one of the most beautiful women,» and he sent (a man) to him to ask: «O Ibrahim, who is this (woman) who (came) with you?» He replied: «(This is) my sister», and then returned to her and said: «Do not refute my words (for), truly, I told them that you are my sister, and I swear by Allah, there is no (now) on earth (not a single) believer but me and you!» Then he sent her to him. When (this king) approached her, she got up (from her place), performed ablution and prayer and said: «O Allah, if I believed in You and Your messenger and took care of myself only for my spouse, do not give power over me to this unfaithful!» - and then he began to wheeze and his legs began to twitch. Abu Salama ibn 'Abdurrahman, who narrated this hadith, reported that Abu Hurayrah (narrated the words of the Messenger of Allah ﷺ) said: «She exclaimed: «O Allah, if he dies, (people) will say that it was I who killed him!» – and then he woke up. And then he (again) approached her, she rose (from her place), performed ablution and prayer and said: «O Allah, if I believed in You and Your Messenger and took care of myself only for my husband, do not let me the power to this infidel!» - and he hoarsely, and his legs began to twitch. Abu Salamah (may Allah Al-

mighty have mercy on him) reported that Abu Hurai-rah said: «She (again) exclaimed: «O Allah, if he dies, (people) will say that it was I who killed him!» - and then he woke up for the second (or: for the third time) and said: «By Allah, you sent me none other than the shaitan! Return her to Ibrahim and give her Azhar,» after which she returned to Ibrahim and said: «Do you know that Allah (shamed) the infidel and gave us a maidservant?» №2217

85) Abu Hurayrah, may Allah be pleased with him, re-ported that the Messenger of Allah ﷺ said: «May Al-lah destroy the Jews! They were forbidden (to eat) fat (of animals), and they began to sell it, eating the mon-ey received for it!» №2224

86) It is reported that Abu Sa'eed al-Khudri, may Allah be pleased with him, once sat with the Prophet ﷺ and said: «O Messenger of Allah! Verily, we have taken captives and love wealth. Do you think it is possible to spew semen outside the womb? And the Messenger of Allah ﷺ said: «Are you doing this? It will not harm you in any way if you do not do this, for, verily, every soul that is destined to appear will certainly appear». №2229

87) It is reported that Abu Musa, may Allah be pleased with him, said: «(Once) I came to the Prophet ﷺ with two people from among the ash'aris and said (to him):« I did not know that they were looking for work. (To this the Prophet ﷺ) said: «We will not appoint (or: We do not appoint) those who themselves achieve this». №2261

88) It is reported that Abu Hurayrah, may Allah be pleased with him, said: - The Messenger of Allah ﷺ said: «Allah will not look at three on the Day of Res-urrection and will not cleanse them, and (prepared) for them a painful punishment: for a person who had excess water by the road and denied it to the traveler; and on a person who takes an oath (of allegiance) to the ruler (guided) only by worldly (interests), remains

pleased when (the ruler) gives him (something) for it, and shows displeasure when he does not give him anything; and on a person who put his goods out after the afternoon prayer and said: «By Allah, besides Whom there is no other true god, I gave so much for it,» which any person (who buys it) will believe, »after which (the Prophet ﷺ) read (the verse that says): «Verily, for those who sell the covenant of Allah and their oaths for an insignificant price, there is no provision in the other world: Allah will not speak to them, and will not look at them on the Day of Resurrection, and will not cleanse them, and (prepared) for them a painful punishment »(Ali 'Imran, 3:77). №2358

89) Abu Hurayrah (may Allah be pleased with him) reported that (once) the Messenger of Allah ﷺ said: «Once upon a time, a man who was walking (on his way) became tormented by a strong thirst. He went down into the well and drank from there, and when he got out, he suddenly saw a dog in front of him, sticking out his tongue and eating wet earth from thirst. (Seeing this) the man said to himself: «This dog is tormented by thirst just as it tormented me,» after which he filled his shoe with water, took it in his teeth, climbed up and watered the dog, and Allah thanked him for this, forgiving him (his sins).» (People) asked: «O Messenger of Allah, are we entitled to a reward for animals?» - to which he replied: «The reward is due for all living things». №2363

90) It is reported that Anas bin Malik, may Allah be pleased with him, said: «(When) the Prophet ﷺ wanted to cut (for the Ansar plots) of land in Bahrain, the Ansar said: «(We will not accept them) until you cut for our brothers from the number of Muhajirs (the same plots) as for us.» (Then the Prophet ﷺ) said (to the Ansar): «After (my death) you will see that preference (will be given to others), so be patient until you meet me!» №2376

91) It is narrated from the words of the wife of the Prophet ﷺ Umm Salama, may Allah be pleased with her, that

once the Messenger of Allah ﷺ heard (noise) an argument at the door of his room, went out to (arguing) and said: «Verily, I am only a man, and (people) come to me (with their) disputes. And it may happen that one of you will be more eloquent than the other, and I will consider that he told the truth, and I will decide in his favour based on this. However, if I (by mistake) decide to give him what rightfully belongs to (another) Muslim, it will be nothing but a part of (the fire of) hell, so let him (himself) take it or refuse it». №2458

92) It is narrated from the words of Ibn 'Abbas, may Allah be pleased with them both, that (once) Umm Hufayd, Ibn 'Abbas's aunt from her mother's side sent dried cottage cheese, ghee and sand lizards as a gift to the Prophet ﷺ, and the Prophet ﷺ ate cottage cheese and butter but did not touch the lizards (because he did not like them). Ibn 'Abbas said: «(However, others) ate them at the table of the Messenger of Allah ﷺ, and if (eating lizards) was forbidden, they would not be eaten at the table of the Messenger of Allah ﷺ». №2575

93) It is reported that Anas, may Allah be pleased with him, said: «The Prophet ﷺ never rejected incense (which was given to him)». №2582

94) It is reported that Abu Bakra, may Allah be pleased with him, said: «(Once) the Prophet ﷺ asked (people):« Shall I tell you about (which) sins are the most serious? - (and repeated this question) three times. They said: «Of course, O Messenger of Allah!» (Then) he said: «(This is) polytheism and disrespect towards parents.» (Saying this, the Prophet ﷺ) was lying on his side, and then he sat down and said: «And, verily, (this is) slanderous speech!» - and he continued to repeat (these words) until we began to say: «Oh if only he would be silent!» №2654

95) It is reported that Abu Bakra, may Allah be pleased with him, said: - (Once) one person began to praise another in the presence of the Prophet ﷺ and (Prophet ﷺ) exclaimed: «Woe to you, you cut your brother's throat,

you cut your throat to your brother!» (He repeated these words) several times, and then he said: «Let one of you who has to praise his brother say:« I consider such and such (such and such, the truth about) he knows (only Allah), and I do not praise anyone before Allah, but (only) consider him such and such, «if he (really) is sure of (what he says) about him». №2662

96) Abu Sa'eed al-Khudri (may Allah be pleased with him) reported that the Prophet ﷺ said: «Performing a big ablution on Friday is obligatory for everyone who has reached puberty». №2665

97) It is reported that al-Bara ibn 'Azeeb, may Allah be pleased with them both, said: - (When) the Prophet ﷺ (decided) to commit 'Imrah in (the month of) Dhul-Qa'da, the people of Mecca refused to let him into (the city) until he agreed with them that he would spend there (only) three days. In (the agreement prepared by the Muslims) they wrote down (the following): «On these conditions, Muhammad, the Messenger of Allah ﷺ agrees (to make peace.» After reviewing the record, the Quraysh) said: «We do not agree with this, because if we had (for sure) it is known that you are the Messenger of Allah, we would not interfere with you, but you are Muhammad ibn 'Abdullah. (To this the Prophet ﷺ) said: «I am the Messenger of Allah, and I am Muhammad ibn 'Abdullah», after which he ordered 'Ali: «Erase (the words)« Messenger of Allah ». ('Ali) said: «No, by Allah, I will never erase (what concerns) you!» Then the Messenger of Allah ﷺ himself took this paper and (ordered) to write: «This is what Muhammad ibn 'Abdullah agreed: (he) will enter Mecca without taking out his weapon from the scabbard, and will not take away with him any of the inhabitants (of Mecca), even if (someone) himself wishes to follow him, and does not prevent any of his companions from staying in (Macca, if the person) so desires. And when (the following year the Prophet ﷺ) entered (Macca) and the (conditioned) period (of his stay there) had already expired, (the Meccans) came

to 'Ali and said (to him): «Tell your friend to leave us, since the (agreed) period has already expired, »and the Prophet ﷺ left (the city). Hamza's daughter ran after him (exclaiming): «O uncle, o uncle!» (The girl) was received by 'Ali, who took her by the hand and said to Fatima, peace be upon her: «Your uncle's daughter is in front of you, take her!» whereupon 'Ali, Zeyd and Ja'far began to argue over her. 'Ali said: «I have more rights to her because she is my uncle's daughter!» Ja'far said: «She is the daughter of my uncle and (besides) I am married to her aunt!» (As for) Zeid, he said: «(She is) my brother's daughter!» - after which the Prophet ﷺ decided (to give the girl) to her aunt and said: «The aunt occupies the same position as the mother.» And then he said to 'Ali: «You are from me, and I am from you», and he said to Ja'far: «You are like me both in appearance and character», while he said to Zeid: «You are our brother and our freedman». №2699

98) It is reported that Abu Bakra, may Allah be pleased with him, said: «I saw (who was) on the minbar the Messenger of Allah ﷺ next to whom (stood) al-Hasan ibn 'Ali, and (the Prophet ﷺ) looked at the people, then at (al-Hasana), saying: «Verily, this son of mine is a Sayyid/lord/, and it may happen that through him Allah will lead to the reconciliation of two large groups of Muslims». №2704

99) It is reported that Abdullah bin Umar said: «I heard the Prophet ﷺ say: «Bad omens are associated with only three things: with a horse, a woman and a house». № 2858

100) It is narrated from Sahl bin Saad that on the day of Khaybar he heard the Prophet ﷺ say: «I will certainly hand this banner to the person through whom Allah will grant us victory.» - Hearing this, the companions of the Prophet ﷺ got up, hoping that the banner would be handed to him, and in the morning they went to the Prophet ﷺ and each of them wanted the banner to be handed to him, but he asked: «Where is Ali?» He was told that his eyes hurt, and he was ordered to call Ali

to him. When he arrived, the Prophet spat in his eyes, and he immediately recovered as if nothing had happened to him, after which he asked: «Should we fight them until they become like us?» Then the Prophet ﷺ said: «Do not hurry until you meet them, and then call them to Islam and inform them of what is obligatory for them. And I swear by Allah, if Allah leads even one person to the straight path through you, it will be better for you than owning red camels!» №2942

101) It is narrated from the words of Ibn Umar that the Prophet ﷺ said: «It is obligatory to listen and obey until you are ordered to do something contrary to the commands of Allah, and therefore if you are ordered to disobey Allah, then you should neither listen nor obey». №2955

102) Abu Hurayrah reported that he heard the Messenger of Allah ﷺ say: «We are the last, but we will be the first. Whoever obeys me obeys Allah, and whoever disobeys me disobeys Allah. Whoever obeys the ruler will obey me, and whoever disobeys the ruler will disobey me. The ruler is nothing but a shield and must be protected and fought under him. If the ruler commands people to fear Allah and adheres to justice, he will receive a reward for this, and if he does otherwise, he will be held accountable for it.» №2956

103) Ibn Masud is reported to have said, «Today a man came to me and asked me a question to which I did not know the answer. He said: «Tell me, what if a well-equipped and energetic person went on a military campaign with our superiors and began to order us what we would not be able to do?» I said: «By Allah, I don't know what to say to you, except that when we were with the Prophet ﷺ, he only had to order something once and we did it. Indeed, any of you will be fine as long as he fears Allah, but if anyone has any doubts about the legality of something, let him ask about it the one who can give him such an answer that will save him from doubt, but the time will soon come when you will not be able to find such people. I swear

by Him besides Whom there is no other deity, truly, thinking about what has already passed in this life and what remains, I can only compare it with a pond, the pure water of which has disappeared, and only turbidity remains!». №2964

104) It is reported that Abu Musa al-Ashari said: «Approaching some wadi along with the Messenger of Allah ﷺ, we loudly pronounced the words «there is no deity but Allah» and «Allah is great», but the Prophet said: «O people, pity yourself because you do not call to the deaf and not to the absent! Verily, He is with you, and He is Hearing, Close! Blessed be His name and high be His majesty!». №2992

105) Abu Hurayrah reported that the Prophet ﷺ said: «Khosroes will perish, and there will be no other Khosroes after him, and the emperor will surely die, and there will be no emperor after him, and their treasures will certainly be divided in the way of Allah!». №3027

106) Abu Hurayrah reported that the Prophet ﷺ called the war a fraud. №3029

107) It is reported from the words of 'Urwa ibn al-Zubair that the mother of the faithful 'Aisha, may Allah be pleased with her, informed him that Fatima, peace be upon her, the daughter of the Messenger of Allah ﷺ turned to Abu Bakr as-Siddiq after the death of the Messenger of Allah ﷺ so that he allocates for her a share of her inheritance from what the Messenger of Allah ﷺ left from the booty that Allah bestowed on him from the fi'a. №3092

108) However, Abu Bakr said to her: «Indeed, the Messenger of Allah ﷺ said: «We leave no inheritance. Whatever we leave behind is alms.» Then Fatimah, the daughter of the Messenger of Allah ﷺ got angry, left Abu Bakr and did not talk to him until her death. She lived after the death of the Messenger of Allah ﷺ for six months. 'Aisha said: «Fatimah asked Abu Bakr to give her her share of what the Messenger of Allah ﷺ left from the property of Khaybar, Fadak and his

alms in Medina. However, Abu Bakr refused her this, saying: «I will not leave anything that the Messenger of Allah ﷺ did. Indeed, I am afraid that if I leave something from his work, I will go astray.» As for the property in Medina, which was considered alms, then 'Umar gave it to the disposal of 'Ali and al-'Abbas. As for Khaybar and Fadak, 'Umar withheld them, saying: «This is the alms of the Messenger of Allah ﷺ, which he got by right and helped him overcome difficulties, and the ruler should dispose of this property.» Az-Zuhri said: «And in this position, they (Khaibar and Fadak) have remained to this day (at the disposal of the ruler)». №3093

109) It is reported from the words of 'Abdullah, may Allah be pleased with him, that (once) the Prophet ﷺ stood up, turning to the people and pointing towards the house of 'Aisha, said: «Trouble is here,» three times. (The Prophet ﷺ:) «Where comes the horn of Shaitan». №3104

110) Ibn al-Hanafiyyah is reported to have said: «If 'Ali had said anything bad about 'Uthman, he would have mentioned the day when some people came to him and complained about the zakat collectors of 'Uthman. Then 'Ali said to me: «Go to 'Uthman and tell him: «This scroll records where the Messenger of Allah ﷺ spent alms, so order your zakat collectors to act under this.» I took this scroll to 'Uthman, but he said: «Take it away.» I returned with him to 'Ali and informed him of this. He said, «Put it where you got it from.»№3111

111) It is reported from the words of 'Ali: «(One day) Fatimah, may Allah be pleased with her, began to complain that her hand hurt because of a hand mill. And when she found out that slaves were brought to the Messenger of Allah ﷺ, she went to him to ask him to give her a maid, but she did not find him and told 'Aisha about this. When the Prophet ﷺ (returned home), 'Aisha told him (that Fatimah came to her), and he came to us when we were already lying in our beds. We wanted to get up, but he said: «Stay where you are»

(and he sat between us), and I even felt the coolness of his feet [skin] chest. Then he said, «Shall I point you to something better than what you asked for? When you go to bed, say the words «Allah is great» / Allahu Akbar / thirty-four times, «Praise be to Allah» / al-hamdu li-Llahi / thirty-three times and «Excellent Allah» / subhana Allah / thirty-three times, and it will be better for you than what you asked for». №3113

112) It is reported that Jabir ibn 'Abdullah al-Ansari, may Allah be pleased with both of them, said: - When one of us had a boy, and he called him al-Qasim, the Ansar said: «We will not call you» Abul- Qasim» and we will not give you (this) pleasure and joy!» Then (this man) came to the Prophet ﷺ and said: «O Messenger of Allah, a boy was born to me, and I named him al-Qasim, and the Ansar said:« We will not call you «Abul-Qasim» and we will not deliver you (this) pleasure and joy!» (To this) the Prophet ﷺ said: «The Ansar did the right thing. You can call (children) by my name, but do not use my kunya, for only I am the qasim (distributor)». №3115

113) It is reported that Hawla (bint Samir) al-Ansariya, may Allah be pleased with her, said: «I heard the Messenger of Allah ﷺ say: «Verily, there are people who dispose of the property of Allah in an inappropriate way, but on the Day of Resurrection they (will get hellish) Fire!» №3118

114) It is reported that Ibn 'Umar, may Allah be pleased with both of them, said: «'Umar ibn al-Khattab expelled the Jews and Christians from the land of Hijaz. As for the Messenger of Allah ﷺ, after the conquest of Khaybar, he wanted to expel the Jews from there, because when he conquered (Khaibar, this land) became the property of Allah, His Messenger ﷺ and Muslims. And he wanted to evict the Jews from there, but they asked the Messenger of Allah ﷺ (to allow them) to stay there on the condition that they (cultivate the land) for half the harvest of dates, and the Messenger of Allah ﷺ said to them: «We will leave you here (on these con-

ditions) as we wish. And they remained (there) until 'Umar evicted them to Taimah and Ariha». №3152

115) It was narrated from the words of Abu Hurayrah, may Allah be pleased with him, that the Prophet ﷺ said: «Allah created Adam, whose height was sixty cubits, and then He said (to him): «Go, greet these angels and listen to how they greet you, (and from now on it will be) your greeting and the greeting of your descendants. And (Adam) said: «Peace be with you / As-salamu 'alai-kum /», they answered (to him): «Peace be with you and the mercy of Allah / As-salamu 'alay-kya wa rahmatu-Llah /», adding (to his greeting words) «and the mercy of Allah.» Each of those who enter Paradise will resemble (in their appearance) Adam, as for people, then (from the time of the creation of Adam) and until now they continue to decrease (in size)». №3326

116) It is reported that Umm Salamah, may Allah be pleased with her, said: «(Once) Umm Sulaym came to the Messenger of Allah ﷺ said: «O Messenger of Allah, verily, Allah is not ashamed (to speak) the truth, (so tell me) should a woman to perform a full bath/ ghusl / if she has a wet dream? The Prophet ﷺ replied: «Yes, if (after waking up) she sees (her) secretions.» (Hearing this,) Umm Salama smiled and asked, «Do women have wet dreams?» (In response to her) The Messenger of Allah ﷺ said: «And why else does the son become like his mother?» №3328

117) It is reported that Anas, may Allah be pleased with him, said: «Having learned about the arrival in Medina of the Messenger of Allah ﷺ 'Abdullah ibn Salam, may Allah be pleased with him, came to him and said:« I (want) to ask you about three (things), which (can) only the prophet know: (tell me) what will be the first omens of this Hour, what will those who find themselves in Paradise taste first of all, and why does the child turn out to be like his father or his uncle on the mother's side? (To this) the Messenger of Allah ﷺsaid: «Jibril only recently informed me about all this,» and 'Abdullah exclaimed: «He is the (only) en-

emy of the Jews from among the angels!» After that, the Messenger of Allah ﷺ said: «As for the first portent of this Hour, then (it will be) a fire that will drive people (to the gathering place) from east to west; as for the first food that the inhabitants of paradise will taste, then it will be a share of the liver of a whale; as for the similarity of the child (here the situation is as follows): if during sexual intercourse a man is ahead of a woman, then (the child turns out to be) like him, if she is ahead of him, then (the child becomes) like her «and (' Abdullah) exclaimed: «I testify that you are the Messenger of Allah!» - after which he said: «O Messenger of Allah, verily, the Jews are deceitful, and if they find out that I converted to Islam before you ask them (about me), they will build a lie on me.» And then (to the Prophet ﷺ) the Jews came, as for 'Abdullah, he entered the house. The Messenger of Allah ﷺ asked (these Jews): «What is the place among you of this 'Abdullah ibn Salam?» They replied: «He is the most knowledgeable of us and the son of the most knowledgeable of us, and he is the best of us and the son of the best of us!» Then the Messenger of Allah ﷺ asked: «What would you say if 'Abdullah converted to Islam?» (In response to this) they exclaimed: «May Allah save him from this!» Then 'Abdullah went out to them and said: «I testify that there is no true god but Allah, and I testify that Muhammad is the Messenger of Allah!» - after which they began to say: «He is the worst of us and the son of the worst of us!» - and (continued) to slander about him (and henceforth)». №3329

118) It was narrated from the words of Abu Hurayrah, may Allah be pleased with him, that the Messenger of Allah ﷺ said: «Treat your wives well, because, verily, a woman was created from a rib and, verily, the most crooked part of the rib is the upper one, and if you try to straighten it, then you will break it, and if you leave it as it is, then it will remain crooked, so treat your wives well». №3331

119) It is reported from the words of Anas ibn Malik that

the Prophet ﷺ said: «Indeed, Allah puts an angel in the womb who says: «O Lord, a drop! Oh Lord, blood clot! O Lord, piece of flesh!» When (Allah) wants to complete his creation, (the angel) asks: «Boy or girl? Unhappy or happy? What are its destiny and term? And (all this) is recorded in the womb of his mother». №3333

120) It is reported from Abu Sa'id, may Allah be pleased with him, that one day 'Ali, may Allah be pleased with him, sent a gold nugget to the Prophet ﷺ, and he divided it into four. These are al-Akra' ibn Habis al-Hanzali al-Mujashi', 'Uyaina ibn Badr al-Fazari and Zeid at-Tai from the Banu Nabhan, (the fourth was) 'Alqama ibn 'Ulyas al-Amiri from the Banu Kilab. (Having learned about this,) the Quraysh and the Ansar were indignant: «Does he give the leaders of the inhabitants of Najd, and leaves us with nothing?» The Prophet ﷺ said: «Indeed, I only incline them (hearts to Islam).» Here came a man with sunken eyes, protruding cheekbones, a prominent forehead, a thick beard and a shaved head. He exclaimed: «Fear Allah, O Muhammad!» (The Messenger of Allah ﷺ) said: «If I disobey Allah, then who is obedient to Him? Allah has entrusted me (to convey His message) to the inhabitants of the earth, and you do not trust me?» One person (perhaps it was Khalid ibn al-Walid) asked the Messenger of Allah ﷺ for permission to execute this person, but (the Messenger of Allah ﷺ) forbade him. And when he left, (the Messenger of Allah ﷺ) said: «Verily, among the descendants or companions of this person there will be people who will read the Book of Allah, but such reading will not go beyond their throat, and they will come out of religion, like an arrow that pierces the game and exits on the other side. They will kill Muslims and leave pagans alive. Indeed, if I find them, I will certainly kill them, as the Adites were killed!» №3344

121) It is reported from the words of Ibn 'Abbas, may Allah be pleased with them both, that (once) the Prophet ﷺ

said: «Verily, you will be gathered barefoot, naked and uncircumcised.» Then he read (the verse in which it is said): «... as We created everything for the first time, so we will repeat it, according to Our promise. Verily, We fulfil (the promise)!» - (after which he said): «The first to be dressed on the Day of Resurrection will be Ibrahim, as for (some of) my companions, they will be taken to the left, and I will exclaim: «My companions, my companions!» (Allah) will say: «They have not ceased to retreat (from the institutions of Islam) since you parted from them!» - and then I will say the same thing that the righteous servant said: «And I was a witness of them while I was among them, and after You gave me rest, You watched over them and You are the Witness to everything. If You punish them, then they are Your servants, and if You forgive them, then, truly, You are the Almighty, the Wise!» №3349

122) It is reported that Ibn 'Abbas, may Allah be pleased with him and his father, said: «When he saw images inside the Kaaba, the Prophet ﷺ did not enter it until they were erased. And when he saw the images of Ibrahim and Isma'il, in whose hands fortune-telling arrows were depicted, he said: «May Allah (Quraysh) destroy them! I swear by Allah, they never guessed with arrows!». №3352

123) It is reported from the words of Ibn 'Abbas, may Allah be pleased with them both, that the Messenger of Allah ﷺ said: «As for Ibrahim, then (if you want to see him, you can) look at (the one who is standing in front of you), as for Musa, he was curly and swarthy and (ridden) on a red camel, the reins of which were made of palm fibres, and I seem to see how he descends into the valley». №3355

124) Abu Hurayra (may Allah be pleased with him) reported that the Messenger of Allah ﷺ said: «Ibrahim, peace be upon him, circumcised at the age of eighty years with the help of a Tesla.» In another version of this hadith, the word «kaddum» is given with one «d». №3356

125) It is narrated from the words of Abu Hurairah, may Allah be pleased with him, that the Messenger of Allah ﷺ said: «Ibrahim never lied, peace be upon him, except for three cases, in two of which (he did it) for the sake of the Almighty and Great Allah. (For the first time) he said: «Truly, I am sick», and (for the second time) he said: «No, the eldest of them did it ...» And when (Ibrahim) together with Sarah (moved), he came to (which -the village where was) one of the tyrants, and (to this tyrant) they said: «Here is a man with one of the most beautiful women.» Then he sent a man to (Ibrahim) who asked (him): «Who is this (woman)?» He replied: «(This is) my sister,» and then he came to Sarah and said: «O Sarah, there is not a single believer on earth but me and you; As for this (king), he asked me (about you), and I told him that you are my sister, do not refute what I said! - and then (the king) sent (people) after her. When she appeared to (this king), he approached her, (wanting) to touch her, but (unexpectedly) hoarsely, and his legs began to twitch. Then he prayed: «Supplication to Allah, and I will not harm you!» - after which she called to Allah, and he was released. Then he again (tried) to touch her, but he had the same or even a stronger attack, and he (again) implored: «Supplication to Allah, and I will not harm you!» - after which she called to Allah, and he was released. Then he called several of his gatekeepers to him and said: «Verily, you did not bring a man to me, but a shaitan!» - and then gave (Sarah) Azhar for service (and let go), and she returned to (Ibrahim), who was praying at that time. He motioned to her with his hand (wanting to ask), «What's the news?» - and she said: «Allah turned the intrigues of the infidel (or: the wicked) against him and gave us Azhar!» (Reporting this hadith to the people,) Abu Hurayrah said: «And she is your mother, O sons of heavenly water». №3358

126) It is reported that 'Abdurrahman ibn Abi Layla said: «Ka'b ibn 'Ujra met me and said: «Should I give you a gift that I heard from the Prophet ﷺ?» I replied, «Of course, give it to me.» Then he said: «(Once) we said

to the Messenger of Allah ﷺ:« O Messenger of Allah, we already know how to greet you, but how can we turn to Allah with supplications for you, O family (of Muhammad ﷺ)? (To this the Prophet ﷺ) said: «Say: «O Allah, bless Muhammad and the offspring of Muhammad, as You blessed the family of Ibrahim, truly, You are Praiseworthy, Glorious! O Allah, send blessings to Muhammad and the offspring of Muhammad, as You sent them to the family of Ibrahim, verily, You are Praiseworthy, Glorious!» №3370

127) It is reported that Ibn 'Abbas, may Allah be pleased with them both, narrated that the Prophet ﷺ often asked for protection for al-Hasan and al-Husayn and said: «Verily, your forefather asked Allah for protection for Isma'il and Ishaq (saying): «I resort to the perfect words of Allah so that they protect you from any shaitan and (poisonous) insect and every evil eye! №3371

128) It is narrated from the words of 'Abdullah bin 'Amr, may Allah be pleased with them both, that the Prophet ﷺ said: «Report (to people what you hear) from me, even if (the matter concerns only one) verse, and convey what the Israelites said, (for) there is no sin in this, but whoever deliberately raises a lie against me, let him (prepare) take his place in the fire». №3461

129) It is narrated from the words of Abu Hurairah, may Allah be pleased with him, that he heard the Messenger of Allah ﷺ say: «(Once upon a time) Allah wished to test three of the Israelites: a leper, a bald man and a blind man. He sent an angel to them, who (assumed a human form) appeared (first) to the leper and asked: «What do you want most of all?» He said: «Good colour, good skin (and to get rid of what is causing) people avoid me.» Then an angel passed over him (with his hand), his illness was gone and he was (again) endowed with good colour and good skin. (Then the angel) asked: «And what kind of property do you like best?» He replied: «Camels (or: cows)», and he was given a pregnant camel, (after which the angel)

said: «May Allah make her blessed for you!» Then (the angel) came to the bald man and asked: «What do you want most?» He said, «Good hair and to get rid of the things that make people avoid me.» Then an angel passed over him (his hand, his ugliness) disappeared and he was (again) endowed with good hair. (Then the angel) asked: «And what kind of property do you like best?» He said: «Cows», and (the angel) gave him a pregnant cow, (after which) he said: «May Allah make her blessed for you!» Then (the angel) came to the blind man and asked: «What do you want most?» He said: «So that Allah restores my sight and I see people.» Then an angel passed over him (with his hand), and Allah restored his sight to him. (Then the angel) asked: «And what kind of property do you like best?» He said, «Sheep,» and (the angel) gave him a pregnant sheep. And after that they gave offspring (a camel and a cow) and gave offspring (a sheep, and after a while) one already had a whole wadi of camels, another had a whole wadi of cows, and the third had a whole wadi of sheep. And then (the angel) appeared to the (former) leper, taking on his (former) appearance, and said (to him): «I am a poor man. On the way, I lost all means, and I have no one to turn to today except Allah, and after (Him) - to you. I conjure you by the One Who gave you a good colour, good skin and wealth, (give me) a camel with which I can complete my journey! (In response, this person) said to him: «Verily, (I have) many debts.» (Then the angel) said, «It seems I know you. Weren't you the leper that people shunned? (And weren't you) a poor man to whom Allah granted (wealth)? (This man) said: «I have inherited this wealth from my ancestors.» (The angel) said: «If you have lied, may Allah restore you to your former appearance!» Then (the angel) appeared to (the one who was) bald, assuming an appearance similar to his former appearance, and said to him the same thing that he had said (to the former leper), and when he gave him the same answer, he said: «If you lied, may Allah restore you to your former appearance!» And (then an angel) appeared to the (former) blind man, taking on a form similar to his former appearance, and said: «I am a poor traveller, and I have lost all means during my journey, and I have no one to turn to today except Allah, and after (Him) to you. I conjure you by the One who restored your sight, (give me one) sheep, which will be enough for me to complete my journey! (Formerly blind) said: «I (really) was blind, and Allah restored my sight, and I was poor, and He gave me wealth, take what you want, and I swear by Allah, today for the sake of Allah I will not burden you with anything whatever you take!» (Then the angel) said: «Keep your possessions for yourself, for, verily, you were only put to the test, and Allah was pleased with you, and He was angry with two of your companions». №3464

130) It is reported that (once) Usama ibn Zayd, may Allah be pleased with them both, was asked: «What did you hear from the Messenger of Allah ﷺ about the plague?» Usama replied: «The Messenger of Allah ﷺ said: «A plague is filth, and it was sent (as a punishment) to a group (of people from among) the Israelites (or: who lived before you), and if you hear that it broke out in any land, do not go there, but if it starts where you will be, do not leave (this land in an attempt) to escape from it. (In the version of this hadith that he cites) Abu-n-Nadr (it is reported that the Prophet ﷺ) said: «And let not desire (leave this land) make you run away from (illness)». №3473

131) 'Aisha, may Allah be pleased with her, reported that at one time the Quraish were concerned about the case of a woman from the Bani Makhzum who committed theft. [Some] began to say: «Who will talk about it with the Messenger of Allah ﷺ?» And [others] said: «Who dares to do this, except Usama ibn Zayd, the favourite of the Messenger of Allah ﷺ?!» And Usama appealed to him [with intercession for her, believing that any intercession is good and acceptable]. The Messenger of Allah ﷺ said: «Are you petitioning for

the abolition of one of the punishments established by Allah ?!» And then he got up and addressed the people with a sermon, after which he said: «Truly, those who lived before you were ruined by the fact that when a noble stole, they left him [did not apply the established punishment to him], and when a weak one stole, they applied to his prescribed punishment. I swear by Allah, if Fatima, the daughter of Mohammed, stole it, I would cut off her hand too!» №3475

132) Abu Hurayrah (may Allah be pleased with him) narrated that the Messenger of Allah ﷺ said: «You will see that people (are like) mines. Those who were the best of them during the pre-Islamic era of ignorance, (remained) the best in Islam, if they learned (the establishment of religion). And you will see that the best of people in this matter is the one who hates it more than others (i.e. power)». №3493

133) It is narrated from the words of Abu Dharr, may Allah be pleased with him, that he heard the Prophet ﷺ say: «Any (person) who declares himself the son of someone other than his father, knowing that (in fact) it (is not so), is necessarily is unfaithful, but as for the one who claims to belong to a people with whose people he has no family ties, then let him (prepare) take his place in the fire». №3508

134) It is reported that Wasil ibn al-Aska', may Allah be pleased with him, said: «The Messenger of Allah ﷺ said: «Verily, the greatest (types) of lies are declaring a person to be the son of not his father, a statement that he saw in a dream what (in fact) did not see, and attributing to the Messenger of Allah what he did not say». №3509

135) It is reported from Jabir ibn 'Abdullah, may Allah be pleased with him, that the Prophet ﷺ said: «An example of me and the rest of the prophets is a man who built a house for himself. And he completed the building, except for one brick. People, entering this house, admired it and said: «(It would be great) if it were not

for the place of one brick». №3534

136) It is reported that (once) Abu Juhaifa (may Allah be pleased with him) said: «I saw the Prophet ﷺ and (I can say that) al-Hasan ibn 'Ali, may Allah be pleased with both of them, looks like him.» (The narrator of this hadith asked Abu Juhaifa, may Allah be pleased with him): «Describe to me (the Prophet ﷺ).» He said: «He was white-skinned, and his black hair (his beard) was already touched by grey hair. And the Prophet ﷺ ordered to give us thirteen camels, but died before we took them». №3544

137) It is reported that (once) Anas, may Allah be pleased with him, was asked: «Did the Prophet ﷺ (his hair) dye?» He replied: «No because he had only a few grey hairs on his temples». №3550

138) It is reported from the words of 'Uqba ibn 'Amir that once the Prophet ﷺ performed the janaz prayer for the fallen at Uhud, after which he climbed the minbar and said: «Verily, I will be ahead of you and will testify about you, and, verily, by Allah, now I see my reservoir, and, verily, the keys to the treasuries of the earth (or: the keys of the earth) were given to me, and, verily, I swear by Allah, I am not afraid that after my death you will become polytheists, but I am afraid that you will compete with each other with a friend (because of worldly goods)!». №3596

139) It is reported that Abu Sa'sa' said: «Once Abu Sa'id al-Khudri, may Allah be pleased with him, said to me:» I see that you love sheep and keep them, take care of them and their food, because Indeed, I heard the Prophet ﷺ say: «Soon the time will come for people when the best possession of a Muslim will be sheep, for which he will walk on the tops of mountains and places of rain, fleeing with his religion from troubles». №3600

140) It was narrated from Ibn Masud that the Prophet ﷺ said: «After me, there will be self-interest (preference will be given to others over them in worldly things),

and deeds that you will blame.» (The Companions) said: «O Messenger of Allah, what will you order us?» To which he said: «Fulfill the rights that lie with you, and ask Allah for what is yours». №3603

141) It is reported from the words of Abu Hurairah, may Allah be pleased with him, that (once) the Messenger of Allah ﷺ said: «This clan (tribe) Quraish will destroy people!» (People) asked: «What will you order us?» (The Prophet ﷺ) said: «(It would be better) for people to stay away from them». №3604

142) It is reported that Abu Hurayrah, may Allah be pleased with him, said: «I heard the truthful and trustworthy (the Prophet ﷺ) say:« My community will perish at the hands of (several) young Quraysh. And Abu Hurayrah said: «If you wish, I will name them: (these are) the sons of such and such and the sons of such and such». №3605

143) Hudhayfa ibn al-Yaman said: «Usually people asked the Messenger of Allah ﷺ about the good, and I asked him about the bad, fearing that it would befall me. I said: «O Messenger of Allah, indeed, we were in ignorance and evil, and then Allah gave us good, but will evil come after this good?» He said yes. Then I asked: «Will good come after this evil?» He said, «Yes, but evil will be mixed with it.» I asked: «What will it be?» He said, «There will be people who will lead others differently than I do, and you will see their deeds and disapprove of them.» I asked: «Will evil come after this good?» He said: «Yes, those who call people to the gates of Hell, and whoever answers their call, they will throw into the Fire!» I asked: «O Messenger of Allah, describe them to us.» He said: «They will be from our midst and will speak our language.» I asked: «What do you tell me to do if I live to see this?» He said: «Do not part with al-Jama'a Muslims and the ruler.» I asked: «And if I don't find either al-jama'a or the ruler ?!» The Prophet ﷺ said: «Then stay away from all these groups, even if you have to bite into the roots of trees with your teeth, and stay in a similar position

until death comes to you!» №3606

144) It is reported that Abu Sa'id al-Khudri, may Allah be pleased with him, said: «Once during the division of military booty after one of the military campaigns, Zul-Khuaysira, a man from the Bani Tamim tribe, approached the Messenger of Allah ﷺ and said: « O Messenger of Allah, be just! The Prophet ﷺ said: «Woe to you, who adheres to justice if I am not just!? You are lost and failed if I do not adhere to justice! Then 'Umar said: «O Messenger of Allah, let him cut off his head!» The Prophet ﷺ replied: «Leave him, for he has comrades, any of you will consider their prayers and fasts insignificant compared to their prayers and fasts, they read the Quran, but it does not fall below their throats, they fly out of religion like that, how an arrow flies through the game, (penetrating it through, with such speed that) nothing is visible on the tip of the arrow, nothing is visible on its «risaf» (part of the arrowhead), nothing is visible on the shaft of the arrow, and on its shank nothing is visible, no entrails, no blood. Their sign will be a black man, one of whose arms will be like a woman's breast or a dangling piece of meat. They will appear when there are disagreements between people.» Abu Sa'eed said: «I testify that I heard this hadith from the Messenger of Allah ﷺ, and I testify that 'Ali ibn Abu Talib fought with such people, and I was with him. He ordered to find a man (described by the Prophet ﷺ), and when he was brought, I looked at him, and he looked exactly as the Prophet ﷺ described him». №3610

145) It is reported that 'Ali (may Allah be pleased with him) said: «When I convey to you something about the Messenger of Allah ﷺ, (know that) I prefer falling from the sky (on the earth) to raising a lie on him when I say about what concerns only me and you, (then know that) war is deceit. I heard the Messenger of Allah ﷺ say: «In the last times there will be young and foolish people who will utter the words of the best creatures, but they will depart from Islam like an arrow shot

from a bow. The faith (of these people) will not go beyond their throats, and therefore, wherever you meet (such), kill them, for, truly, he who kills them on the Day of Resurrection will receive a reward for this». №3611

146) It is reported that 'Aisha, may Allah be pleased with her, said: «One day Fatima came to the Prophet ﷺ, whose gait was similar to the gait of the Prophet ﷺ. The Prophet ﷺ said to her: «Welcome to my daughter!», Then he sat her to the right (or: ... to the left) of himself, and then he said something in her ear, and she began to cry. I asked her, «Why are you crying?» Then he said something in her ear again, and she laughed, and I said, «I've never seen joy come so close to sadness as I do today.» And then I asked her about what he said to her, and she replied: «I will not betray the secrets of the Messenger of Allah ﷺ!» When the Prophet ﷺ died, I asked her about it again. №3623
147)   She replied: «He said to me: «Each year, Jibril recited the Quran (in full) with me once, and this year he repeated it with me twice, and I consider this nothing more than (an indication that) my term already close. You will be the first member of his family to follow me.» And I cried, and he said: «Are you not glad that you will be the mistress of women in Paradise (or: mistress of believing women)?», so I laughed». №3624

148) It is reported from the words of Sa'd ibn Abi Waqqas that the Prophet ﷺ said to 'Ali: «Do you not agree to take the same place with me that Harun occupied with Musa?» №3706

149) It is reported that Abu Hurayrah, may Allah be pleased with him, said: «Verily, people say:« Abu Hurayrah (transmits) many (hadith)!» Indeed, I was inseparable from the Messenger of Allah ﷺand (thought only of how little) to eat, (after which nothing distracted me from the Prophet ﷺ). I did not eat bread, did not wear silk (robes), and neither men nor women served me. It happened that I fell on the stones with my stomach

due to (strong) hunger. And it happened that I asked a person to read some verse, which I already knew (however, I did it) so that he would invite me (to himself) and feed me. The best attitude towards the poor was Ja'far ibn Abi Talib, who invited us to his place and fed us with what was available in his house. And it so happened that he brought us a leather waterskin, in which there was nothing, but we cut it and licked what (remained)». №3708

150) It is reported that Abu Bakr (may Allah be pleased with him) said: «Honor Muhammad 鬱 with his family members». №3713

151) It is reported from the words of Misuar ibn Mahram that the Messenger of Allah 鬱 said: «Fatimah is a particle of myself, and whoever angers her will cause my anger». №3714

152) It is reported that al-Bara, may Allah be pleased with him, said: «I heard the Prophet 鬱, on whose shoulder sat al-Hasan ibn 'Ali, said:» O Allah, verily, I love him, love him You too!». №3749

153) It is reported that (once) a man asked Ibn 'Umar, may Allah be pleased with both of them, about whether a person wearing ihram could kill flies. (In response to him, Ibn 'Umar) said: «The people of Iraq ask about flies after they killed the son of the daughter of the Messenger of Allah 鬱, and the Prophet 鬱 said: «In this world, they are like two basilicas to me!». №3753

154) It was narrated from Misuar bin Mahram, may Allah be pleased with both of them, that the Messenger of Allah 鬱 said: «Fatimah is a particle of myself, and whoever angers her will provoke my anger». №3767

155) Abu Wail (Shaqiq ibn Salama) said: «When 'Ali sent 'Ammar and al-Hasan to Kufa to mobilize (the people of Kufa), 'Ammar delivered a sermon and said, 'Indeed, I know that 'Aisha is the wife of the Prophet 鬱 in this world and the next world, however, Allah tested you to (know) you will follow Him or her». №3772

156) It was narrated from Usayd ibn Hudair, may Allah be pleased with them, that one of the Ansar said: «O Messenger of Allah, will you appoint me as a ruler, as you appointed such and such?» To which he said: «After me, you will meet self-interest (preference will be given to others over them in worldly things), be patient until you meet me near the pond». №3792

157) It was narrated from Anas ibn Malik, may Allah be pleased with him, that the Prophet ﷺ said to one of the Ansar: «Verily, after me, you will meet self-interest (preference will be given to others over them in worldly things), be patient until you meet me at the reservoir, and your meeting at the pond». №3793
158) It is reported from the words of 'Ali ibn Abi Talib, may Allah be pleased with him, that the Prophet ﷺ said: «The best woman (of this world at one time) was Maryam, and the best woman (of this community) is Khadija». №3815

159) It is reported that 'Aisha, may Allah be pleased with her, said: «None of the wives of the Prophet ﷺ I was jealous of him so much as Khadija, who died before he married me because I often heard how he remembered her. And Allah ordered him to please the news of the house of hollow pearls (which awaits her in Paradise). And when he slaughtered sheep, he sent as a gift to her friends a sufficient amount (meat)». №3816

160) It is reported that 'Aisha, may Allah be pleased with her, said: «(One day) Hal bint Khuwaylid, the sister of Khadija, asked permission to enter the Messenger of Allah ﷺ who was reminded of how she asked permission of Khadija, which worried him, and he exclaimed: «O Allah, (this is) Hala!» ('Aisha, may Allah be pleased with her) said: «This caused jealousy in me, and I said:« Why do you remember a long-dead (toothless) old woman with red gums from the number of old women (of the tribe) Quraish, when did Allah give you something better instead of her?!» №3821

161) It is reported from the words of Qays ibn 'Ubad that

'Ali ibn Abi Talib, may Allah be pleased with him, said: «I will be the first to kneel before the Merciful to litigate on the Day of Judgment.» Qays ibn 'Ubad said: «It was about them that the verse was sent down: «Here are two litigating groups that were arguing about their Lord'» (Surah al-Hajj, verse 19). He said: «These are those who fought on the day of the Battle of Badr: Hamza, 'Ali and 'Ubaida (or: Abu 'Ubaida ibn al-Harith) and Sheiba ibn Rabi'a, 'Utba ibn Rabi'a and al -Walid ibn Utba». №3965

162) Qays ibn 'Ubadah is reported to have said: «I heard Abu Dharr swear that these verses: 'These are two litigious groups that were quarrelling about their Lord' (Surah al-Hajj, verse 19) was sent down regarding those who fought on the day of the Battle of Badr: Hamza, 'Ali, 'Ubaida ibn al-Harith, 'Utba, Sheiba, the two sons of Rabi'a and al-Walid ibn 'Utba». №3969

163) It is reported that Ibn 'Abbas, may Allah be pleased with him and his father, said (regarding the words of Allah Almighty): «Who exchanged the mercy of Allah for unbelief» (Surah «Ibrahim», verse 28): «By Allah, these are disbelievers (from among) the Quraysh. 'Amr said: «These are the Quraysh, and Muhammad is the mercy of Allah.» And regarding the words of the Almighty: «... and cast their people into the Abode of perdition» (Surah «Ibrahim», verse 28) Ibn 'Abbas said: «This is a fire (into which they will enter after their death) on the day of Badr». №3977

164) It is narrated from the words of Abu Talha, may Allah be pleased with him, who took part in the battle of Badr along with the Messenger of Allah ﷺ, that (the Prophet ﷺ) said: «Angels do not enter (such) a house where there is a dog or an image», having in the sight of the image of that in which there is a spirit. №4002

165) It is reported from the words of 'Aisha that Fatima, peace be upon her, the daughter of the Prophet ﷺ sent a man to Abu Bakr, asking her to give her her inheritance from the Messenger of Allah ﷺ from the prop-

erty granted to him by Allah without a fight, which was in Medina and Fadak, and also that what is left of the fifth part /hummus/ Khaybar. However, Abu Bakr said: «Indeed, the Messenger of Allah ﷺ said: «We leave no inheritance. Whatever we leave behind is alms, and the members of Muhammad's family subsist from these funds.» I swear by Allah, I will not change the position of the alms of the Messenger of Allah ﷺ, as it was during the time of the Messenger of Allah ﷺ. I will deal with this property as the Messenger of Allah ﷺ did.» So Abu Bakr refused to give Fatimah any of it. Fatima was angry with Abu Bakr, left him and did not talk to him until her death, and she lived after the death of the Prophet ﷺ for six months. When she died, her husband 'Ali buried her at night without informing Abu Bakr about it, and he performed the funeral prayer for her. When Fatima was alive, people respected 'Ali very much, but after her death, 'Ali noticed that they had changed their attitude towards him. Then he began to try to reconcile with Abu Bakr and decided to swear allegiance to him because until that time he had still not done so. 'Ali sent a man to Abu Bakr, saying: «Come to us, but let no one come with you,» not wanting the presence of 'Umar. 'Umar said to Abu Bakr, «No, by Allah, you will not enter them alone.» Abu Bakr said, «What can they do to me? By Allah, I will go to them!» When Abu Bakr came, 'Ali uttered the words of witness (shahada) and said: «We know about your virtues, and what Allah has endowed you with, and we do not claim the good that Allah has given you, but you did not consult us in the matter of government, and we believed that we had a right to this because of our close relationship with the Messenger of Allah ﷺ. After that, Abu Bakr's eyes filled with tears, and he said: «By the One in Whose Hand is my soul, keeping in touch with the relatives of the Messenger of Allah ﷺ is more beloved to me than even with my relatives. As for the problem that has arisen between me and you regarding that property, then I will do my best to spend it in a good way, and

I will not leave a single deed that I saw the Messenger of Allah ﷺ doing without doing it. On this 'Ali said to Abu Bakr: «I promise to give you an oath in the afternoon.» Having performed the midday prayer /zuhr/, Abu Bakr went up to the minbar and said the words of tashahhud, and then mentioned the story of 'Ali, that he did not give him an oath, and his excuse that he mentioned. Then 'Ali (got up), said the words of istighfar (a petition for forgiveness), said the words of tashahhud, exalted the right of Abu Bakr and said that he did not induce him to what he did, the desire to compete with Abu Bakr or the expression of dissatisfaction with what he endowed his Allah. 'Ali added, «But we believe that we also have some right in this matter and that he (Abu Bakr) did not consult us in this matter, so we got angry.» The Muslims rejoiced at this and said, «You did the right thing.» After 'Ali swore allegiance to Abu Bakr, the Muslims befriended him. №4240

166) It is reported that Buraidah, may Allah be pleased with him, said: «The Prophet ﷺ sent 'Ali to Khalid to bring (him from Yemen) a fifth of the spoils of war, and I hated 'Ali, and after he performed a full ablution, I said to Khalid, «Won't you pay attention to this?» When we came to the Prophet ﷺ, I told him about it, and he asked: «O Buraida, do you hate 'Ali?» I said yes. (Then the Prophet ﷺ) said: «You should not hate him, for, verily, from this fifth part, he is due more (of what he took)!» №4350

167) It is reported that Abu Sa'eed al-Khudri, may Allah be pleased with him, said: «' Ali ibn Abi Talib, may Allah be pleased with him, sent the Messenger of Allah ﷺ from Yemen an unrefined gold nugget in (a bag of) tanned leather and (the Prophet ﷺ) divided it into four. (Parts of this nugget were received) 'Uyayna ibn Badr, Akra' ibn Habis and Zeid al-Khail, as for the fourth, it was either 'Alqamah or 'Amir ibn at-Tufayl. (Having learned about this,) one of the companions (of the Prophet ﷺ) said: «We had more rights to (this

gold) than they had!» This reached the Prophet ﷺ, and he said: «Do you not trust me, even though He who is in heaven trusts me, and that I receive messages from heaven in the morning and evening?» (After that, a man with sunken eyes, wide cheekbones, a prominent forehead, a thick beard and a shaved head, on which he wore a highly gathered izar, rose from his seat and who exclaimed: «O Messenger of Allah, fear Allah!» (To this the Prophet ﷺ) said: «Woe to you, but of all those living on earth, is it not right for me to fear Allah most of all ?!» Then this man left, and Khalid ibn al-Walid said: «O Messenger of Allah, should we cut off his head?» (The Prophet ﷺ) said: «No, for he may be among those who pray.» Khalid exclaimed: «And how many are those who pray, in whose tongue (not at all) what is in the heart!» (In response to him) The Messenger of Allah ﷺ said: «Indeed, I was not ordered to penetrate the hearts of people, nor cut their wombs!» And then (the Prophet ﷺ) looked after this man and said: «Verily, among the descendants of this man there will be people who will read the Book of Allah with soft voices, but their throat (their reading) will not spread further, and they will depart from religion like that like an arrow fired from a bow!» (The narrator of this hadith said:) «And I think that (the Prophet ﷺ) said: «Indeed if they appear when I am alive, I will certainly begin to kill them like they killed Thamud!».№4351

168) It is reported that 'Abdullah ibn al-Zubayr, may Allah be pleased with both of them, said: «(When) a (group) of riders from (a tribe) of Banu Tamim arrived at the Prophet ﷺ, Abu Bakr said:» Appoint (them) the ruler of al- Ka'ka'a ibn Ma'bad ibn Zuraru», and as for 'Umar, he said: «No, appoint al-Akra'a ibn Habis!» Abu Bakr exclaimed: «You only wanted (to say something) against me!» 'Umar said: «I did not want this at all!» - and then they began to argue loudly, in connection with which (the following verse) was sent down: «O you who believe! Do not (try) to get ahead of Allah and His messenger, (but) fear Allah, (for) verily, Allah

is Hearing, Knowing!» (Surah «al-Khujurat, verse 1)».
№4367

169) It is reported from the words of Abu Hurairah, may Allah be pleased with him, that the Prophet ﷺ said: «Faith/iman / is in Yemen, and confusion/fitna / is where the horn of Shaitan rises». №4389

170) It is narrated from the words of Sa'd ibn Abi Waqqas, may Allah be pleased with him, that, having gone (on a campaign) to Tabuk, the Messenger of Allah ﷺ left (in Medina) instead of himself 'Ali, who asked: «Do you (want) to leave me among women and children? - (to which the Prophet ﷺ) said: «Do you not agree to take the same place with me that Harun occupied with Musa, with the only difference that there will be no more prophets after me?» №4416

171) CIt is reported that Abu Bakra, may Allah be pleased with him, said: «Allah made it so that the words that I heard from the Messenger of Allah ﷺ benefited me in the days (preceding) of the camel fight after I almost joined to those who gathered around the camel and did not fight with them. (The fact is that) when the Messenger of Allah ﷺ became aware that the Persians handed power over themselves to the daughter of Chosroes, he said: «People who handed power over themselves to a woman will never succeed». №4425

172) It is reported that (once) Ibn 'Abbas, may Allah be pleased with him and his father, said: «When death approached the Prophet ﷺ, there were men in the house, and the Prophet ﷺ said: «Come, and I will write down what later you will never go astray.» And some of them began to say: «Verily, the Prophet ﷺ is broken by illness! You have the Quran! The Book of Allah is sufficient for us!» Those present in the house disagreed and began to argue with each other. Some of them said: «Bring (paper), let the Prophet (peace be upon him) write something for you, thanks to which you will not go astray.» Some began to express other opinions. When there was too much noise and contro-

versy, the Messenger of Allah ﷺ said: «Leave (me).» 'Ubaydullah narrated that Ibn 'Abbas, may Allah be pleased with him, said: «Verily, the whole trouble is that because of their noise and polemics, the Messenger of Allah ﷺ did not write them that paper». №4432

173) It is reported that 'Aisha, may Allah be pleased with her, said: «During the illness (of the Prophet ﷺ) we put medicine in his mouth, but he gave us a sign (wishing to say) that this should not be done. We said: «(This is because no one) the sick person wants (to take) medicine», but, waking up, (the Prophet ﷺ) asked: «Didn't I forbid you to give me medicine?» We said: «(We thought) the sick people do not like (to take) medicines», and (the Prophet ﷺ) said: «Let them give medicine before my eyes to everyone present in the house, except for al-'Abbas, for he was not among you!». №4458

174) It is reported that al-Aswad said: «Once in the presence of 'Aisha, some people mentioned that the Prophet ﷺ bequeathed 'Ali to be his successor. 'Aisha said, «Who said that? Truly, dying, he lay on my chest, and he asked to bring a basin, and then fell on his side and gave up his soul, and I did not even feel that he had died. So, when did he bequeath this to 'Ali!?». №4459
175) It is reported that Talhah said: «(Once) I asked 'Abdullah ibn Abi Awf, may Allah be pleased with them both:« Did the Prophet ﷺmake a will? He replied: «No.» I asked, «So why were people ordered to make wills (or: were they told to make wills)?» He said: «(The Prophet ﷺ) made his will the Book of Allah». №4460

176) It is reported that 'Aisha, may Allah be pleased with her, said: – (Once) the Messenger of Allah ﷺ recited an ayah (which says): «He is the One who revealed the Book to you. There are clear verses in it that form the basis of (this) Book, while others are not (quite) clear. As for those (people) in whose hearts there is a deviation (from the truth), then they follow what is (quite) clear is not, trying to plunge (others) into temptation

and wanting to give this (their) interpretation, while (the true The interpretation of this is known only to Allah. As for those who are established in knowledge, they say: «We believed in this (for) all this is from our Lord», and only those who have understanding listen to admonitions, »and then the Messenger of Allah ﷺ said:« If you see those who follow from (of the Quran) to that which is not (quite) clear, (know that) these are those whom Allah has named, so beware of them!» №4547

177) It is reported from the words of Ibn Abu Mulayika, may Allah Almighty have mercy on him, that in one house (or: in one room) two women were engaged in piercing (leather for sewing shoes. Accidentally) injuring their hands with an awl, one of them went outside, and then accused this other, and their case was submitted to Ibn 'Abbas, may Allah be pleased with them both, who said: «The Messenger of Allah ﷺ said:» If people were given (what they claim) based on (only) their claims, then the lives and property of (many other) people would be lost.» Remind her of Allah and read (the verse where it is said): «Verily, for those who sell the covenant of Allah ...» (The transmitter of this hadith said): - And when she was reminded, she confessed, and Ibn 'Abbas said: «The Prophet ﷺ said: «The defendant should take an oath». №4552

178) Ibn Abbas (may Allah be pleased with him) reported that the Messenger of Allah ﷺ said: «You people will be gathered before Allah on the Day of Judgment naked, barefoot and uncircumcised. The first person to be dressed on this day will be Ibrahim. Look! Many of my followers will be taken to the left (to hell). I will say: «Lord, these are my companions!» They will answer me: «You don't know what they did after your death.» Then I will say, as the righteous servant, Jesus, said: «I was responsible while I was among them...» (5:117). Then they will say to me: «O Muhammad, they have not ceased to deviate since you left them!» №4740

179) It is reported that Abu Sa'eed al-Khudri, may Allah be pleased with him, said: - (Once) we said: «O Messenger of Allah, (we know that) this is a greeting, (which should be addressed to you,) but how can we turn to Allah with supplications for you? (In response to us, the Prophet ﷺ) said: «Say: «O Allah, bless Muhammad, Your servant and Your messenger, as You blessed the family of Ibrahim, and send blessings to Muhammad and the family of Muhammad, as You sent them to Ibrahim! №4798

180) It was narrated from the words of Abu Hurayrah, may Allah be pleased with him, that the Messenger of Allah ﷺ said: «The Almighty and Great Allah said: «The Son of Adam offends Me by blaspheming the time / dahr /, while I am the time, everything is in My power, and by (My will) the day succeeds the night!» №4826

181) It is reported from the words of Anas bin Malik, may Allah be pleased with him, that shortly before the death of His Messenger, Allah Almighty continuously sent down revelations to him ﷺ when the revelations (sent down) most of all, He reposed him and the Messenger of Allah ﷺ died. №4982

182) Zayd ibn Thabit, may Allah be pleased with him, said: «Abu Bakr, may Allah be pleased with him, called me to him and said: «Verily, you wrote revelations for the Messenger of Allah ﷺ. Take care of the Quran.» And I set to work and found the last two verses from the Surah at-Tauba from Abu Khuzayma al-Ansari. I haven't found any other than him. (These were the words:) «A messenger from your midst has come to you. It is hard for him that you are suffering. He is trying for you. He is kind and merciful to believers. And if they turn away, then say: «Allah is enough for me! There is no god but Him. I trust only in Him, for He is the Lord of the great Throne». №4989

183) It is reported from Masruk that 'Abdullah (ibn Mas'ud), may Allah be pleased with him, said: «I swear by Him besides Whom there is no god worthy of worship, no

matter what verse was sent down, I know who it was sent down and where he was sent down. If I knew (the whereabouts) of the one who knows the Book of Allah more than I do and that he (can) be reached (on) a beast of burden, then I would certainly go to him». №5002

184) It is narrated from the words of 'Aisha, may Allah be pleased with her, that every night, before going to bed, the Prophet ﷺ joined his hands in front of him (palms inward), then blew on them, then read «Say:« He, Allah, One...», «Say: «I resort to the Lord of the dawn...» and «Say: «I resort to the Lord of people...», and then ran (palms) all over the body, wherever he could reach, starting from the head, face and front of the body and did it three times. №5017

185) Abu Hurayrah (may Allah be pleased with him) reported that the Messenger of Allah ﷺ said: «One should not envy anyone except two: a man whom Allah taught the Quran and who reads it night and day, and his neighbour hears him and says:« Oh, that the same thing was given to me that was given to such and such, and I would do the same as he does! - and to a person to whom Allah has given wealth and who spends it properly, and (some) person says: «Oh, if I were given the same thing that was given to such and such, and I would do the same, what does he do!» №5026

186) It was narrated from the words of 'Uthman, may Allah be pleased with him, that the Prophet ﷺ said: «The best of you is the one who studies the Quran and teaches it (others)». №5027

187) It is narrated from the words of Abu Musa, may Allah be pleased with him, that (once) the Prophet ﷺ said to him: «O Abu Musa, you were given a pipe from among the pipes of the family of Dawud». №5048

188) It is reported that Abu Sa'eed al-Khudri (may Allah be pleased with him) said: «I heard the Messenger of Allah ﷺ say: «There will be among you people whose prayers, fasting and deeds will make you despise your

prayers, fasting and deeds, (however) they will recite the Quran in such a way that the recitation does not extend beyond their throats, and they will depart from religion like an arrow shot from a bow, when (the shooter) looks at the blade, but does not see anything, looks at the unfeathered part of the arrow, but does not see anything, looks at the plumage, but does not see anything, and then looks at the heel of the arrow (hoping to see something)». №5058

189) It was narrated from the words of Abu Musa, may Allah be pleased with him, that the Prophet ﷺ said: «A believer who reads the Quran and acts (by its regulations) is like a sweet lemon with a pleasant smell and taste, and a believer who does not read the Quran, but comes in (by its regulations), like a date, pleasant to the taste, but not having a smell. The hypocrite who reads the Quran is like reyhan, which has a pleasant smell but tastes bitter, and the hypocrite who does not read the Quran is like a coloquint, which tastes bitter (or: disgusting) and smells bitter». №5059

190) Jundub bin 'Abdullah (may Allah be pleased with him) reported that the Prophet ﷺ said: «Read the Quran while your hearts are in agreement regarding it, and when (between you) disagreements arise, leave it». №5060

191) It was narrated from the words of Abu Hurayrah, may Allah be pleased with him, that the Prophet ﷺ said: «A woman is taken as a wife because of four (things): because of her wealth, because of her origin, because of her beauty and because for her religion, pursue the one who adheres to religion, otherwise you will lose!» №5090

192) It was narrated from the words of Usama bin Zayd, may Allah be pleased with them both, that the Prophet ﷺ said: «I will not leave behind a temptation that is more harmful to men than women». №5096

193) Abu Hurayrah (may Allah be pleased with him) reported that the Prophet ﷺ said: «You should not marry

a woman without consulting her, and you should not marry a girl without asking her permission (for this).» (People) asked: «O Messenger of Allah, how do we know about her permission?» (The Prophet ﷺ) said: «By her silence». №5136

194) Hansa bint Hizam al-Ansariya (may Allah be pleased with her) narrated that when her father married her in a second marriage against her will, she came to the Messenger of Allah ﷺ and he dissolved this marriage. №5138

195) It was narrated from the words of Abu Hurairah, may Allah be pleased with him, that the Prophet ﷺ said: «Let the one who believes in Allah and the Last Day not offend his neighbour! And (always) treat women well, because, indeed, they were created from a rib, and its upper part is distinguished by the greatest curvature; if you try to straighten (a rib), you will break it, and if you leave it (alone), it will remain crooked, (and therefore always) treat women well!» №5185

196) It is narrated from the words of Usama, may Allah be pleased with him, that the Prophet ﷺ said: «I stopped at the gates of paradise and saw that most of those who entered there were poor, as, for the rich, they were detained when the inhabitants of hell had already been commanded (plunge) into hell. And I stopped at the gates of hell and saw that most of those who entered there were women». №5196

197) It is reported that Asma bint Abu Bakr, may Allah be pleased with both of them, said: «During the lifetime of the Messenger of Allah ﷺ, we slaughtered a horse in Medina and ate it». №5511

198) It is reported that Sa'eed bin Jubair (may Allah Almighty have mercy on him) said: «(Once) when I (along with others) was in the company of Ibn 'Umar, he passed by young men (or: a group of people) who were tied to something chicken and began to shoot at it. When they saw Ibn 'Umar, they fled, and Ibn 'Umar said: «Who did this? Indeed, the Prophet ﷺ cursed

those who did this!» In another version of this hadith, it is reported that Ibn 'Umar, may Allah be pleased with both of them, said: «The Prophet ﷺ cursed (such people) who cut off parts of the body of still-living animals!» №5515

199) It is narrated from the words of Abu Musa, may Allah be pleased with him, that the Prophet ﷺ said: «Verily, a righteous comrade and a bad (comrade) are like a seller of musk and (a man) blowing bellows. As for the seller of musk, he (may) either give you (something of his goods), or you will buy something from him, or you will feel the aroma (coming from) him. As for the puffing fur, it will either burn through your clothes, or you will smell (coming from) a stench from it.» №5534

200) It is reported that Anas, may Allah be pleased with him, said: «The Prophet ﷺ forbade men to use saffron». №5846

201) It is reported that Abu Hurayrah, may Allah be pleased with him, said: «Once I was with the Messenger of Allah ﷺ in one of the markets of Medina. We walked together and he said, «Where is that rascal?» He repeated this three times and added: «Call al-Hasan ibn 'Ali.» Al-Hasan ibn 'Ali came with a necklace of beads around his neck. The Prophet ﷺ extended his arms and al-Hasan also extended his arms and they embraced. The Prophet ﷺ said: «O Allah, verily, I love him, love him and love those who love him.» Abu Hurayrah, may Allah be pleased with him, said: «After these words of the Messenger of Allah ﷺ, I loved no one more than al-Hasan ibn 'Ali». №5884

202) It is reported that Ibn 'Abbas, may Allah be pleased with them both, said: «The Prophet ﷺ cursed men who resemble women and women who resemble men». №5885

203) It is narrated from the words of Abu Hurairah, may Allah be pleased with him, that (The Prophet ﷺ said): «Five (things) are natural / fitra / or: Five (things)

are natural ... /: circumcision, shaving off pubic hair, plucking armpit hair, cutting nails and trimming moustaches». №5889

204) Nafi' narrated from the words of Ibn 'Umar, may Allah be pleased with them both, that the Prophet ﷺ said: «Be different from the polytheists: let go of beards and trim moustaches.» And every time Ibn 'Umar performed Hajj or 'Umrah, he took his beard into a fist and what stood out (for a fist), he cut off. №5892

205) It is reported that Ibn 'Umar (may Allah be pleased with them both) said: «I heard the Messenger of Allah ﷺ forbade qaza'.» The transmitter (of this hadith) said: «Kaza' is leaving strands of hair in different places while shaving a child's head,» while pointing his hand to his forehead and both sides of the head. №5920

206) It is reported from the words of Anas, may Allah be pleased with him, that the Prophet ﷺ did not reject incense (which people gave him). №5929

207) It is reported from the words of 'Abdullah bin 'Amr, may Allah be pleased with them both, that (once) one person asked the Prophet ﷺ: «Which (manifestation) of Islam is the best?» - (to which the Messenger of Allah ﷺ) replied: «(The best thing is) that you treat (people) and greet those whom you know and whom you do not know». №6236

208) It is reported from the words of Ibn 'Abbas, may Allah be pleased with both of them, that the Messenger of Allah ﷺ said: «Many people are deprived of two favours: health and free time». №6412

209) It is reported that 'Abdullah (ibn Mas'ud), may Allah be pleased with him, said: «(Once) the Prophet ﷺ drew a rectangle, (then) he drew a line in the middle of (its) that goes beyond its (limits, then) he drew (several) small lines (reaching) to the (line) that was in the middle, after which he said: «This is a man; what surrounds him (or: what surrounded him) is his term; what goes beyond (the rectangle) is its hopes, and

these little lines are the vicissitudes of fate (which befall it), and if one passes it, it will grab the other with
its teeth, but if it passes it (the second), it will grab it
with its teeth (first)». №6417

210) It was narrated from the words of Abu Hurayrah, may
Allah be pleased with him, that the Prophet ﷺ said:
«Allah accepts the excuses of a person, postponing his
term until he lives to sixty years». №6419

211) Narrated Ibn Aban, may Allah be pleased with him:
«I brought water to Uthman ibn 'Affan to perform ablution when he was sitting in his place. He correctly
performed ablution and said: «I saw the Prophet ﷺ
perform ablution in this place, and he performed it
correctly and said:« Who will perform ablution, as I
did this time (it was done), and then go to a mosque
and perform a two-rak'at prayer, and then sit down,
his past sins will be forgiven. And the Prophet ﷺ said
(further added): «Do not delude yourself (thinking
that your sins will be forgiven because of your prayer,
thereby neglecting sins)». №6433

212) It is reported that Abdullah (bin Mas'ud), may Allah be pleased with him, said: «(Once) the Prophet ﷺ
asked (people):« Which of you loves the wealth of his
heir more than his (own) wealth? They said: «O Messenger of Allah, there is no one among us who does
not love his (own) wealth more.» (Then) he said: «But,
verily, the wealth (of each) is what he (spent), and what
he put aside is the wealth of his heir!» №6442

213) It was narrated from the words of Abu Hurairah, may
Allah be pleased with him, that the Prophet ﷺ said: «It
is not the abundance of property that brings wealth,
(true) wealth is the wealth of the soul». №6446

214) It is reported that Sa'd [ibn Abu Waqqas], may Allah be
pleased with him, said: «Indeed, I was the first among
the Arabs who shot an arrow in the path of Allah.
And it happened to us to make a military campaign
when we had no other food than acacia leaves and this
as-samur, from which our stools resembled sheep's

droppings, not mixing (with each other) [meaning that the stools were hard and dry]. And then [people from the tribe] Bani Asad began to blame me for [my] Islam [i.e. they complained to 'Umar about me, expressing several claims against me]. [If they are right], then I was lost, and all my efforts [at that difficult time] were in vain». №6453

215) It is reported from the words of Ibn Abbas that the Messenger of Allah ﷺ said: «Seventy thousand people from among the members of my community will enter paradise without calculation: these are those who do not ask others to speak them, do not believe in bad omens, judging by the flight of birds and trust in their Lord». №6472

216) It was narrated from Sahl bin Sa'd (may Allah be pleased with him) that the Messenger of Allah ﷺ said: «Whoever guarantees me for what is between his jaws and between his legs, I will guarantee (that he will enter into) paradise». №6474

217) Ibn 'Abbas, may Allah be pleased with both of them, reported that the Prophet ﷺ, transmitting the words of his Almighty and Great Lord, said: «Verily, Allah wrote down good and bad deeds, after which he explained it: «For the one who decides to do a good deed but does not do it, Allah will record with Himself (the completion of) a whole good deed; if (a person) decides (to do a good deed) and does it, Allah will record for him (commission) from ten to seven hundred and many more good deeds; after the one who decides to commit an evil deed, but does not commit it, Allah will record (completion) of a whole good deed, and if he decides (to commit an evil deed) and commits it, Allah will record (behind him) one bad dead». №6491

218) It is reported that Anas (may Allah be pleased with him) said: «Indeed, you commit such deeds that are thinner than a hair in your eyes, while during the life of the Prophet ﷺ we considered them to be among the deadly sins / mubikat /.» Abu 'Abdullah (Imam Al-

Bukhari) said: «Under them (i.e. mortal sins) is meant everything that leads to death / al-muhlikat /». №6492

219) It is reported that Ibn 'Umar, may Allah be pleased with them both, said: «I heard the Messenger of Allah 🕮 say: «Indeed, people are like a hundred camels, of which there is hardly one fit for riding». №6498

220) It is reported that Abu Qatada ibn Rib'i al-Ansari said that (once) a funeral stretcher was carried past the Messenger of Allah 🕮, and he said: «(One) will rest, and (others) will rest from the other.» (People began to) ask: «O Messenger of Allah, what does it mean to «rest» and what does it mean to «rest from another»? (In response to this, the Prophet 🕮) said: «The believing slave will rest from the suffering and torment of this world (going) to the mercy of Allah, as for the wicked slave, then (other) slaves, and cities, and trees, and animals». №6512

221) Abu Hurairah (may Allah be pleased with him) said: «Once upon a time two people, one of whom was a Muslim and the other a Jew, quarrelled with each other. The Muslim said: «I swear by Him Who chose Muhammad from all the worlds!» And the Jew said: «I swear by Him Who chose Musa among all the worlds!» At that moment, the Muslim became angry and hit the Jew in the face, and then the Jew went to the Messenger of Allah 🕮 and told him about what happened between him and the Muslim. After which the Prophet 🕮 said: «Do not give preference to me over Musa, for, truly, on the Day of Resurrection, people will be amazed, and I will come to my senses first and see Musa (who will) hold on to the edge of the Throne. And I don't know if Musa will be smitten like others and will come to his senses before me, or if he will be among those for whom Allah will make an exception.». №6517

222) It is reported from the words of 'Aisha, may Allah be pleased with her, that (once) the Messenger of Allah 🕮 said: «People will be gathered barefoot, naked and

uncircumcised.» 'Aisha said: «I asked: «O Messenger of Allah, will men and women begin to look at each other?» - (to which the Prophet ﷺ) said: «It will be too hard for them to think about it!» №6527

223) Abu Hurairah reported that the Prophet ﷺ said: «The first person to be called on the Day of Resurrection will be Adam. He will be shown his offspring, who will be told: «This is your father Adam» (Adam) will answer: «Here I am in front of You and ready to serve You (O Lord)!» (Allah) will say (to him): «Bring out those of your offspring who are destined to be in Gehenna.» (Adam) will ask, «O Lord, how many should I bring out?» (The Lord) will answer: «Get out of every hundred ninety-nine.» (People) asked (the Prophet ﷺ): «O Messenger of Allah, if ninety-nine is taken from every hundred, then what will be left of us?» He replied: «Indeed, my community among the rest of the nations is like a white hair on the (skin) of a black bull.». №6529

224) It was told to us by Sa'id ibn Abu Maryam, who said: It was told to us: Muhammad ibn Mutarrif, who said: It was told to us: Abu Hazim, from Sahl ibn Saada, said: The Prophet ﷺ said: «Indeed, I will be the first of you (to be) at the reservoir and whoever passes by me drinks from it, and whoever drinks from it will never feel thirsty after that. People whom I know will certainly come to me, and they know me, and then they will separate me from them.». №6583

225) Abu Hazim said: An-Numan ibn Abu Ayayash heard me, and said: thus did you hear from Sahl? I said yes. Then he (An-Numan) said: I testify that I heard Abu Sa'id al-Khudri add to him: «And I will say they are truly from us.» And it will be said: «You do not know what they changed after you.» Then I will say: «Get out, get out those who changed after me.» Ibn Abbas, may Allah be pleased with him, said: «Sukhkan» means to move away. It is said: (ﻗَﻴِﺤَﺲ) (far) [al-Hajj 31]: further, «sahakahu» and «ashakahu»-distant. №6584

226) It is narrated from the words of Abu Hurayrah, may Allah be pleased with him, that the Prophet ﷺ said: «(Once) I saw in a dream (that they brought to me) a crowd (of people), when I recognized them, some kind of man and said, «Hurry up!» I asked: «Where?» He said: «By Allah, into the fire!» I asked, «What's the matter with them?» He said: «After your (death) they apostatized (from your religion)!» And then (they brought to me) another crowd (of people), when I recognized them, some person stood between them and me and said: «Hurry!» I asked: «Where?» He said: «By Allah, into the fire!» I asked, «What's the matter with them?» He said: «After your (death) they apostatized (from your religion)!» - and I did not see any of them escape, except those of them that were like camels grazing without supervision». №6587

227) Sa'id ibn Abi Maryam told us, from Nafi'a ibn 'Umar, he said: Ibn Abi Muleyka told us, from Asma bint Abi Bakr, may Allah be pleased with her, she said: «The Prophet ﷺ said:» Being by the pool (Howd), I will see which one of you will come to me. But, some people will be turned away from me. Then I will say: «O Lord, they are mine and from my community», but it will be said: «Did you not feel what they did after you. I swear by Allah, they did not stop turning back. And on this, Ibn Abu Muleyka said: «O Allah, we ask You for protection from turning back or from being tested in our faith.» (you backed away from them) [Al-Mu'minun: 66]: «turned back». №6593

228) It is reported that 'Abdullah (bin Mas'ud), may Allah be pleased with him, said: «The truthful and trustworthy Messenger of Allah ﷺ said to us:» Verily, each of you is formed in the womb of his mother for forty days in the form of a drop of semen, then he stays (there) for the same amount in the form of a clot of blood and the same amount in the form of a piece of flesh, and then angel is sent to him, who blows the spirit into him. And he receives a command to write down four things: the lot (of a person), his (life), his deeds, and

also whether he will be happy or unfortunate. And I swear by Allah, besides Whom there is no true god, indeed, any of you can do the deeds of the inhabitants of paradise until he is only one cubit from paradise, after which (it will come true) written to his family, and he will begin to do deeds of the inhabitants of the fire, and enter (the fire). And, verily, any of you can do the deeds of the inhabitants of the fire until he is only one cubit from the fire, after which (it will come true) what is written in his family, and he will begin to do the deeds of the inhabitants of paradise and fall into (paradise)». №6594

229) Anas ibn Malik, may Allah be pleased with him, reported that the Prophet ﷺ said: «Allah puts an angel in the womb who says: «O Lord, a drop! Oh Lord, blood clot! O Lord, piece of flesh!» When Allah wishes to complete his creation, (the angel) says: «O Lord, a boy or a girl? Unhappy or happy? What are its destiny and term? And that's how it's all written in his mother's womb». №6595

230) Abu Hurairah (may Allah be pleased with him) narrates that the Messenger of Allah ﷺ said: «Every person is born in his natural state/fitra/, and only then his parents make him a Jew or a Christian, just like you help animals in childbirth. Have you seen among them an animal (born) with a severed limb? And only then do you do something with them, as a result of which they have injuries. The people asked: «O Messenger of Allah, what do you say about the one who died in childhood?» He said: «Allah knows what they would do». №6599

231) It is reported that Hudhaifah, may Allah be pleased with him, said: «Once the Prophet ﷺ turned to us with a sermon and told us about everything that will happen until the Day of Judgment. Whoever remembered what he said, he remembered, and whoever forgot, he forgot. And, seeing something of what he predicted, which I forgot (over time), I remember the prediction itself, just as a person remembers a familiar person

whom he met after a long separation.». №6604

232) Abu Hurayrah (may Allah be pleased with him) narrates that the Prophet ﷺ said: «Turn to Allah for protection from the difficulties of trial, from an extremely
difficult situation, bad predestination and malevolence
of enemies». №6616

233) It is reported that Harisa ibn Wahb, may Allah be
pleased with him, said: «I heard (once) the Prophet
ﷺ say:« Shall I inform you about the inhabitants of
Paradise? (It is) every weak and despised, (however)
when he swears (in anything), Allah will surely fulfil
his oath. (Should I not inform you) about those who
will be in the fire? (This is) every greedy /javvaz/, rude
/'utull/ and proud». №6657

234) It is reported that ('Abdullah) ibn 'Abbas, may Allah
be pleased with him and his father, said: «Once, a man
said to the Prophet ﷺ: «I circumambulated the Kaaba
/ tawaf / before I threw the stones.» (The Prophet ﷺ)
replied: «No problem.» Another said, «I shaved my
head before I slaughtered the sacrificial animal.» (The
Prophet ﷺ) replied: «No problem.» Another said, «I
slaughtered the sacrificial animal before I threw the
stones.» (The Prophet ﷺ) replied: «No problem».
№6666

235) Abu Hurairah, may Allah be pleased with him, reported that the Prophet ﷺ said: «Whoever has eaten out
of forgetfulness during fasting, let him finish his fast,
for, verily, it was Allah who fed and watered him».
№6669

236) It is reported from the words of 'Umar bin al-Khattab,
may Allah be pleased with him, that during the life of
the Prophet ﷺ there was one person, whose name was
'Abdullah, nicknamed the Donkey. He made the Messenger of Allah ﷺ laugh, and as for the Prophet ﷺ, he
happened to be ordered to beat him for drinking wine.
Once he was brought to the Prophet ﷺ, they began to
beat him on his orders, and one man exclaimed: «O
Allah, curse him! How often he was brought!» - (to

which) the Prophet ﷺ said: «Do not curse him, for, by Allah, I know that he loves Allah and His Messenger!» №6780

237) Narrated Ibn Abbas: I taught (the Quran) some Muhajirs (immigrants), among whom was Abdur Rahman bin Auf. When I was at his house in Mina, and he was with Umar ibn al-Khattab during the last Hajj of Umar, Abdur-Rahman approached me and said: «If you saw a man who came today to the leader of the believers (Umar), saying: «O leader of the faithful! What do you think of someone who says: «If Umar dies, I will swear allegiance to such and such a person, as I swear by Allah, the swearing of allegiance to Abu Bakr was nothing but an instantaneous sudden action that was subsequently confirmed. Umar became angry and then said: «By the will of Allah, tonight I will stand before the people and warn them against those people who want to deprive others of their rights (a matter of government). Abdur-Rahman said: «I said: «O leader of the believers! Do not do this, for the time of the Hajj gathers the rabble and the ruins, and it is they who will gather around you when you get up to address the people. And I'm afraid that you will stand up and say something and some people will circulate your statement and may not say what you said and may not understand its meaning and may misinterpret it, so you should wait, until you get to Medina, for that is the place of emigration and the place of the Traditions of the Prophet, and there you can get in touch with the scholars and nobles and present your ideas to them with confidence, and learned people will understand your statement and put it in its place.» Umar then said, «By Allah! If it is the will of Allah, I will do this in the first speech that I will make before the people in Medina.» Ibn Abbas added: «We reached Medina towards the end of the month of Dhul-Hijjah and when it was Friday, we quickly set off (to the mosque) as soon as the sun went down and I saw Said bin Zayd bin Amr bin Nufail sitting in the corner of the pulpit and I also sat next to him so that my knee touched his

knee, and soon Umar ibn al-Khattab came out, and when I saw that he was coming towards us, I said to Said ibn Zayd ibn Amr ibn Nufail: «Today Umar will say this, which he has never said since. he was elected caliph. Sa'eed rejected my statement with astonishment and said, «What do you think Umar will say that is similar to something he has never said before?» In the meantime, Umar sat on the pulpit and when the callers to prayer had finished their call, Umar stood up and, glorifying and praising Allah as He deserved, said, «Now I am going to tell you something. which (Allah) wrote for me to say. I don't know; perhaps it portends my death, so that whoever understands and remembers this must tell others, wherever his journey may lead him; Allah sent Muhammad with the Truth and sent down the Holy Book to him and among what Allah sent down was the Verse of Rajam (stoning a married person (male and female) who commits illegal sexual intercourse and we recited this Verse and I understood and memorized it The Messenger of Allah (ﷺ) applied the punishment of stoning and we are after it. I am afraid that after a long time someone will say: «By Allah, we do not find the verse of Rajam in the Book of Allah», and thus they will go astray with way, leaving the obligation which Allah has sent down, the required evidence is available or there is a conception or confession.And then we read among the verses in the Book of Allah: «O people! the part that you call the descendant of someone other than your real father.» Then The Messenger of Allah (ﷺ) said: «Do not praise me excessively, as they praised Jesus, the son of Mary, but call me the slave of Allah and His apostle.» (O people!) I was informed that one of you says: «By Allah if Umar dies, I will give a damn your allegiance to such and such a person.» It is given suddenly and successfully. No doubt it was so, but Allah saved (people) from his evil, and there is no one among you who has the qualities of Abu Bakr. Remember that whoever gives an oath of allegiance to any of you without consulting other Muslims must not support either that person or the person to whom the oath of allegiance was given, otherwise, they will both be killed. And, no doubt, after the death of the Prophet (ﷺ) we were informed that the Ansar did not agree with us and gathered in the barn of the Bani Sada. Ali, Zubair and all who were with them came out against us, and the settlers gathered together with Abu Bakr. №6830

238) It is narrated from the words of Ibn 'Abbas, may Allah be pleased with them both, that the Prophet ﷺ said: «The most hated people for Allah are three: a deviant who is in the sanctuary/haram/, a person striving to preserve the customs of jahiliyyah in Islam, and one who seeks (a way) to shed someone's blood without having the right to do so». №6882

239) Abu Hurayrah (may Allah be pleased with him) reported: «I heard the Messenger of Allah ﷺ say: «If someone looks (at what is being done) in your house without your permission, and you (for this) throw a stone at him and gouge out his eye, there will be no sin on you». №6888

240) It was narrated from 'Abdullah ibn 'Amr, may Allah be pleased with him, that the Prophet ﷺ said: «Whoever killed an unbeliever who concluded a peace treaty with Muslims will not even feel the fragrance of Paradise. And indeed, its fragrance spreads for a distance of forty years». №6914

241) It is reported that Ibn Mas'ud (may Allah be pleased with him) said: «A man asked: «O Messenger of Allah, will we be punished for what we did during the time of Jahiliyyah?» (The Prophet ﷺ) said: «The one who does good deeds in Islam will not be asked for what he did during the time of the Jahiliyyah, but the one who does bad deeds in Islam will be asked for both the first and the last». №6921

242) Anas ibn Malik, may Allah be pleased with him, narrated that the Messenger of Allah ﷺ said: «The good dream of a righteous person is one of the forty-six parts of the prophecy». №6983

243) It is narrated from the words of Abu Sa'eed al-Khudri, may Allah be pleased with him, that he heard the Prophet ﷺ say: «If any of you see such dreams that he likes, (it means that) they) only from Allah, so let him praise Allah for (such dreams) and tell them (to others), but if he sees something else that he does not like, then this is only from the shaitan, let him turn for protection to Allah from the evil of this and does not tell anyone (such dreams), and then it will not harm him». №6985

244) Abu Hurayrah (may Allah be pleased with him) said: «I heard the Prophet ﷺ say: «He who sees me in a dream will see me in reality, and the devil cannot (can) take my form.» Abu 'Abdullah (Al-Bukhari) said: «(Muhammad) ibn Sirin said:« If he sees him in his (true) image and appearance». №6993

245) Hasan (al-Basri) said: - In the night of unrest, I went out with my weapons, and (after a while) I met Abu Bakra. He asked (me), «Where are you (going)?» I said: «I want to help the son of the uncle of the Messenger of Allah ﷺ (i.e. ‹Ali).» He said: «The Messenger of Allah ﷺ said:» If two Muslims cross swords, then they will both be from among the inhabitants of the Fire. (He) was asked: «Everything is clear with the murderer, but why is the murdered one too?» He said: «He also wanted to kill his comrade!». №7083

246) Abu Wail (Shaqiq ibn Salamah) said: Once Usama (ibn Zayd) was asked: «Why don't you talk to this (i.e. 'Uthman ibn 'Affan)?» (In response to them, Osama) said: «I have already spoken to him (in private), but I do not want to be the first to open the door (to evil and confusion). And if a person becomes a ruler over two people, then I am not the one who says to him: «You are the best (of people)» after I heard the words of the Messenger of Allah ﷺ who said: «(On the Day of Resurrection) they will bring a person and throw him into the fire, where he will turn like a donkey turning the millstones of a mill. And the inhabitants of the Fire will gather around him, and they will say: «O so-and-

so! Have you not commanded what is right and forbid what is wrong?» (To this) he will say: «Indeed, I encouraged to do what was good, but I did not do it, and I withheld from what was blamed, but I did it!». №7098

247) Abu Wail (Shaqiq ibn Salama) said: «' Ammar stood on the minbar of Kufa, mentioned 'Aisha and her journey (to Basra) and said: «Verily, she is the wife of your Prophet ﷺ in this world and in the other world, however, she - your test». №7101

248) Shaqiq ibn Salamah said: «Once I was sitting with Abu Mas'ud, Abu Musa and 'Ammar, and Abu Mas'ud said: «If I wanted, I would say something about any of your associates, except you. Ever since you began to accompany the Prophet ﷺ, I have not seen anything from you so reprehensible to me than your haste in this matter! 'Ammar replied: «O Abu Mas'ud! Ever since you began to accompany the Prophet ﷺ, I have not seen from you and your friend anything so reprehensible for me than your non-participation in this matter! Abu Mas'ud was a rich man, and said: «O servant, give me two robes,» - and then he gave one to Abu Musa, and the other to 'Ammar, and said: «Go in these robes to Friday prayer». №7107

249) Sufyan (ibn 'Wayna) said: - I met Abu Musa in Kufa Israel and he told us that he came to ('Abdullah) ibn Shubruma and said (to him): «Take me to 'Isa so that I turn to him with the exhortation,» and Ibn Shubruma seemed to fear for Israel and did not do what he asked. (Israel) said: «Hasan (al-Basri) told us the following:» When al-Hasan ibn 'Ali, may Allah be pleased with him and his father, went to Mu'awiyah with an army, 'Amr ibn al-'As said Mu'awiya: «I see a detachment that will not retreat (from the battlefield) until the opposing side retreats (from the battlefield).» Mu'awiya replied: «And who will then take care of the children of Muslims?» He replied: «I am.» At this time, 'Abdullah ibn 'Amir and 'Abdurrahman ibn Samur said (to al-Hasan): «We will meet with Mu'awiya and tell him about the truce.» Hasan (al-Basri) said: «I heard

Abu Bakr, may Allah be pleased with him, say: «At the time when the Prophet ﷺ was preaching, al-Hasan (ibn 'Ali) came, and the Prophet ﷺ said: «This is my son - master, and perhaps through him Allah will reconcile the two groups of Muslims». №7109

250) Hudhayfa ibn al-Yaman, may Allah be pleased with him, said: «Verily, in the time of the Prophet ﷺ there was hypocrisy, and today it is unbelief after faith». №7114

251) Narrated from 'Abdurrahman ibn Samurah, may Allah be pleased with him: «The Prophet ﷺ said to me:» O 'Abdurrahman ibn Samurah, do not seek power, for if it is granted to you at your request, then you will be left in it to yourself, and if it is given to you without asking you, then you will be helped in (related to) it. And if you swear something, but then you see that something else is better (what you swore to do), then expiate (breaking) your oath and do what is better». №7146

252) It is reported that Hasan al-Basri said: - Once we came to visit Ma'kil ibn Yasar, may Allah be pleased with him, and (at that moment) 'Ubaydullah came to us, and then Ma'kil said to him: «I will tell you hadith that I heard from the Messenger of Allah ﷺ that he said: «Allah will surely make Paradise forbidden for any ruler who rules over Muslims and dies deceiving them». №7151

253) It is reported that Abu Mas'ud al-Ansari, may Allah be pleased with him, said: «Once a man came to the Messenger of Allah ﷺ and said: «O Messenger of Allah, I swear by Allah, I miss the (collective) morning prayer only because that so-and-so spends it with us for too long.» (Abu Mas'ud, may Allah be pleased with him, said): «And I never saw the Prophet ﷺ exhorting people, was angrier than on that day. He said: «O people! Indeed, (some of you) repel (others from prayers)! Let the one who spends it with people make it easier, because among them (may) be old, weak and

those who have an urgent business!». №7159

254) ('Abdullah) ibn 'Umar, may Allah be pleased with
him and his father, said: «Salim, the freedman of Abu
Khuzayfa, led the prayer of the first Muhajirs and
Companions of the Prophet ﷺ in the mosque of Quba,
and among them were Abu Bakr, 'Umar, Abu Salama,
Zeid and 'Amir ibn Rabi'a». №7175

255) It is reported that (once) people said ('Abdullah) ibn
'Umar, may Allah be pleased with him and his father:
«Indeed, when we enter our rulers, we say to them not
what we say when we leave them», - (to which) Ibn
'Umar, may Allah be pleased with him and his father,
said: «We considered such hypocrisy!» №7178

256) 'Abdullah (ibn Mas'ud), may Allah be pleased with
him, narrates that the Prophet ﷺ said: «(Whoever)
takes an obligatory oath (by Allah) to thus appropriate
property, and he uttered it falsely, he will meet Allah angry with him.» Then Allah sent down: «Verily,
for those who sell their covenant with Allah and their
oaths cheaply, there is no share in the Hereafter. Allah
will not speak to them, will not look at them on the
Day of Resurrection and will not purify them. A painful suffering is prepared for them »(Surah Ali 'Imran,
verse 77). №7183

257) 'Abdullah ibn 'Umar, may Allah be pleased with him
and his father, said: «(At one time) the Prophet ﷺ sent
Khalid ibn al-Walid on a campaign against (the tribe
of) Bani Jazim, (and Khalid called them to Islam),
however, they did not say: «We have already accepted
Islam / Aslam-na /», but began to say: «We have already retreated! We've already retreated! /Saba-on/».
Then Khalid began to kill (some of these people), and
he captured someone and gave each of us captives,
(and one day) he ordered each of us to kill his captives,
and then I said (to him): «By Allah, I will not kill my
prisoner, just as none of my comrades will do this!»
And we told the Prophet ﷺabout this and said twice:
«O Allah, verily, I am not involved in what Khalid ibn

al-Walid did!». №7189

258) 'Ubadah ibn as-Samit, may Allah be pleased with him, said: «We swore an oath to the Messenger of Allah ﷺ that we will listen and obey him in prosperous and difficult times, and we will not try to deprive those to whom it will belong according to right, and that we will stand or speak for the truth, wherever we may be, not fearing the rebuke of the rebuke for the sake of Allah». №7199

259) It is reported that Jabir bin Samurah, may Allah be pleased with him, said: - I heard the Prophet ﷺ say: «There will be twelve rulers ...», after which he uttered some word that I did not hear, and my father said: «He said: «... and they will all be from (the tribe) Quraish». №7222

260) It is reported that Abu Hurairah said: «The Messenger of Allah ﷺ said: «By the One in Whose hand is my soul, (it happened that) I wanted to order to collect firewood, then to order to call (people) to prayer, then to order someone to be imam, and then appear to those people (who did not come to prayer) and burn their houses to the ground! I swear by Him in Whose hand is my soul, if any of them knew that he would receive here a bone with a piece of fatty meat, or a pair of good sheep's hooves, he would certainly come to the evening prayer!» №7224

261) It is narrated from the words of Anas ibn Malik, may Allah be pleased with him, that he said: «If I had not heard the Prophet ﷺwho said:« (In no case) wish yourself death, I would certainly wish it». №7233

262) It is reported that Abu Hurairah, may Allah be pleased with him, said: - When the Messenger of Allah ﷺ died, Abu Bakr became the caliph. Some of the Arabs returned to disbelief. Then 'Umar ibn al-Khattab said to Abu Bakr (may Allah be pleased with them both): «How can you fight with these people? Indeed, the Messenger of Allah ﷺ said: «I was ordered to fight with these people until they say: 'There is no deity

worthy of worship except Allah. And the property and life of the one who uttered these words become inviolable, and cannot be taken away except by the law [Sharia], and only Allah can demand an account from him. Abu Bakr, may Allah be pleased with him, said: «By Allah, I will certainly fight with those who separate prayer from zakat, because taking zakat from the property is the right [Sharia]! And by Allah, if they refuse to give me at least the fetters of the camel that they gave to the Messenger of Allah ﷺ I will fight them because of this! Then 'Umar (may Allah be pleased with him) said: «By Allah, it was Allah Himself who inspired Abu Bakr with the idea of fighting, and I realized that this was the right decision.» Ibn Bukeir and Abdullah narrate from Leys: «... a kid». And this is a more reliable version. №7285

263) It is reported that 'Abdullah Ibn 'Abbas, may Allah be pleased with him and his father, said: - (At one time) 'Uyayna ibn Hisn ibn Khuzayfa ibn Badr came (to Medina) and stayed with his nephew al-Hurr ibn Qays ibn Hisn, who was among those who were brought closer to him by 'Umar, may Allah be pleased with him. Readers of the Quran took part in the meetings of 'Umar. They were his advisors, whether they were old or young. 'Uyaina said to his nephew: «O son of my brother, you are in a high position under this ruler, so ask him to accept me.» He replied, «I will ask him for permission for you.» Ibn 'Abbas said: «Al-Hurr asked permission for 'Uyayn. And when 'Uyayna entered 'Umar, he said: «O Ibn al-Khattab, I swear by Allah, you do not give us much and rule us unjustly!» (Hearing these words,) 'Umar, may Allah be pleased with him, became so angry that he even wanted to punish him, but Al-Hurr said to him: «O Commander of the Faithful, verily, Allah Almighty said to His prophet:» Show condescension, lead do what is right, and turn away from the ignorant»—as far as this is concerned, he is precisely among the ignorant.» And by Allah after al-Hurr recited this verse, 'Umar did not do anything that would be contrary to its meaning, since he

steadfastly adhered to (the provisions of) the Book of Allah». №7286

264) It was narrated from Abu Sa'id al-Khudriy, may Allah be pleased with him, that the Prophet ﷺ said: «You will certainly follow the customs / Sunan / of those who were before you, span by span and cubit by cubit. And even if they climb into the hole of the monitor lizard, then you will follow them.» We asked: «O Messenger of Allah, are they Jews and Christians?» The Prophet ﷺ replied, «Who else?» №7320

265) It is reported that 'Ubaydullah ibn 'Abdullah said: - Ibn 'Abbas narrated to me, may Allah be pleased with him and his father, saying: «I taught the Quran 'Abdur-Rahman ibn 'Awf, and now during the last Hajj, which I made ' Umar, 'Abdur-Rahman ibn 'Auf, being in Mina, said: «Oh, if you saw the commander of the faithful today! A man came to him and said: «Indeed, such and such says: If the ruler of the faithful died, then we would swear allegiance to such and such.» 'Umar said: «I will certainly go out (to the people) tonight and will warn against this group who want to take (power) of the Muslims.» 'Abdur-Rahman ibn 'Awf said: «Don't do that. Indeed, the season (Hajj) gathers ordinary people, and there are more of them than those who are with you, and I am afraid (that if you say something today), they will misunderstand them and spread these words to everyone. ends. Wait until you arrive in Medina - the abode of Hijra and Sunnah, you will stay with the companions of the Messenger of Allah ﷺ from among the Muhajirs and Ansar, and they will keep what you said and understand your words as they should be understood. Then 'Umar said: «By Allah, I will certainly pronounce these words first of all in Medina.» Ibn 'Abbas said: «When we arrived in Medina, 'Umar said: «Indeed, Allah sent Muhammad ﷺ to the people with the truth and sent down the Book to him, and among what He sent down to him was the verse about stoning». №7223

266) It is reported that once 'Aisha, may Allah be pleased

with her and her father, said to 'Abdullah ibn al-Zubayr, may Allah be pleased with him and his father: «Bury me next to my companions (i.e. the wives of the Prophet ﷺ), and do not bury me at home next to the Prophet ﷺ. Indeed, I do not want to be praised (because of this)». №7327

267) It is reported that Jarir ibn 'Abdullah (may Allah be pleased with them both) said: «The Messenger of Allah ﷺ said:« Allah will not have mercy on the one who does not show mercy to people». №7376

268) Shu'ba reported that Mu'awiya ibn Qurra narrated from 'Abdullah ibn Mughaffal that he said: «I saw the Messenger of Allah ﷺon the day of the conquest of Mecca, sitting on his camel, reciting the surah al-Fath» or it's part in a singsong voice.» However, then Mu'awiyah (ibn Qurra) recited (the Quran) in the same way as Ibn Mughaffal recited it, saying: «If (I did not fear) that people would gather (around me), then I would recite (the Quran) in a chant-like that, like Ibn Mughaffal, recited (it) in a singsong voice, imitating the Prophet ﷺ. I (Shu'ba) asked Mu'awiya: «How did he chant it?» He said «Aah» three times (imitating the tone of his voice). №7540

«Sahih» Muslim

Muslim ibn al-Hajjaj was born in 817 according to the Christian calendar in Nishapur and died in 874 in the same place. During his travels in Iraq, the Arabian Peninsula, Syria and Egypt, Muslims collected about 300,000 hadiths. Sahih Muslim is divided into 43 books containing a total of 7190 hadiths, of which 2200 hadiths without repetition. Imam Muslims regularly attended the classes of al-Bukhari and maintained close contact with him. Interestingly, Muslim ibn al-Hajjaj was able to meet with Imam Bukhari in his hometown of Nishapur. Imam Muslim did not provide a title for his book Sahih so there was controversy regarding this and several of them are mentioned:

– «al-Jami'» (arab. الجامع - he was mentioned by al-Fairuzabadi, Ibn Hajar al-'Asqalani, Haji Khalifa, al-Kanuji, etc.);

– «al-Musnad» or «al-Musnad as-Sahih» (arab. المسند وأ المسند الصحيح – this is how Imam Muslim himself called it, pointing it out of the book [in other places], saying: «I did not put it in this book of mine» Musnad «nothing but with an argument», «If the hadith experts wrote hadiths for two hundred years, then they would revolve around this» Musnad,» I compiled this «al-Musnad as-Sahih» from three hundred thousand heard hadiths»);

— «Al-Musads as-Sahih al-Mukhtasar M. Asan-Sunan b-nakly al-'adl 'an al-al-'adl' an al-Rasuli-Llyakhi ﷺ» (Arab. المسند الصحيح المختصر من السنن بنقل العدل عن العدل عن رسول الله - this is how the book of Ibn Khair al-Ishbili and at-Tajibi was called, but it is more preferable that this is still not a title, but a description of the book);

— «as-Sahih» or «Sahih Muslim» (arab. وأ صحيح مسلم صحيح - this name was mentioned by Ibn al-Asir, Ibn Halakan, al-Dhahabi, Ibn Kathir and others, and this is the most famous and common name).

269)   Abu Hurayrah reported that the Messenger of Allah ﷺ said: «In the last days, people will appear in my community who will tell you things that neither you nor your fathers heard before. Beware of them!» №6

270)   It is reported that Abu Hurairah, may Allah be pleased with him, said: «(Once) the Messenger of Allah ﷺ said: «Ask me!» And when they approached him to ask questions, suddenly a man came up to him, who sat at his knees and said: «O Messenger of Allah, what is Islam?» He replied: «(Islam is when) you do not worship anyone other than Allah, stand up prayer, pay zakat and fast in Ramadan.» (This man) said: «You told the truth.» (Then) he said: «O Messenger of Allah, what is iman?» (The Prophet ﷺ) said: «(The essence of iman is) that you believe in Allah, in His angels, in His Book, in meeting with Him and in His messengers, and that you believe in the Resurrection, and that you believe in predestination Total». (This man) said: «You told the truth.» (Then) he said: «O Messenger of Allah, what is ihsan?» He replied: «(The essence of ihsan is) that you fear Allah as if you see Him, and if you do not see Him, then (remembering that) He truly sees you.» He said, «You told the truth.» (The man again) asked: «O Messenger of Allah, when will this

Hour come?» He said: «The one who is asked about it knows no more than the questioner, but I will tell you about his symptoms. When you see that a woman will give birth to her mistress, this is one of his signs, and when you see that barefoot and naked, deaf and blind people will rule the earth, then this will be one of his signs, and when you see that shepherds , (who once pastured) sheep and goats, will boast to each other (the size and number of their) houses, then this will be one of his signs. (As for the knowledge of the time of its occurrence, it is one of) the five hidden (things), and which only Allah knows, »after which he ﷺ read the (next) verse: «Verily, (only) Allah knows (when this hour will come, and (only) He sends down rain, and (only) He knows what is (hidden) in the wombs. A man does not know what he will gain tomorrow, and a man does not know in what land he will die. Indeed, Allah is All-Knowing, All-Aware!» (Surah Luqman, verse 34). (Abu Hurairah) said: «Then this man left, and the Messenger of Allah ﷺ ordered:« Return this person to me. People began (searching) for him, but they did not find anyone, and then the Messenger of Allah ﷺ said: «It was Jibril who wanted to teach you since you do not ask». №99

271) It is narrated from the words of Malik ibn Anas that Abu Suhayl ibn Malik narrated from the words of his father that he heard Talha ibn 'Ubaydullah, may Allah be pleased with him, say: «(Once) to the Messenger of Allah ﷺ A man from Najd appeared with dishevelled hair. We heard his loud voice but did not understand what he was saying until he approached the Messenger of Allah and it turned out that he was asking about Islam. The Messenger of Allah ﷺ said: «(Compulsory are) five prayers during the day and night.» He asked: «Should I (pray) beyond that?» (The Prophet ﷺ) said: «No, unless you (yourself wish) to make an additional prayer.» (Then the Messenger of Allah ﷺ) said: «(It is obligatory to observe) fasting during the month of Ramadan.» He asked, «Should I (fast) beyond that?» (The Prophet ﷺ) said: «No, unless you (wish to fast)

additionally.» (Talha said): - And then the Messenger of Allah ﷺ told him (about the need) to pay zakat, and he asked: «Do I have to (pay anything) beyond this?» (The Prophet ﷺ) said: «No, unless you wish it.» (Talha said): - And after that, the man turned (and went to the exit) with the words: «By Allah, I will not add anything to this and I will not take anything away!», - As for the Messenger of Allah ﷺ, he said: «He will succeed if he speaks sincerely!» №100

272) It is reported that Ibn Shihab said: «Sa'id ibn al-Musayyab told me that Abu Hurayrah, may Allah be pleased with him, informed him that the Messenger of Allah ﷺ said:« I was ordered to fight with these people until then until they say: «There is no god worthy of worship except Allah / La ilaha illa-Allah /», - and whoever says La ilaha illa-Allah (thus) will protect his property and his life from me, unless (not does anything for which it will be possible to deprive him of his property or life) by right, and then (only) Allah (will be able to demand) an account from him». №125

273) It is reported that Abu Hurayrah, may Allah be pleased with him, said: «(Once, when) we, along with several people, among whom were Abu Bakr and 'Umar, may Allah be pleased with them both, were sitting around the Messenger of Allah ﷺ he stood up, (left) us and did not return for a long time. (After some time) we began to fear that (something would happen to him), we got worried and got up (from our seats). Feeling the anxiety first, I went in search of the Messenger of Allah ﷺ (and searched for him) until I came to the wall (garden), which belonged to the Ansar from the Bani an-Najjar clan. I went around (this wall) in search of a gate, but did not find it, but I found a stream that flowed from a well located outside (the garden) and disappeared behind its walls. Then I curled up into a ball like a fox, entered (and saw) the Messenger of Allah ﷺ who asked: «Abu Hurairah?» I said, «Yes, O Messenger of Allah.» He asked, «What happened?» I said, «You were among us, and then you left and did

not return for a long time. We began to fear that something might happen to you, and we were seized with
anxiety, and I was the first to worry. Then I came to
this garden and huddled like a fox, and (the rest follow) me. Then (the Prophet ﷺ) addressed (to me): «O
Abu Hurairah!», gave me his sandals and said: «Go
with these sandals of mine and rejoice with the news
of Paradise (anyone) whom you meet outside this garden and who will testify, that there is no god worthy of
worship except Allah, being convinced of this in the
heart. The first person I met was 'Umar, who asked:
«What are these sandals, O Abu Hurairah?» I replied:
«These are the sandals of the Messenger of Allah ﷺ
who sent me with them so that I would rejoice with the
news of Paradise (any person) whom I meet and who
will testify that there is no god (worthy of worship)
except Allah, being convinced of this by the heart ».
Then 'Umar slapped me on the chest with his hand
so that I sat down on the ground, and said: «Come
back, O Abu Hurairah!» Almost crying, I returned to
the Messenger of Allah ﷺ as for 'Umar, he came after
me. The Messenger of Allah ﷺ asked me: «What is
the matter with you, O Abu Hurairah?» I said: «I met
'Umar and told him what you sent me with, and he hit
me in the chest so that I sat on the ground and said:
«Come back!» The Messenger of Allah ﷺ said to him:
«O 'Umar, what prompted you to do this?» ('Umar)
said: «May my father and mother be a ransom for you,
O Messenger of Allah! Have you (indeed) sent Abu
Hurairah with your sandals so that he will rejoice with
the news of Paradise (any person) whom he meets
and who will testify that there is no god worthy of
worship except Allah, being convinced of this in his
heart? (The Prophet ﷺ) said: «Yes.» (Then 'Umar) exclaimed: «Do not (do this), for, verily, I am afraid that
people (only) will rely on this, so let them engage in
deeds (of worship)!» - and the Messenger of Allah ﷺ
said: «Let (do)». №147

274)   It is reported that Tariq ibn Shihab said: «Marwan
(ibn al-Hakam) was the first who began to read the

khutba before prayer on the day of the holiday. (When he began to read), a man approached him and said: «The (Festive) prayer should be performed before the khutba.» (Marwan) said: «Now they don't do that anymore.» (Hearing this), Abu Sa'id (al-Khudri may Allah be pleased with him) said: «As for this (man), he has fulfilled his duty, for I heard the Messenger of Allah ﷺ say: «Let one of you whoever sees (something) blamed will change it with his own hands. If he cannot (do) this, (let him change what is condemned) with his tongue, and if he cannot (even this), then with his heart, which will be the weakest (manifestation) of faith». №177

275) It is narrated from the words of 'Abdullah ibn Mas'ud (may Allah be pleased with him) that the Messenger of Allah ﷺ said: «Whatever Prophet Allah sent before me to this or that people, he always had apostles and companions from his people who followed his sunnah and those who carried out his orders, and they were replaced by those who said what they did not do and did what they (were) not ordered to do. He who wrestles with such with his hand is a believer, and he who wrestles with them with his tongue is a believer, and he who wrestles with them with his heart is a believer, and behind this, there is no faith and the size of a mustard seed!» Abu Rafi' said: «I told (this hadith) to 'Abdullah ibn 'Umar, but he did not accept it from me. Arriving Ibn Mas'ud stopped in Qana and 'Abdullah ibn 'Umar took me to him to visit him and I went with him. When we sat down, I asked Ibn Mas'ud about this hadith and he told it to me as I told it to Ibn 'Umar». №179

276) It is reported that Abu Hurairah (may Allah be pleased with him) said: «The Messenger of Allah ﷺ said:« You will not enter Paradise until you believe, and you will not believe until you begin to love each other, so do not indicate whether me to you what will lead you to mutual love if you do this? Spread greetings with the world/salaam / among yourselves!» №194

277) Narrated from the words of Tamim ad-Dari (may Allah be pleased with him) that the Prophet ﷺ said: «Religion is a manifestation of sincerity.» We asked: «Concerning whom?» He said: «(Towards) Allah, and to His Book, and His Messenger, and to the leaders of Muslims and all Muslims in general». №196

278) It is reported that Abu Hurairah (may Allah be pleased with him) said: «The Messenger of Allah ﷺ said:« If the son of Adam reads (verse, after which reading is performed) prostration and prostration, then the shaitan leaves, crying and exclaiming: «Oh woe to him...» (In the version narrated from the words of Abu Qurayb, it is reported that the shaitan says: «Oh woe to me!) I was ordered to bow to the ground, but I refused, and now (hellish) Fire awaits me!» №244

279) It is reported that Abu Sufyan said: - I heard Jabir (ibn 'Abdullah, may Allah be pleased with him) say: «I heard the Prophet ﷺ say: «Verily, between a person and polytheism and unbelief - abandoning prayer». №246

280) It is narrated from the words of 'Abdullah ibn Mas'ud (may Allah be pleased with him) that the Prophet ﷺ said: «A person will not enter Paradise, in whose heart (remains) arrogance (at least weighing) with a speck of dust.» (Hearing this, one) the man exclaimed: «But a man wants his clothes and shoes to be beautiful!» (To this the Prophet ﷺ) said: «Verily, Allah is beautiful, and He loves the beautiful, (as for) arrogance, then this is the rejection of the truth and a manifestation of contempt towards people». №265

281) Hudhayfah (may Allah be pleased with him) reported that the Messenger of Allah ﷺ said: «The gossiper will not enter Paradise». №290

282) It is reported that Abu Hurayrah (may Allah be pleased with him) said: «The Messenger of Allah ﷺ said: «On the Day of Resurrection, Allah will not speak to three, will not purify them (Abu Muawiyah said: «... and will not look at them»). (These three are) a lecherous old

man, a ruler who is a notorious liar, and a proud poor man». №296

283)   It is reported that Abu Hurairah (may Allah be pleased with him) said: «One day, people from among the companions of the Prophet ﷺ came (to him) and asked him: «Verily, (sometimes) we feel that in our souls (something is happening), which we dare not even speak of.» (The Prophet ﷺ) asked: «So you had to feel it?» They answered: «Yes», (and then) he said: «This and (indicates) the purity of faith» №340

284)   Hudhayfah (may Allah be pleased with him) reported: «(Once when) we were with 'Umar (ibn al-Khattab), he asked: «Which of you heard that the Messenger of Allah ﷺ spoke about trials?» People began to say: «We heard him (words).» ('Umar) said: «Probably you mean (his words) about the disaster (related) to the family, property or neighbour of a person», and they said: «Yes». Then he said: «This is expiated by prayer, fasting and sadaqah. And who heard that the Prophet ﷺ spoke of (a calamity) that would rage like a raging sea?» Hudhaifa said: «Then the people fell silent, and I said:« I. ('Umar) said: «You? Your father (worthy of praise)!» (After that) Hudhayfah said: «I heard the Messenger of Allah ﷺ say: «Hearts will be tempted (one after another), like a (reed) mat, (which is woven, attaching) the stalk to the stem, and a black dot will appear in the heart that sinks into them. As for the heart, which considers them unpleasant for itself, then a white dot will appear in it, (and after a while) two (kinds of) hearts will arise: (one will be) white and like a smooth stone, and not a single temptation will harm (such heart) as long as heaven and earth exist; (others will be) black and (dyed in) ashen/aswadu murbadd/colour, like an inverted/mujahhiyan/ jar, and (such a heart) will not know what is approved (sharia) or reject what is condemned, but will only plunge into its desires ». Hudhaifah said: «And I said (to 'Umar): 'You are separated from (such temptations) by a locked door that is about to break. (Umar) said: «So it will

break, will you lose your father? If it opens, then may-be (closes again).» I said: «No, it (can only) break», and I told him that this door is a person who will be killed or die a natural death, and these are words in which there is no mistake. Abu Khalid said: «I asked Sa'd: «O Abu Malik, what is aswadu murbadd?» He said, «Bright white on black.» I asked: «What is a Mu-jahhiyan?» He said, «Tipped over». №369

285) Abu Hurairah (may Allah be pleased with him) report-ed: «The Messenger of Allah ﷺ said: «Islam began as foreign and will return as foreign as it began. And Tuba (a tree in Paradise) - foreign / guraba /» №372

286) It is reported that Abu Dharr (may Allah be pleased with him) said: «(Once) I asked the Messenger of Al-lah ﷺ: «Have you seen your Lord?» He replied, «There was light! How could I see Him?» №443

287) It is reported that Husayn ibn 'Abdu-r-Rahman said: – (Once), when I was with Sa'id ibn Jubair, he asked: «Which of you saw a star fall yesterday?» I answered: «I am,» and then I said: «However, I did not pray, for I was stung.» He asked: «And what did you do?» I re-plied: «I asked that a spell be read over me.» He asked, «What prompted you to do this?» I replied: «The ha-dith that al-Sha'bi narrated to us.» He asked: «What did ash-Shabi tell you?» I replied: «He told us that Bu-raidah ibn al-Husayb al-Aslamy said: «Spells are read only from the evil eye and poison.» (Husayn narrated that after that) Sa'id ibn Jubayr said: - It is wonder-ful when a person learns what he hears, however, Ibn 'Abbas narrated to us that (once) the Prophet ﷺ said: «I was shown (all religious) communities , and I saw (one) prophet with whom there were several people, and (another) prophet with whom there was (only) one person or two, and such a prophet with whom there was no one at all. Suddenly a great crowd of people appeared in front of me, and I thought that they were my community, but I was told: «This is Musa and his people, but look at the horizon.» I looked (there), and it turned out that there were many people there, after

which they told me: «(Now) look at the other (edge) of the horizon» and there were also many people there, and then they told me: «This is your community , and among them are seventy thousand (persons) who will enter Paradise without calculation and torment.» After that (the Prophet ﷺ) got up and entered his house, and people began to talk about those who would enter Paradise without calculation and torment. One of them said: «Perhaps these are the people who were the Companions of the Messenger of Allah.» Another said: «Maybe they will be (people) who were born in Islam and did not worship anyone but Allah,» and they expressed (many other assumptions. After a while) the Messenger of Allah ﷺ came out to them and asked: «What are you say?» - and they told him (what it was about). Then he said: «These are those (people) who themselves do not utter conspiracies and do not turn to others for this, do not believe in bad omens, judging by the flight of birds, and trust in their Lord.» After that, 'Ukkasha ibn Mihsan got up from his seat and said: «Ask Allah to number me among them.» (The Prophet ﷺ) replied: «You are from among them.» And then another person got up from his seat and (also) said: «Ask Allah to number me among them», (but this time the Prophet ﷺ) said: «'Ukkasha ahead of you in this». №527

288) It is reported that Musab ibn Sa'd said: «(Once) 'Abdullah ibn 'Umar went to visit Ibn 'Amir when he was ill and (Ibn 'Amir) said: «O Ibn 'Umar! Won't you turn to Allah with a prayer for me!?» (Ibn 'Umar) said: «I heard the Messenger of Allah ﷺ say: «Prayer is not accepted without purification, and alms from a stolen trophy / gulul / are not (accepted),» and you were the governor of Basra». №535

289) It is reported that Ibn al-Mughaffal said: «(First) the Messenger of Allah ﷺ ordered to kill dogs, and then (cancelled his command), saying: «What do they care about dogs?» Subsequently, he allowed dogs to be kept for hunting and guarding sheep and said: «If a dog

licks any vessel, wash it seven times, and wipe it with earth on the eighth». №653

290) It is narrated from the words of Ishaq ibn Abu Tal-ha that Anas ibn Malik said: «(Once upon a time) Umm Suleim, the grandmother of Ishaq, came to the Messenger of Allah ﷺ at the time when 'Aisha was with him, and asked:« O Messenger Allah, (what do you say) about a woman who (first) sees in a dream the same thing as a man, and then sees that the same thing happens to her as happens to men? (Hearing her words), 'Aisha exclaimed: «O Umm Suleim, you are a disgrace to women, may your right hand be covered with dust!» (As for the Prophet ﷺ, then) he said to 'Ai-sha: «It is you (disgrace to women), let your right hand be covered with dust! Yes, Umm Suleim if a woman sees this, let her perform a full ablution». №709

291) It is reported that Abu Mas'ud said: «Usually (before the beginning of) the prayer, the Messenger of Allah ﷺ took us by the shoulders and said: «Align yourself and do not violate uniformity, otherwise there will be no agreement between your hearts. Let mature and sensible men from among you follow me, then those who follow them, and then those who follow them.» Abu Mas'ud said: «Now you have gone to the extreme in your disagreements». №972

292) It was narrated from the words of 'Abdullah ibn 'Amr, may Allah be pleased with him, that the Messenger of Allah ﷺ said: «The time of the midday prayer contin-ues until the time of the afternoon prayer begins. The afternoon prayer time continues until the sun turns yellow. The sunset prayer time continues until the evening dawn disappears. The evening prayer time continues until midnight, and the morning prayer time continues until the sun rises. When the sun has risen, refrain from praying, for verily, it rises between the two horns of Shaitan». №1388

293) It is reported that Abu Dharr, may Allah be pleased with him, said: «(One day) the Messenger of Allah ﷺ

asked me:« O Abu Dharr, verily, after me, there will be rulers who will kill the prayer, so perform (every obligatory) prayer in (the best for her) time, and if you pray at the (best for her) time, then (this prayer will be counted as) additional, otherwise, you have already reached the (goal) of your prayer». №1466

294) It is narrated from the words of Sa'eed ibn Jubair that Ibn 'Abbas, may Allah be pleased with both of them, said: a time when he was not afraid and not being on the road. Abu az-Zubair said: I asked Sa'id (ibn Jubayr): «Why did he do that?» He replied: «I asked Ibn 'Abbas in the same way as you asked me, and he said:« He did not want to complicate (life) for anyone (from members of) his community». №1629

295) It is reported that 'Aisha, may Allah be pleased with her, said: «Usually the Messenger of Allah ﷺ performed a prayer in two rak'ats (before the obligatory) morning prayer, shortening them (so much) that I even said (to myself): «Yes, I read whether he is in them the «Mother of the Quran»?» №1684

296) Ubay ibn Kaab, may Allah be pleased with him, said: «Once the Messenger of Allah ﷺ asked me: «O Abu-l-Munzir, do you know which verse from the Book of Allah is the greatest?» I said, «This is the verse which says: 'Allah - there is no deity worthy of worship except He, the Living, the Sustainer of life.'» After that, the Prophet ﷺ clapped his hand on my chest and said: «May you be happy in knowledge, O Abu al-Mundhir!» №1885

297) 'Uqba ibn 'Amir al-Juhani, may Allah be pleased with him, said: «The Messenger of Allah ﷺ forbade us to pray and bury our dead in three periods of time: during sunrise until it rises; during the standing of the sun at its zenith, until it slopes towards sunset; during sunset, until the sun disappears (behind the horizon)». №1929

298) It is narrated from the words of Abu Hurairah that the Prophet ﷺ said: «When Friday comes, at each door of

the mosque (located) are angels who record (coming) one by one, when the imam sits down (on the minbar, the angels) fold their scrolls and appear (in the mosque) to hear the (words) of remembrance (of Allah). The person who comes (to the mosque) in advance will be like the one who sacrifices (to Allah) a camel; (the one who comes to prayer later) will be like the one who sacrifices (to Allah) a cow; (the one who comes even later) will be like the one who sacrifices (to Allah) a ram; (the one who comes even later) will be like the one who sacrifices (to Allah) a chicken, (and the one who comes even later) will be like the one who sacrifices (to Allah) an egg». №1984

299) It is reported that Abu Hurairah, may Allah be pleased with him, said: «The Messenger of Allah ﷺ said: «If any of you perform Friday prayer, let him perform after it (and an additional prayer in) four rak'ahs». №2036

300) It is narrated from the words of 'Ata (ibn Abu Rabah) that Jabir ibn 'Abdullah, may Allah be pleased with him, said: «Once I was present with the Messenger of Allah ﷺ at a festive prayer, and he began with a prayer before a sermon, without calling / azan/ and announcements about the beginning of prayer /iqama/. Then he stood up, leaning on Bilal, and ordered (the people) to fear Allah, called them to obedience to Him, and began to exhort them and remind them. Then he approached the women, began to exhort them and remind them, and said: «Give alms, for verily, most of you are the fuel of hell.» Then a dark-cheeked woman stood up among these women and said: «Why O Messenger of Allah?» He replied: «Because you complain a lot and are ungrateful towards your husbands.» (Jabir) said: «And they began to give as alms their jewels, throwing earrings and rings into Bilal's clothes». №2048

301) It is reported that Anas said: «(Once) when we were with the Messenger of Allah ﷺ, rain overtook us. The Messenger of Allah ﷺ (a little) opened the (out-

er) clothes so that (drops of) rain began to fall on his (body). We asked: «O Messenger of Allah, why did you do this?» - and he said: «Because he was recent with his Lord». №2083

302) It is reported that Abu Hurayrah, may Allah be pleased with him, said: - The Messenger of Allah ﷺ said: «Inspire your dying people (so that they pronounce the words)« There is no god worthy of worship except Allah » / La ilaha illa-l-Lah /». №2125

303) It is narrated from the words of Abu Malik al-Ash'ari, may Allah be pleased with him, that the Messenger of Allah ﷺ said: «The members of my community did not abandon the four things that were done during the Jahiliyyah: from (the habit) to be proud of their origin, denigrate the origin (of others), turn to the stars with prayers for rain and lament for the dead. He also said: «If (a woman) who lamented loudly over the deceased does not repent of this until her death, then on the Day of Resurrection she will be resurrected in a robe of liquid resin and a shell of scabs». №2160

304) It is reported that Jabir, may Allah be pleased with him, said: «The Messenger of Allah ﷺ forbade covering the grave with plaster, sitting on it and erecting (any) structure over it». №2245

305) Muharib ibn Disar reported from the words of Ibn Buraida that his father (Burayda), may Allah be pleased with him, said: «The Messenger of Allah ﷺ said: «(Before) I forbade you to visit the graves, but (from now on) visit them, and I forbade you (to eat) the meat of sacrificial animals for more than three days, but (from now on you can) keep it as long as you like, and I forbade you to make a drink from dates in anything other than large wineskins/sika/, (from now on you you can) drink (drinks that are prepared) in any wineskins, but do not drink anything intoxicating!» Ibn Numair in his version said: «From 'Abdullah ibn Buraid, who transmitted from his father.» In another version of this hadith, the Prophet ﷺsaid: «... and whoever wants to

visit the graves, let him visit, for, verily, they will remind him of death!» №2260

306) It is reported that Jabir said: «One person from (kind) Bani 'Uzra (bequeathed) to release his slave after his death. This reached the Messenger of Allah ﷺ and he asked (the man): «Do you have any other property besides this (slave)?» He said, «No.» Then (the Prophet ﷺ) began to ask: «Who will buy it from me?» - and (this slave) for eight hundred dirhams was bought by Nu'aym ibn 'Abdullah al-'Adawi. (After that) the Messenger of Allah ﷺ brought (this money to the former owner of the slave) and gave it to him, and then said: «Start with yourself and give sadaqah to yourself. If there is anything left, (spend it) on your family; if there is anything left (and after that, spend it) on your relatives; if there is anything left (and after that, spend it) so and so.» (and he began to make signs with his hand, wishing) to say: «(Expand funds) in front of you, (and also) to the right and left». №2313

307) Abu Hurayrah (may Allah be pleased with him) reported that the Messenger of Allah (peace and blessings of Allah be upon him) said: «There is a duty on every joint of a person to give alms every day on which the sun rises. If you judge fairly between the two, it will be charity. If you help a person to get on his mount, or lift his things on the mount, it will be charity. And a good word is also charity. And every step you take on the path to prayer is charity. And if you remove from the road that which hinders (passers-by), this will also be alms». №2335

308) It is reported that Jarir ibn 'Abdullah, may Allah be pleased with him, said: «Once at the beginning of the day, when we were with the Messenger of Allah ﷺ, half-naked people came to him, dressed in striped pieces of woollen cloth, in which they made holes for their heads, and girded with swords, and most of them, but most likely all of them were from the Mudar tribe. Seeing their need, the Messenger of Allah ﷺ changed his face and went (to his house), and then he went out

and gave the order to Bilal, who first called for prayer, and then announced its beginning. And (the Prophet ﷺ) made this prayer, and then turned to the people with a sermon and said: «O people! Fear your Lord, who created you from one person, and created from him a couple for him, and scattered from them (over the earth) a multitude of men and women. And be afraid of Allah (name) in which you ask each other, (and be afraid of breaking) family ties (in fact,) verily, Allah is Watching over you!» And then (he recited) another verse from (the number of the last verses) of Surah «The Gathering» (saying): «O you who believe! Fear Allah, and let a man see what he has prepared for tomorrow », - (after which he called):« Let a person donate their dinar, or their dirham, or their clothes, or sa' wheat or sa' dates, - (and he went on the listing) until he said: «… or at least half a date.» (Jarir) said: «And after that, one man from among the Ansar brought such a heavy purse of silver that he could hardly hold it in his hand, and other people followed him one by one, and at last, I saw that on two heaps were formed on the ground (one of which was) food (and the other -) clothes. And I also saw that the face of the Messenger of Allah ﷺ shone as if gilded, and then the Messenger of Allah ﷺsaid: «Whoever initiates any good custom in Islam will receive a reward for it, as well as a reward for those who begin to adhere to this custom after him, which will not diminish their rewards one iota. The one who initiates some bad custom in Islam will bear both the burden of this sin itself and the burden of the sins of those who will adhere to this custom after it, which will not reduce the burden of their sins one iota!» №2351

309) It is reported from 'Abdullah ibn 'Amr al-'As that the Messenger of Allah ﷺ said: «The one who converted to Islam and was endowed with food sufficient to (maintain) life succeeded, and Allah made him pleased with what He bestowed on him». №2426

310) 'Abidah (as-Salmani) narrated that (once) 'Ali (ibn

Abu Talib) mentioned the Kharijites and said: «Among them, there is a man with a defect in his hand (or: with a small hand), and if you did not begin to show cruelty, then I would tell you what Allah promised in the language of Muhammad ﷺ to those who would kill them. ('Abidah) said: «I asked: «And you heard this from (himself) Muhammad ﷺ!?» He replied: «Yes, I swear by the Lord of the Kaaba! Yes, I swear by the Lord of the Kaaba! Yes, I swear by the Lord of the Kaaba!» №2465

311)   It is reported from the words of Abu Qatada al-Ansari, may Allah be pleased with him, that (once) the Messenger of Allah ﷺ was asked about fasting on Monday and he said: «On this day I was born and (on this) day I was sent down (first revelation)». №2750

312)   Abu Bakr ibn Abu Shayba told us: Husain ibn 'Ali told us from Zaid, who narrated from 'Abdul-Malik ibn 'Umayr with this isnad in the mention of fasting from the Prophet ﷺ the same hadith. «Once the Prophet ﷺ was asked: «What is the best prayer after the prescribed one, and what is the best fast after the fast of the month of Ramadan?» fasting, after (fasting) the month of Ramadan - fasting of the month of Allah Muharram». №2757

313)   It is reported that Aisha, may Allah be pleased with her, said: «In the last ten (days) of Ramadan, the Prophet ﷺ was always inseparable in the mosque (and this continued) until the Great and Almighty Allah laid him to rest, and after him also his wives began to act». №2784

314)   It is reported that 'Aisha, may Allah be pleased with her, said: «Wishing to be alone, the Messenger of Allah ﷺ (first) performed the morning prayer, and then came to the place of his seclusion, where, at his command, they set up a tent. (Once, when) he decided to spend the last ten days of Ramadan in seclusion, (in the place of his seclusion), at the command of Zainab, a tent was set up for her, and (some) other wives of the

Prophet ﷺ (also) ordered to put (there) tents for them. Having performed the morning prayer, the Messenger of Allah (unexpectedly) saw several tents and said: «Did they (did it) out of piety?» - after which, at the command (of the Prophet ﷺ), his tent was removed, and he did not retire to the mosque in Ramadan but spent the first ten days of Shawwal there». №2785

315)   It is narrated from the words of Ibn 'Umar, may Allah be pleased with both of them, that (after the completion of the rites of the Hajj), the Messenger of Allah ﷺ said: «O Allah, have mercy on those who shave off their hair.» (People) said: «(Supplication) for those who shortened, O Messenger of Allah!» He (again) said: «O Allah, have mercy on those who shave their hair.» (People) said: «(Supplication) for those who shortened, O Messenger of Allah!» He (again) said: «O Allah, have mercy on those who shave their hair.» (People again) said: «(Supply) and for those who shortened, O Messenger of Allah!» - (and then) he said: «And those who shortened». №3146

316)   It is reported that 'Ata said: - When under Yazid ibn Mu'awiya (Kaaba) burned down during her (siege by the army) from Sham, and what happened to her happened, Ibn al-Zubair left her (in this form), until in the season (hajj to Mecca) people began to come whom he wanted to inspire (or: whose anger he wanted to inflame) (and direct) against (warriors) from Sham. When people began to leave (Mecca), he turned (to them): «O people, give me advice regarding the Kaaba. (Should) I destroy it and rebuild it, or (better) put in order what (remains) of it? Ibn 'Abbas said: «It is clear to me (which) opinion about her (is correct). I believe that you (should) put it in order, (preserve) what was left of it, and leave the house in which people converted to Islam, and the stones in which people converted to Islam, and the Prophet ﷺ was entrusted with the prophetic mission. Ibn al-Zubayr said: «If one of you had a house burned down, he would not be satisfied until he renovated it, so what about the House of your

Lord? Indeed, I will ask my Lord for three (days) to help me make the right choice, and then I will make a (final) decision on this matter. When these three (days) expired, he decided to destroy (Kaaba), but people began to avoid him, (fearing) that the first one who climbed it would be (struck) by heaven (punishment). (However, after a while, a man went upstairs and began to throw stones from there. Seeing that nothing happened to him (happened there), one by one (began to approach) people. They began to disassemble (the masonry and did not stop) until they reached (the level of) the ground. Then Ibn az-Zubayr set up pillars there and hung curtains on them, (which were not removed) until the (walls) of the building were raised. Then Ibn al-Zubair said: «Indeed, I heard 'Aisha say that the Prophet ﷺ said: «If it were not for (the circumstance that) people (very) recently (got rid of) disbelief, and not for the lack of funds for construction, I would add to it five cubits from al-Hijr and arranged in it a door through which people would enter (the Kaaba, as well as) another door through which they would leave from there. Today I have something to spend, and I'm not afraid of people. And he added to it five cubits from al-Hijr, (as a result of which) the foundation was opened, and people looked at it, and then he erected a (new) building on it. (Formerly) the length of the Kaaba was eighteen cubits, but (Ibn az-Zubair) considered (that this was not enough) and made it ten cubits longer. (In addition), he arranged two doors in it, through one of which (it was necessary to enter the Kaaba), and through the other - to leave. When Ibn az-Zubair was killed, al-Hajjaj wrote a letter to 'Abdul-Malik ibn Marwan, in which he informed him about (everything, including) that Ibn al-Zubair erected a (new) building on the foundation (of the Kaaba) which was seen by the pious (witnesses) from among the inhabitants of Mecca. 'Abdul-Malik wrote to him (in reply): «We have nothing to do with anything (of what) Ibn al-Zubayr did. Leave what he lengthened, and what he added (to the Kaaba) from al-Hijr, return (to its previous state) and repair the door that he (arranged) », after which (al-Hajjaj) destroyed (that what Ibn Az-Zubair built), and returned the building (previous appearance). №3245

317) It is reported from the words of Qaza'a that during the tour of the House (Kaaba), 'Abdul-Malik ibn Marwan exclaimed: «May Allah destroy Ibn al-Zubair, who builds a lie on the mother of the faithful! He says: «I heard her say that the Messenger of Allah ﷺ said: «O 'Aisha if it were not for (the circumstance that) your tribesmen (very) recently (got rid of) disbelief, I would certainly have destroyed this House (Kaaba) and added (part of) al-Hijr to it because your tribesmen made the building too short. (Kaza'a said): «(Hearing this), al-Harith ibn 'Abdullah ibn Abu Rabi'a said: «Do not speak like that, O Commander of the Faithful, for I heard the mother of the Faithful speak of this» (To this ' Abdul-Malik) said: «If I had heard (your words) before destroying (Kaaba), I would certainly have left it (in the form that I gave it) Ibn al-Zubayr!» №3248

318) 'Aisha, may Allah be pleased with her, said: «Once I asked the Prophet ﷺ: «Is the wall part of the Kaaba?» He said yes. I asked, «So why didn't they attach it to the Kaaba?» He replied, «Because your people were short of funds.» I asked: «Why is her door raised (above the ground)?» He replied: «Your tribesmen made it so that they let in whoever they want, and do not give (to enter the Kaaba to anyone) who they don't want. If your tribesmen were not (so) close to the Jahiliyyah and I would not be afraid that their hearts would not like (such), I would attach this wall to the Kaaba, and lower the door to (level) the ground». №3249

319) It is reported that Abu Nadra said: «While I was with Jabir ibn Abdullah, a man came up and asked that Ibn Abbas and Ibn Zubayr disagreed about entering into a temporary marriage. Then Jabir replied: «During the time of the Prophet ﷺ it was allowed, but then Umar forbade us from it, so we abstain». №3250

320) It is reported that Abu Hurairah, may Allah be pleased with him, said: - (Once) the Messenger of Allah ﷺ turned to us with a sermon (in which, among other things) said: «O people, Allah charged you with the duty of Hajj, so perform it! » One man asked: «Every year, O Messenger of Allah?», but he remained silent until he (repeated his question) three times, and then the Messenger of Allah ﷺ said: «If I say:« Yes, »it will certainly become (for you) obligatory, but you, after all, cannot (do this)!» And then he said: «Spare me (from questions about) what I (did not speak to you), for, truly, those who lived before you perished because they asked many questions and did not agree with their prophets! When I command you to do something, (simply) make of it what you can, and when I forbid you to do something, refuse it». №3257

321) It is reported that Ali bin Abi Talib, may Allah be pleased with him, said at the time of Khaibar about the prohibition of temporary marriage and the eating of meat of domestic donkeys. №3263

322) It is narrated from the words of Muhammad ibn Ibrahim that Abu Salama ibn 'Abdurrahman said: «(Once) I asked 'Aisha, the wife of the Prophet ﷺ:« What was the marriage gift of the Messenger of Allah ﷺ? She said: «(As a) marriage gift (he gave each of) his wives twelve okiya's and (one) ashsh (silver)». (Then 'Aisha) asked: «Do you know what oursh is?» I answered: «No.» Then she said: «Half an okiya, but in total it was equal to five hundred dirhams. Such a marriage gift the Messenger of Allah ﷺ (made each of his) wives». №3489

323) It was narrated from the words of Abu Hurairah, may Allah be pleased with him, that the Messenger of Allah ﷺ said: «If a woman spends the night not on the bed of her husband, the angels will curse her until morning». №3538

324) It is reported that Abu Hurairah (may Allah be pleased with him) said: «The Messenger of Allah ﷺ said: «I

swear by Him in Whose hand is my soul if any of the men call his wife to bed, and she refuses him, the one who abides in heaven, will not cease to be angry with her until (her husband again) is pleased with her!» №3540

325) It is reported that Abu Sa'eed al-Khudri (may Allah be pleased with him) said: «The Messenger of Allah ﷺ said: «Indeed, on the Day of Resurrection, one of the greatest (violations) of Amanat before Allah will be (how) a man spends the night with (his) wife and then divulges her secret. And Ibn Numair (in his version) said: «Verily, the greatest...». №3543

326) It was narrated from the words of Abu Hurairah, may Allah be pleased with him, that one day Sa'd ibn 'Ubad al-Ansari, may Allah be pleased with him, asked: «O Messenger of Allah, tell me, can a person kill an outsider if he finds him with his wife? and the Messenger of Allah ﷺ said: «No!» Sa'd said, «Yes, I swear by Him Who honoured you with the truth!» And then the Messenger of Allah ﷺsaid: «Listen to what your master says». №3761

327) Abu Hurayrah, may Allah be pleased with him, reported that (one day) Sa'd ibn 'Ubadah (may Allah be pleased with him) asked: «O Messenger of Allah, if I find a stranger with my wife, I will not hurry until I bring four witnesses?» (The Messenger of Allah ﷺ) said: «Yes!» №3762

328) Abu Hurayrah reported that the Messenger of Allah ﷺ said: «A child will not be able to repay his parent in full unless he finds him (someone's) slave, after which he ransoms and frees him». №3799

329) It is reported that Jabir (may Allah be pleased with him) said: «The Messenger of Allah ﷺ said:« If a Muslim plants a tree, then everything that will be eaten from it will be sure (counted) for him as sadaqah/ alms/, and everything that will be stolen from him, it will be reckoned to him as sadaqah, and everything that the animals eat from him will be reckoned to him

as sadaqah, and everything that the birds eat from him will be reckoned to him as sadaqah, and if someone harms him, it will be counted him like sadaka». №3968

330) It is reported that Rafi' ibn Khadij (may Allah be pleased with him) said: «I heard the Prophet ﷺ say: «The worst earnings (are money) received by a harlot (for adultery), money (received for) a dog, and the earnings of a barber». №4011

331) It is reported that Abu al-Zubayr said: «I asked Jabir about the sale of dogs and cats and he said: «The Prophet ﷺ strictly forbade this / zajara /!» №4015

332) It is reported that Jabir ibn 'Abdullah, may Allah be pleased with both of them, said: «(First) the Messenger of Allah ﷺ ordered us to kill dogs, and even when a woman came from the desert with her dog, we killed her (dog). And then the Prophet ﷺ forbade us to kill them and said: «You should (kill only) completely black dogs with two (white) spots (above the eyes, for), verily (every such dog) is a shaitan». №4020

333) It was narrated from the words of Abu Qatada al-Ansari, may Allah be pleased with him, that he heard the Messenger of Allah ﷺ say: «In no case do not give a lot of oaths (concluding) a trade deal, for, truly, (at first) it will promote the sale (of goods, but) then it will destroy (profit)». №4126

334) It is reported that Abu Mas'ud al-Badri, may Allah be pleased with him, said: «(Once) while beating my slave with a whip, I heard a voice behind me:» Know, O Abu Mas'ud ... «, - but did not understand to whom it belonged, as he was overcome with anger. When (the person who spoke with this) voice approached me, it turned out that it was the Messenger of Allah ﷺ who said: «Know, O Abu Mas'ud! Know, O Abu Mas'ud!» And I threw away the whip (which I held) in my hand, and he said: «Know, O Abu Mas'ud, that Allah can do more with you than you with this slave!», - and then I said: «After that, I will never hit a slave!» – (as for the

Prophet ﷺ then) he exclaimed: «Truly if you didn't do this, you would surely be scorched by fire! (or: ... the fire would touch!)» №4306

335) It is reported that Jabir ibn Samura said: «I heard the Messenger of Allah ﷺ say: «The affairs of the people will go well when they are ruled by twelve rulers. Then the Prophet ﷺ said something that I did not understand». №4478

336) It is reported that Abu Hurairah, may Allah be pleased with him, said: «The Messenger of Allah ﷺ said: «Verily, Allah desires (that you do) three (things) and does not want (that you do) three (others). He wants you to worship Him and not worship anything else along with Him, and that you all hold on to the rope of Allah and not be divided, and He does not want you (engaged in) gossip, (asked) many questions and (in vain) squandered (own) funds». №4481

337) It is narrated from the words of Suleiman ibn Buraida that his father (Burayda, may Allah be pleased with him) said: «When appointing someone to command an army or detachment, the Messenger of Allah ﷺ personally ordered him to fear Allah and treat Muslims well (who go to campaign) with him, and then he said: «Go on a campaign in the name of Allah and the path of Allah and fight with those who do not believe in Allah. Go on a campaign and do not deceive, do not act treacherously, do not disfigure the bodies of the slain (enemies) and do not kill children. When you meet enemies from among the polytheists, call them to three things, and if they agree with anything, then accept it from them and (leave) them. Then invite them to Islam, and if they answer you (with consent), accept (this) from them and (leave) them. Then call them to migrate from (the places where they live to where they are) the Muhajirs, and inform them that if they do this, they will enjoy all the rights of the Muhajirs and perform the same duties. If they refuse to move from there, inform them that they will be in the position of Muslims from among the Bedouins, and they will be

subject to the provisions of Allah, like all believers, but their share of military spoils and everything that Muslims receive from the infidels in a peaceful way (fai), they will receive only if they participate in jihad along with (other) Muslims. If they refuse, demand from them the payment of jizya, and if they answer you (with consent), accept (this) from them and (leave) them. If they refuse, then turn to Allah for help and fight them. If you besiege (enemies who have taken refuge) in a fortress and they want to obtain from you (guarantees) the protection of Allah and His Prophet, do not guarantee them the protection of Allah and His Prophet, but guarantee them your protection and the protection of your companions, for if you break the promise to guarantee them your protection and the protection of your companions, it will be a lesser sin than breaking the promise to guarantee them the protection of Allah and His Prophet. If you besiege (enemies who have taken refuge) in a fortress, and they want to be subject to the influence of the decrees of Allah, do not apply the effect of the decrees of Allah to them, but take them under your authority, for you do not know whether you will correctly determine the decree Allah, which applies to them». №4522

338) It is reported that Abu Musa (al-Ash'ari), may Allah be pleased with him, said: «When sending one of his companions on any assignment, the Messenger of Allah ﷺ said:« Bring joy and do not scare away. Lighten, don't burden». №4525

339) It is reported that Abu at-Tayyah said: - I heard Anas ibn Malik, may Allah be pleased with him, said: «The Messenger of Allah ﷺ said: «Facilitate, and do not create difficulties, calm (people), and do not inspire disgust (to Islam)». №4528

340) It is reported from the words of 'Aisha, may Allah be pleased with her, that (after the death of the Prophet ﷺ) Fatimah, the daughter of the Messenger of Allah ﷺ sent to Abu Bakr as-Siddiq (a man) ask him (to give her) the inheritance of the Messenger of Allah ﷺ from

what that Allah granted him in Medina and Fadak, as well as from the rest of the fifth part (of the booty captured in) Khaibar. (In response to this) Abu Bakr said: «The Messenger of Allah ﷺ said: «(Our property) cannot (can) be inherited, and what we left is sadaqah, and (part of the income) from this property (goes to) subsistence for the family of Muhammad. I swear by Allah, I will not change (the order of spending) the sadaqah of the Messenger of Allah ﷺ (established) during (his) life, and I will certainly (spend) it in the same way as the Messenger of Allah ﷺ did.» (Thus), Abu Bakr refused to give anything to Fatimah, who became angry with him because of this, left (him) and did not speak to him until her death, and she survived the Messenger of Allah ﷺ by six months. When she died, her husband 'Ali ibn Abu Talib (may Allah be pleased with both of them) buried her at night, without notifying Abu Bakr, and he performed the funeral prayer for her. During the life of Fatimah, may Allah be pleased with her, to 'Ali (many came), when she died, ('Ali stopped meeting) with noble people, he began to look for (ways) of reconciliation with Abu Bakr and (wished) to take an oath to him, (which he hasn't done in all) these months. He sent to Abu Bakr (a man) to tell him the following: «Come to us, but let no one else come with you» (for 'Ali did not want 'Umar ibn al-Khattab to be present). (Having learned about this), 'Umar said to Abu Bakr: «By Allah, you (should not) come to them alone!» (To this) Abu Bakr said: «What can they do to me? By Allah, I will go to them!» When Abu Bakr came to them, 'Ali ibn Abu Talib uttered the words of evidence of monotheism, and then said: «O Abu Bakr, truly, we recognized your dignity and what Allah endowed you with, and did not envy the good (bestowed) on you Allah, but you began (to dispose of it), and we believed that we had the right (to something) as relatives of the Messenger of Allah Muhammad, »and he spoke until Abu Bakr's eyes filled with tears. Then Abu Bakr spoke and said: «By the One in Whose hand is my soul, kinship with the Messenger of Allah ﷺ is dearer to me than maintaining ties with my relatives! As for the disagreements regarding this property that arose between me and you, then I did not miss anything (from what) I had to (should have done), and I always acted in the same way as the Messenger of Allah ﷺ acted before my eyes. Then 'Ali said to Abu Bakr: «(I will swear) to you in the afternoon.» Having completed the midday prayer, Abu Bakr went up to the minbar and uttered the words of evidence of monotheism, then said that 'Ali had not yet taken the oath to him, and then mentioned how ('Ali) explained the reason for this and asked (Allah) to forgive (him). After that, 'Ali ibn Abu Talib uttered words of evidence of monotheism, then duly expressed respect to Abu Bakr (as he said to the Caliph) that it was not envy of Abu Bakr and not the denial of what Almighty and Great Allah gave him preference (over others). ('Ali also said): «But we believed that we had some kind of inheritance in (what belonged to the Prophet ﷺ), but you began to dispose of it without us, and we became angry (with you).» Rejoicing at this, the Muslims said: «You did the right thing!» - and began (to love even more) 'Ali after he, (like the rest, took the oath). №4580

341) It is reported from the words of Abdullah ibn Amr, may Allah be pleased with him, it is reported that the Messenger of Allah ﷺ said: «Verily, the righteous with Allah will be on the minbars of light, on the right hand of the Merciful, both of whose hands are right. These are those who adhere to justice in their decisions, families and in what they manage». №4721

342) Abu Bakr ibn Abu Shayba told us: He told us: Abu al-Ahwas and Waqi', and Abu Sa'id al-Ashaj told me, he said: He told us: Waqi', and Abu Qurayb and Ibn Numeir told us. They said: Abu Mu'awiya told us, and Ishaq ibn Ibrahim and 'Ali ibn Hashrama told us, they said: 'Isa ibn Yunus told us, they are all from al-A'mash, and 'Uthman ibn Abi Sheyba told us, the words belong to him, we were told by Jarir, from al-

A'mash, from Zayd ibn Wahb, from 'Abdullah, said: The Messenger of Allah ﷺ said: «Truly after me, there will be self-interest (preference will be given to others over them in worldly things), and deeds that you will condemn. (The Companions) said: O Messenger of Allah, what will you command those of us who find this? To which he said: «Fulfill the rights that lie with you, and ask Allah for what is yours.». №4755

343) It is reported that Umm Salama - the wife of the Prophet ﷺ said: «The Messenger of Allah ﷺ said:« When the young month of Dhul-Hijja appears, let the one who has a sacrificial animal (which he wants) to slaughter, in no case cut his hair, no nails until he makes a sacrifice!» №5121

344) It is reported that Abu at-Tufayl 'Amir ibn Vasilya said: - (Once, when) I was with 'Ali ibn Abu Talib, a man came to him and asked: «What did the Prophet ﷺ say to you in secret (from the others)?» ('Ali) got angry and said: «The Prophet ﷺ did not say anything only to me, hiding it from people, but he said four words to me.» (This man) asked: «What, O Commander of the Faithful?» ('Ali) said: «He said: 'Allah has cursed the one who curses his father, and Allah has cursed the one who sacrifices to other than Allah, and Allah has cursed the one who gives shelter to a person who introduces (to the religion) something new, and Allah has cursed the one who changes the landmarks». №5124

345) Abu al-Zubayr reported from the words of Jabir that one day a man who came from Jaishan ((a city that is) in Yemen) asked the Messenger of Allah ﷺ a question about a drink prepared from Indian millet and called «mizr», which they drank at home (at home). The Prophet ﷺ asked: «Does this (drink) intoxicate?» He said: «Yes», and then the Messenger of Allah ﷺ said: «Everything intoxicating is forbidden. Verily, the Great and Almighty Allah has promised to water (a person) who uses intoxicating drinks, (with what is called) «tynat al-habal». (People began to) ask: «O

Messenger of Allah, what is «tynat al-khabal»?» (The Messenger of Allah ﷺ) said: «(This) is the sweat (or juices) of the inhabitants of the Fire». №5217

346) It is reported that Ibn 'Abbas, may Allah be pleased with them both, said: «(Once) I gave the Messenger of Allah ﷺ to drink (water) from Zamzam, which he asked for and he drank it standing near the Home (Al-lah)». №5283

347) 'Abdullah ibn Abu Qatada narrated from the words of his father: «The Prophet ﷺ forbade breathing into a vessel (while drinking)». №5285

348) It is reported that Anas (may Allah be pleased with him) said: «When the Messenger of Allah ﷺ drank water, he took three breaths and exhaled, and said: «It is healthier, more pleasant and healthier to drink like this.» Anas said: «While drinking, I also take three breaths in and out». №5287

349) It is reported that Jabir said: «I heard the Prophet ﷺ say: «Verily, the shaitan is next to each of you, no matter what he does, without leaving (a person) even while eating. And if one of you drops a piece, let him remove what sticks to it and eat it without leaving it to the devil. When he has finished (eating), let him lick the fingers of his hands, for, verily, he does not know in what (piece) of his food (hidden) grace». №5303
350) It is reported that 'Aisha, may Allah be pleased with her, said: «The Messenger of Allah ﷺ said:» O 'Aisha, those people who do not have dates at home will remain hungry, O 'Aisha, those people will remain hungry who have no dates at home,» repeating this twice or thrice». №5337

351) It is reported from the words of Ibn 'Abbas, may Allah be pleased with both of them, that (once) the Messenger of Allah ﷺ, who saw a golden ring on the hand of one person, took it off, threw it away and said: «One of you himself strives for a hot coal from the flame (hell) and puts it on his hand!» And when the Messenger of Allah ﷺ left, someone said to this man: «Take

your ring and use it (somehow),» (to which) he replied (as follows): «No, by Allah, I will never take (this ring), since the Messenger of Allah ﷺ threw it away». №5472

352) It is narrated from the words of Ibn Shihab, (narrated) from Anas ibn Malik (may Allah be pleased with him) that «one of the days he saw on the hand of the Messenger of Allah ﷺ a silver ring.» (Anas) said: «And the people also made (for themselves) rings of silver and put them on (on their fingers), but the Prophet ﷺ threw away his ring, and then the people also threw away their rings». №5483

353) It is narrated from the words of Anas ibn Malik (may Allah be pleased with him) that the Prophet ﷺ forbade (wearing clothes dyed with saffron). №5506

354) It is reported that Sa'eed ibn Abul-Hasan said: - A man came to Ibn 'Abbas (may Allah be pleased with him) and said: «I create these images, so give me advice (regarding this).» (Ibn 'Abbas) said: «Come closer to me,» and he approached him. (Ibn 'Abbas again) said: «Come closer to me», and when he came even closer, (Ibn 'Abbas) put his hand on his head and said: «Shall I tell you what I heard from the Messenger of Allah ﷺ? I heard the Messenger of Allah ﷺ say: «Every (man) who creates images (will be) in the Fire, where for each image he draws, he will be (attached) to him who will torment him in Gehenna.» (After that, Ibn 'Abbas) said: «If you absolutely must do this, (depict) trees and what has no soul». №5540

355) Abu Hurayrah (may Allah be pleased with him) reported that the Messenger of Allah ﷺ said: «The bells are the pipes of Shaitan». №5548

356) It is reported that Asma bint Abu Bakr (may Allah be pleased with them both) said: «A woman came to the Prophet ﷺ and said: «O Messenger of Allah, I have a daughter-bride who had measles, (from which) she began to fall out hair, so why not tie it up for me (false hair in place of the fallen out)?» - (to which the Proph-

et 🕮) said: «Allah cursed both the tie-up and the one who asks to tie up (someone else's hair)». №5565

357) It is reported that al-Mughira ibn Shu'ba said: - When I arrived in Najran, (the people of the Book) began to ask me: «Why do you read (in the Quran):» O sister of Haruna! (Surah «Maryam», verse 28), although Musa (lived) so and so many years earlier than 'Isa?!» When I came to the Messenger of Allah 🕮, I asked him about this, and he said: «Verily, they addressed (to people) by the names of their prophets and the righteous who lived before them». №5598

358) It is narrated from the words of Ibn 'Umar that Umar had a daughter whose name was 'Asia and the Messenger of Allah 🕮 (changed her name) and called her Jamila. №5605

359) Muhammad ibn 'Amr ibn 'Ata said: «I called my daughter Barra (pious), but Zainab bint Abu Salama said to me:« The Messenger of Allah 🕮 forbade giving this name. My name was also Barra, but the Messenger of Allah 🕮 said: «Do not praise yourselves, Allah knows best which of you is pious», then the people asked: «What should we call her?» He said, «Call her Zainab» №5609

360) It is narrated from the words of Ibn 'Abbas, may Allah be pleased with them both, that the Prophet 🕮 said: «The evil eye is the truth, and if anything could get ahead of predestination, then it would be an evil eye, and therefore if you are asked to commit a complete ablution, do it». №5702

361) Safiyya (bint Abu 'Ubayd) narrated from the words of one of the wives of the Prophet 🕮 that the Prophet 🕮 said: «The prayer of the one who comes to the soothsayer and asks him about something will not be accepted for forty nights». №5721

362) It is reported that Abu Sa'eed al-Khudri said: «The Messenger of Allah 🕮 said: «Verily, in Medina, there lives a group of jinn who converted to Islam, and who-

ever sees one of them (in the form of a snake), let him ask him (leave your house) for three days, and if after that (the snake) appears again, it kills it, for, verily, it is a shaitan!» №5841

363) It is narrated from the words of Abu Umama ibn Sahl ibn Hunayf that his father said that the Messenger of Allah ﷺ said: «Let none of you says: «I am bad» / Habusat nafsi / - but let him say: «I deserve censure» / Lakisat nafsi/». №5880

364) Abu Hurayrah (may Allah be pleased with him) reported that the Messenger of Allah ﷺ said: «Let the one who is offered basil not reject it, for it is easy to wear and has a pleasant smell». №5883

365) It is reported that Nafi' said: «When burning incense, Ibn 'Umar, may Allah be pleased with both of them, used an aloe tree not mixed with any other incense, and a camphor tree, (pieces) of which he threw (into the fire) along with (pieces) of aloe, after which he said: «So the Messenger of Allah ﷺ burned incense». №5884

366) It is narrated from the words of Abu 'Umar Shaddad that he heard Wasil ibn al-Ask' say: «I heard the Messenger of Allah ﷺ say:» Verily, Allah chose the clan of Kinan from among the sons of Isma'il, then from the clan, Kinana chose the Quraysh, from among the Quraysh he chose the clan of Hashim, and from the clan of Hashim he chose me». №5938

367) It was narrated by Abu Hazim who said: - I heard Sahl say: «I heard the Prophet ﷺ say: «I will be the first of you (to be) at the reservoir, and whoever comes to it will be able to drink from it, and whoever drinks from it will never feel thirsty. People whom I know will certainly come to me, and they know me, and then they will separate me from them.» Abu Hazim said: «An-Numan ibn Abu 'Ayyash heard when I told them this hadith, and asked: «Is this how you heard when you said, Sahl?» And I answered: «Yes». №5968

368) It was narrated from the words of 'Abdullah bin 'Amr bin al-'As, may Allah be pleased with him, who reported that the Prophet ﷺsaid: «It will take a month to go around my reservoir, its angles are equal to each other, its water is whiter than milk, its fragrance is more pleasant than the aroma of musk, and the jugs standing on its banks are (in their number) as the stars of heaven, and each of those who have drunk its water will never feel thirsty again». №5971

369) He said: and Asma bint Abi Bakr said: «The Messenger of Allah ﷺ said: «Being at the reservoir (Haud), I will see which one of you will come to me. But some people will be taken away from me. Then I will say: «O Lord, they are mine and from my community,» but it will be said: «Did you not feel what they did after you. By Allah, they did not stop turning back after you.» Said: And so Ibn Abu Muleykah said: «O Allah, we ask You for protection from being turned back or from being tested in our faith». №5972

370) We were told by Abu Bakr ibn Abu Shayba, Abu Quraib and ibn Numeir, who said: Abu Mu'awiya told us from A'mash from Shaqiq from 'Abdullah, said: The Messenger of Allah ﷺ said: «I will be the first of you (to be) at the reservoir, and I will certainly fight for the people, but they will (anyway) overcome me, and then I will say: «Oh Lord, my companions, my companions!» And it will be said: «Verily, you do not know what they did after you». №5978

371) It is reported that Anas (ibn Malik, may Allah be pleased with him) said: «(One day) the Messenger of Allah ﷺ was on one of his trips, and a black slave named Anjala urged camels by singing, and the Messenger of Allah ﷺ said to him: «Oh Anjala, (carry) slower, (as if you are carrying) bottles». №6036

372) It is reported that Jabir ibn Samura (may Allah be pleased with him) said: «I made the first prayer together with the Messenger of Allah ﷺ, and then he went to his family, and I went with him. On the way, he met a

group of children, and he began to stroke each of them in turns on the cheeks. «When he stroked my cheeks,» Jabir said, «I felt that a wonderful aroma emanated from his hands as if he had just taken them out of a chest of incense». №6052

373) It is narrated from the words of Musa ibn Talha that his father (Talha ibn 'Ubaidullah, may Allah be pleased with him) said: «(Once) I, along with the Messenger of Allah ﷺ, passed next to palm trees, on the tops (of which sat) people, and he asked: «What are these (people) doing (there)?» (To him) they said: «They pollinate (palms), transferring pollen from the male (trees) to female.» The Messenger of Allah ﷺ said: «I don't think it will bring any benefit.» (Talhah) said: «They were told (his words), and they stopped (doing it), and then the Messenger of Allah ﷺ was informed about this and he said:« If it benefited them, let them do it (in the future). I only assumed (something), so do not blame me for the assumption. If I convey to you something from Allah, hold on to it, for verily, I do not build a lie on the Almighty and Great Allah!» №6126

374) According to Jabir ibn 'Abdullah, the Messenger of Allah ﷺ said: «They showed me paradise and I saw the wife of Abu Talha there. Then I heard some rustling in front of me and it turned out that it was Bilyal». №6321

375) Umar is reported to have said: «I heard the Messenger of Allah ﷺ say: «The best of my followers will be a man named Uwais al Qarni. He will take care of his mother and will be white due to a small point of leprosy. Ask him to ask Allah for forgiveness for you» №6491

376) It is reported that 'Abdullah ibn Dinar said: «Once 'Abdullah ibn 'Umar met a certain Bedouin on the way to Mecca, greeted him with peace (salaam), put him on his donkey and gave him his turban. Then we said to him: «May Allah correct you! These are the Bedouins, they are content with little.» 'Abdullah replied: «The father of this (Bedouin) was a friend of (my father) 'Umar ibn al-Khattab. And I heard the

Messenger of Allah ﷺ say: «The highest piety (is that) a person keeps in touch with those whom he loved, whom his father loved». №6513

377) Narrated Anas ibn Malik (may Allah be pleased with him) that the Messenger of Allah ﷺ said: «Give up hatred towards each other, do not envy each other, do not turn your back on each other, and be brothers, O slaves Allah! It is not allowed for a Muslim to leave his brother (for a period) exceeding three days!» №6526

378) Abu Hurayra (may Allah be pleased with him) reported: The Messenger of Allah ﷺ said: «Do not envy each other, do not raise the price, give up mutual hatred, do not turn your back on each other, do not interrupt each other's trade and be brothers, Oh servants of Allah, indeed a Muslim is a brother to a Muslim, and therefore none of the Muslims should either oppress another, or treat him with contempt, or leave him without help, and piety is hidden here!», - and (the Messenger of Allah ﷺ) pointed out three times (hand) on his chest (after which he said): «There will be enough harm to that person who despises his brother in Islam, and for every Muslim, (should be) inviolable is the life, property and honour of another Muslim!» №6541

379) It is reported that Abu Hurayrah, may Allah be pleased with him, said: «The Messenger of Allah ﷺ said: «Verily, Allah does not look at your bodies or your appearance, but He looks at your hearts», after which he pointed his finger to himself on the chest». №6542

380) It is narrated from the words of Abu Hurairah, may Allah be pleased with him, that the Messenger of Allah ﷺ said: «The gates of Paradise open on Mondays and Thursdays, and (sins) are forgiven (sins) to every slave (of Allah) who did not worship anything along with Allah, except for such a person, whom hatred (shared) with his brother, and then they say: «Wait with these two until they are reconciled with each other, wait with these two until they are reconciled with

each other, wait with these two until they are reconciled with each other!» №6544

381)   It is reported that Abu Hurayrah, may Allah be pleased with him, said: «The Messenger of Allah ﷺ said: «Indeed, on the Day of Resurrection, Allah will say:« Where are those who loved each other for the sake of My greatness? Today, on the Day when there will be no (other) shadow but My shadow, I will cover them in My shadow!» №6548

382)   It is reported that Abu Hurairah said: - The Messenger of Allah ﷺ said: «Indeed, on the Day of Resurrection, the Great and Almighty Allah will say: «O son of Adam, I was sick, and you did not visit Me!» (The person to whom He will turn) will say: «O my Lord, how can I (can) visit You when You are the Lord of the worlds?!» (Allah) will say: «Did you not know that such and such My servant fell ill, and you did not visit him? Didn't you know that if you visited him, you would find me next to him? O son of Adam, I asked you to feed Me, but you did not feed Me!» (Man) will say: «O my Lord, how can I (can) feed You when You are the Lord of the worlds?!» (Allah) will say: «Did you not know that such and such a servant of mine asked you to feed him, and you did not feed him? Didn't you know that if you had fed him, then (then) you would certainly have found it with Me? O son of Adam, I asked you for water, but you did not give Me drink!» (Man) will say: «O my Lord, how can I (can) give You drink when You are the Lord of the worlds?!» (Allah) will say: «So-and-so My servant asked you for water, but you did not give him a drink! Didn't you (know) that if you had given him a drink, then (then) you would certainly have found it with Me?» №6556
383)   It is reported from the words of Ibn 'Umar (may Allah be pleased with both of them) that the Messenger of Allah ﷺ said: «A Muslim is a brother to a Muslim, and he (should not) neither oppress nor betray him. Whoever (helps) his brother in his need, Allah (will help) in his own need, whoever delivers a

Muslim from sorrow, Allah will deliver from one of the sorrows of the Day of Resurrection, and whoever covers a Muslim, Allah will cover on the Day of Resurrection». №6578

384) It is narrated from the words of Abu Hurairah (may Allah be pleased with him) that the Messenger of Allah ﷺ said: «Charity/sadaqah / does not reduce wealth in any way, Allah will not add to (His) slave (forgiving others) anything but glory, but any (from those who) show modesty for the sake of Allah, Almighty and Exalted Allah will always exalt». №6592

385) It is narrated from the words of Abu Hurairah (may Allah be pleased with him) that (once) the Messenger of Allah ﷺ asked: «Do you know what slander / giba / is?» (People) said: «Allah and His Messenger know (about it) better.» (The Prophet ﷺ) said: «(This is when) you mention your brother in such a way that he would not like it.» (He) was asked: «Tell me if what I say is inherent in my brother?» (The Prophet ﷺ) said: «If what you say is inherent in him, then you slander about him, and if this is not in him, then you will slander / bukhtan /». №6593

386) It is reported that Abu Hurairah said: «The Messenger of Allah ﷺ said: «If any of you fights with his brother (by faith), let him not touch his face, for Allah created Adam in His image». №6655

387) It is reported that Abu Hurairah said: «Abu al-Qasim ﷺ said:« If anyone points any iron (weapon) at his brother, the angels will curse him until he stops, even if it is his father's brother and mother». №6666

388) It is reported from the words of Abu Sa'eed al-Khudri and Abu Hurairah that the Messenger of Allah ﷺ said: «(Almighty Allah said): «Greatness is My izar and pride is My cape / rida / whoever disputes them with Me, that I will torment!». №6680

389) It is narrated from the words of Jundab ibn 'Abdullah, may Allah be pleased with him, that the Messenger of

Allah ﷺ said: «(Once) a man said:« By Allah, Allah will not forgive such and such! said, «Who swears by me that I won't forgive so-and-so? Indeed, I have already forgiven so-and-so, and I have made your deeds in vain!» №6681

390) It was narrated from the words of Abu Hurayrah, may Allah be pleased with him, that the Messenger of Allah ﷺ said: «The souls (are like) warriors called into the army and those of them who recognize each other unite, those who do not recognize contradict each other». №6708

391) It is reported that the mother of the faithful 'Aisha said: «(Once) the Messenger of Allah ﷺ was called to the funeral of a deceased boy (son) of one of the Ansar. I said: «O Messenger of Allah, this sparrow from among the sparrows of paradise has a Tuba! He did no evil, and it did not reach him.» Then he said: «Maybe something else, O 'Aisha! Indeed, Allah created the inhabitants for Paradise while they were still in the loins of their fathers, and created the inhabitants for the Fire while they were still in the loins of their fathers!» №6768
392) It was narrated from the words of Abu Hurairah, may Allah be pleased with him, that the Messenger of Allah ﷺ said: «Whoever calls to the right path will receive a reward equal to the rewards of (all) those who follow him, which will not reduce their rewards one iota, and he who called (others) to error, will bear the (burden) of sin, equal (in terms of the weight of the burden) of the sins of those who follow him, which will not alleviate (the weight of) their sins». №6804

393) It is reported that Abu Hurairah (may Allah be pleased with him) said: «The Messenger of Allah ﷺ said: «Whoever saves a believer from one of the sorrows of this world, Allah will deliver from one of the sorrows of the Day of Resurrection, whoever alleviates the situation of the insolvent (the debtor), Allah will ease his position both in this world and in the next world, and whoever covers a Muslim, Allah will cover

in this world and the next world. Allah will help (His) slave as long as the slave himself helps his brother. Whoever embarks on any path in search of knowledge, Allah will facilitate the path to paradise for this, and when people gather in one of the houses of Allah, where they read and study the Book of Allah together, calmness will surely descend on them, and mercy will cover them, and surround them angels and Allah remembers them among those who are before Him, and whoever is hindered by his deeds, his origin will not help to move faster». №6853

394) It was narrated from Anas ibn Malik, may Allah be pleased with him, that the Messenger of Allah ﷺ said: «Verily, Allah is pleased with such a slave who, having eaten food, praises Him for it, or, having a drunk drink, praises Him for it». №6932

395) It is reported that Hanzala al-Usayyidi, who was one of the scribes of the Messenger of Allahﷺ, said: «Once I was met by Abu Bakr, may Allah be pleased with him, who asked: «How are you, O Hanzala?» (In response to him) I said: «Hanzala has become a hypocrite!» He exclaimed: «Glory be to Allah! What are you saying?!» I said: «When we visit the Messenger of Allah ﷺ, who reminds us of heaven and hell, we seem to see both, but when we leave him and begin to deal with our wives, children and earning a livelihood, then we forget a lot!» Abu Bakr, may Allah be pleased with him, said: «But, by Allah, something similar is happening to us!», - (after which) Abu Bakr and I went to the Messenger of Allah ﷺ and I said (to him): «Hanzala became hypocrite, O Messenger of Allah!» He asked: «What is it (expressed)?» I said: «O Messenger of Allah, when we come to you and you remind us of heaven and hell, then we seem to see both with our own eyes, when we leave you and begin to take care of our wives, children and earning food, then we forget a lot!» (After listening to me,) the Messenger of Allah ﷺ said: «By the One in whose hand my soul is, if you were constantly in the state in which you are with

me and always remembered (Allah), then the angels would shake hands with you, (wherever you are -) in bed or on the road, however, O Hanzala, there is a time for everything, »repeating (these words) three times». №6966

396) It is reported that Anas ibn Malik (may Allah be pleased with him) said: «The Messenger of Allah ﷺ said: «Paradise is surrounded by hatred, and (Hell) Fire is surrounded by passions». №7130

397) It is reported from the words of 'Iyad ibn Himar al-Mujashi'i that once during his sermon the Messenger of Allah ﷺ said: «Verily, my Lord ordered me to teach you what you did not know and what He taught me today. (He said), «Any property that I have given to a slave is lawful (for him). Verily, I created all My slaves as hanifs, but the devils began to appear to them, who turned them away from their religion, declared forbidden what I allowed them, and ordered them to worship along with Me that for which I did not give any arguments. Almighty and Great Allah looked at (people) living on earth, hated (all) them, Arabs and non-Arabs, except for the remaining people of the Book, and said: «I sent you (to people) to test you and subject (them) trial through you, and I have sent down to you a Scripture that cannot be washed away with water, and which you will read in your sleep and while you are awake.» And indeed, Allah ordered me to burn the Quraysh, and I said: «My Lord, in this case they will break my head (and it will be like crumbled) bread!» (Allah) said: «Drive them out as they drove you out, and attack them, and We will help you, and spend (your means), and We will spend on you, and send (against them) an army, and We let us send five such (armies), and fight those who disobey you, (by the hands) of those who obey you.» (And Allah) said: «Three will become the inhabitants of Paradise: a just and almsgiving ruler who is assisted, a merciful person whose heart shows gentleness towards every relative and (every) Muslim, and also a modest (person)

burdened with children, showing abstinence». (And Allah) said: «Five will become the inhabitants of the Fire: the weak one who is devoid of intelligence, those of you who will follow everything (indiscriminately), neither seeking (to benefit) the family, nor (acquire) wealth, the treacherous one who shows treachery (for the sake of satisfying any) desire, even if it concerns trifles, and a person who deceives you morning and evening in (related to) your family and your property. In addition, He mentioned stinginess (or: deceit) and a person who has a bad temper and speaks vile words». №7207

398) It is reported that Jabir, may Allah be pleased with him, said: «I heard the Prophet ﷺ say:« Every slave (of Allah) will be resurrected in that (state) in which he will meet death». №7232

399) It is reported that al-Ahnaf ibn Qays said: «One day, I went out wanting to help this man and I (on the way) was met by Abu Bakr, who said: «Where are you going, O Ahnaf?» I said: «I want to help the son of the uncle of the Messenger of Allah ﷺ meaning 'Ali». Then he said to me: «O Ahnaf, come back, for verily, I heard how once the Messenger of Allah ﷺ said:« If two Muslims come together (in battle, crossing) their swords, then both the killer and the killed will be in Fire (hell).)». I asked (or: Someone said): «O Messenger of Allah, (it will be fair if it gets there) this killer, but why is he killed?!» He replied: «After all, he wanted to kill his comrade!» №7252

400) It is reported that 'Aisha (may Allah be pleased with her) said: - (Once) I heard the Messenger of Allah ﷺ say: «Night and day will not pass until al-Lat and al-'Uzza (again) will begin to worship», and said (to him): «O Messenger of Allah, and when Allah sent down (verse where it says):« He is the One Who sent His messenger with the guidance and the religion of truth to exalt it above any (other) religion, even if this is hateful to the polytheists» (at-Tawba, 9:33), I thought that it would happen.» (To this the Prophet

🕸) said: «From this (it will happen) what Allah wills, and then Allah will send a good wind and give rest to everyone (person) in whose heart there will be faith (at least by weight) of a mustard seed, (after which) will remain those in whom there will be no good, and they will return to the religion of their fathers». №7299

401) It is reported that Abu Hurayrah, may Allah be pleased with him, said: «The Messenger of Allah 🕸 said:« This world is a prison for the believer and Paradise for the disbeliever». №7417

402) It is reported from the words of 'Abdullah ibn 'Amr ibn al-'As (may Allah be pleased with both of them) that (once) the Messenger of Allah 🕸 asked (his companions): «What kind of people will you become if you are granted victory over Persia and Byzantium? 'Abdurrahman ibn 'Auf said: «We will say what Allah has commanded us.» The Messenger of Allah 🕸 said: «Maybe something else (happen) and you will (first) compete with each other, then envy each other, then turn away from each other, then hate each other (or he said something like that), and then move to the dwellings of the (weak among) Muhajirs and make some of the masters of others?» №7427

403) It is reported that once during a sermon, an-Numan ibn Bashir (may Allah be pleased with them both) said: which people got, said: «And I saw how the Messenger of Allah 🕸 bent (from hunger) for a whole day, during which he could not find even bad dates to get enough of them!» №7461

404) It is reported that Suhayb (ibn Sinan), may Allah be pleased with him, said: «The Messenger of Allah 🕸 said:« How wonderful is the position of a believer! Verily, everything in his position is good for him, and this is not given to anyone except the believer: if something pleases him, he thanks (Allah), and this becomes good for him, but if grief befalls him, he manifests patience, and this (also) becomes good for him». №7500

405) It is reported from the words of Suhayb, may Allah be pleased with him, that the Messenger of Allah ﷺ said: Among those who lived before you there was one king who had (in-service) a sorcerer. Having grown old, he said to the king: «Truly, I am already old, send a young man to me so that I can teach him witchcraft,» and he sent a young man to him to teach him. On the way (to the house of the sorcerer to the young man) he met a monk. He sat down next to him and listened to what he had to say, and he liked it. And (after that) every time the young man went to the sorcerer, he passed by this monk (lingering to) sit with him, and when he came to the sorcerer, he beat him. (The young man) complained about this to the monk, who said: «If you are afraid of the sorcerer, say: «I was detained at home,» and if you are afraid of your loved ones, then say: «I was detained by the sorcerer.» And then one day, being in a similar position, (the young man) suddenly encountered a huge beast that did not allow people (to walk freely along this road), and said: «Today I will find out who is more worthy - a sorcerer or a monk.» After that, he grabbed a stone and exclaimed: «O Allah, if You love the deeds of a monk more than the deeds of a sorcerer, then kill this beast so that people can walk (freely)!» And he threw (a stone) at the beast and killed him, and people (gave the opportunity) to walk (on this road). Then (the young man) came to the monk, (about everything) he told and he said to him: «O son, today you have already surpassed me, for I see what you have achieved, and, verily, trials await you, but when you undergo them, don't point at me.» And after that, the young man began to heal the blind and lepers, curing people also of other ailments. One of the king's associates, who was blind, heard about (him). He came to him with numerous gifts and said: «All this will be yours if you heal me.» (In response, the young man said to him): «Truly, I do not heal anyone - only Allah Almighty heals, and if you believe in Him, I will turn to Allah with a prayer and He will heal you.» And he believed in Allah Almighty and

Allah Almighty healed him, and then he came to the king and sat down in front of him as usual. The king asked him: «Who gave you back your sight?» He replied, «My Lord.» (The king) asked: «Do you have (another) master besides me?» He said: My Lord and your Lord is Allah». Then the king (ordered) to seize him, after which he subjected him to torment until he pointed to this young man, and he was brought to the king, who said to him: «O son, it came to me that you achieved in your witchcraft (of such heights that you can) heal the blind and the lepers and do (many other things).» (To this the young man) said: «Truly, I do not heal anyone - only Allah Almighty heals.» Then the king (ordered) to seize him, after which he tortured him until he pointed to the monk. Then this monk was brought to him, to whom it was suggested: «Renounce your religion!» - but he refused. Then (the king ordered to bring) a saw, it was put to the middle of the head (of a monk) and he sawed it so that one half fell (to the ground). After that (to the king) they brought his entourage, to whom (also) it was proposed: «Repudiate your religion!» - but he refused. Then he put a saw to the middle of his head and sawed it until one half of it fell (to the ground). After that (to the king) a young man was brought, and he was (also) asked: «Renounce your religion!» - but he refused. Then (the king) gave him to his servants and said: «Take him to such and such a mountain and go up with him, and when you reach the top (let him go), if he renounces his religion, and if not, then throw him down!» They took him there and climbed the mountain (where) he exclaimed: «O Allah, deliver me from them as you wish!» - and then the mountain began to move, they rolled down and (the young man again) appeared to the king. The king asked: «And what did those who were with you do?» (Young man) said: «Allah Almighty delivered me from them!» Then (the king) gave him to (other) his servants and said: «Take him (to the sea), put him on a ship and take him to the middle of the sea, and if he renounces his religion (then let him go), and if not, leave him (in water)!» And they brought him (where they were ordered, where the young man) said: «O Allah, deliver me from them as you wish!» - after which the ship capsized and (the servants of the king) drowned, and (the young man again) appeared to the king. The king asked him: «And what did those who were with you do?» (The young man replied): «Allah Almighty delivered me from them!» - and then he said to the king: «Truly, you cannot kill me until you do what I command you!» (The king) asked: «What is this?» (The young man) replied: «Gather the people on one hill and tie me to the trunk of a palm tree, then take an arrow from my quiver, put it in the middle of the bow and say:« In the name of Allah, the Lord of this young man! »- and then shoot, and, truly, you can kill me only if you do (all this)». And (the king) gathered people on one hill, tied (the young man) to the trunk of a palm tree, took out an arrow from his quiver, put it in the middle of the bow, said: «In the name of Allah, the Lord of this young man!» - and shot an arrow that hit (the young man) in the temple. He grabbed his temple with his hand and died, and then the people said: «We believed in the Lord of this young man!» After that, (his close associates) came to the king and said to him: «What do you say about what you were afraid of? We swear by Allah, what you feared happened to you, for people believed!» And then the king ordered (to dig) ditches at the (city) gates, and they dug them and kindled a fire in them, and then (the king) said: «Throw into the fire everyone who does not renounce his religion!» / or: ... and they said to such a person: «Throw yourself!» / And (servants) carried out (his command) until a woman approached (to the fire) with her son. She stopped (in front of the fire, not wanting) to be there, and then the boy said to her: «O mother, be patient, for verily (religion) yours is true!» №7511

406) 'Ata narrated that Ibn 'Abbas, may Allah be pleased with them both, said: «Once upon a time, people from among the Muslims met a man (herding) a small flock of his sheep, and he said:» Peace be upon you / as-

Salam 'Alaikum /», they seized and killed him, and they took away these sheep, and then a verse was sent down, which says: «And do not say to the one who (turns) to you (with greetings and wishes) peace: «You do not you are a believer» (an-Nisa, 4:94). №7548

407) Ibn 'Abbas, may Allah be pleased with him, said: «(In the pre-Islamic period) a woman went around the Kaaba naked, saying:« Who will give clothes for ta-waf? »To cover her private parts. And then she said: «Today, all or part will be exposed; but what is naked I will not make lawful.» It was in this connection that the verse was sent down: «Put on your ornaments at every mosque» (surah «al-Araf», verse 31)». №7551

«Sunah» Tirmidhi

Imam Abu Isa Muhammad ibn Savrat at-Tirmidhi was born in 209 after the Hijra and died in 279 in Termez (the territory of modern Uzbekistan). He received good religious education, studied hadith from the hadith scholars of Termez and Balkh, and Islamic law (fiqh) from the jurists of the Hanafi madhhab. At the age of 27, he went on Hajj. As he writes in his book, every night Tirmidhi made a detour around the Kaaba, repented of his sins, prayed (dua) to turn away from the earthly world, correct his condition and memorize the Quran. Returning from the Hajj, Tirmidhi began to read books to know Allah and prepare for the afterlife, and also began to look for a mentor for himself, wandering around different lands. At the same time, he led an ascetic lifestyle - he fasted, performed many prayers, gained a taste for solitude, wandered alone, and often visited ruins and cemeteries. But, as he writes, he did not find sincere friends who could help him, until he finally saw the Messenger of Allah (peace be upon him) in a dream, after which the veils between him and Allah were opened.

According to al-Qattani, at-Tirmidhi called his book «al-Jami al-Kabir», but there are many people who call it «Sunan at-Tirmidhi». It contains 3962 hadiths and has been divided into fifty chapters, per the principles of Islamic law. When writing a book, at-Tirmidhi first gave the title of the section, and then cited one or two hadiths on the proposed topic. Further, he gives the opinions of jurists on a particular issue. The main focus of the book is on legal issues. Subsequently, these hadiths were used in issuing a legal opinion (fatwa). «Jami» at-Tirmidhi became an important source for various points of view of various theological and legal schools (madhhabs). His teacher, Imam al-Bukhari, highly appreciated the level of knowledge of Imam at-Tirmidhi. Even though Imam al-Bukhari was older than Imam at-Tirmidhi and higher than him in terms of knowledge, he transmitted some hadiths from him. He said to his disciple Imam at-Tirmidhi: «I have benefited from you more than you from me»

Hakim Tirmidhi tried to harmonize religious (nakli) sciences with rational ones (akli), to substantiate religious sciences from a rational point of view. This is reportedly why he was nicknamed «Hakim», which translates as «wise man».

408) Waqi' told us from Israel, (narrated) from Simak, (narrated) from Mus'ab ibn Sa'd, (transmitted) from the words of Ibn 'Umar (may Allah be pleased with them both), that the Prophet ﷺ said: «It is not accepted prayer without purification, and (not accepted) alms from stolen trophies / gulul /. In his (version of this) hadith, Hannad said: «Except with purification». №1

409) It is reported from the words of 'Ali (may Allah be pleased with him) that the Prophet ﷺ said: «The key to prayer is purification, the entrance to it is takbir, and the exit from it is taslim.» Abu 'Isa (at-Tirmidhi) said: «This hadith is the most authentic and the best report on this subject.». №3

410) It is reported that Anas ibn Malik said: «When the Prophet ﷺ entered the latrine, he said:« O Allah! I resort to Your protection » /Allahumma inni a'uzu bika

/. Shu'ba said: «Sometimes he said: «I resort to Your protection from the male and female devils» /A'uzu bika minal-khubsi wal-habisi/ or /hubusi wal-habais/. №5

411) It is reported that Abu Ayyub al-Ansariyy said: - The Messenger of Allah ﷺ said: «When you go out of need, then the time of defecation and urination does not turn to the qibla either with your face or back, but turn to the east or west.» Abu Ayyub said: «When we went to al-Sham, we found that their toilets were built in the direction of the qibla, and we turned away from it and asked Allah for forgiveness». №8

412) It is reported that 'Aisha said: «If someone tells you that the Prophet ﷺ urinated while standing, then do not believe him. He did not urinate except while sitting. Abu 'Isa (at-Tirmidhi) said: «The hadiths transmitted from 'Umar, Buraydah and 'Abdurrahman ibn Hasan also belong to this chapter.» Abu 'Isa (at-Tirmidhi) said: «The Hadith of 'Aisha is the best and most reliable in this chapter.» The hadith of 'Umar is narrated from 'Abdul-Karim ibn Abul-Muharik from Nafi'a from the words of Ibn 'Umar, who reported that 'Umar said: «Once the Prophet ﷺ saw me when I was urinating while standing and he said: «O 'Umar, do not urinate while standing!» And I didn't pee standing up after that». №12

413) It is narrated from the words of Hudhaifah that one day the Prophet ﷺ went to a dump where people threw garbage and urinated while standing. I brought him water for ablution and followed him behind him, but he called me so that I was at his heels. And (then) he performed ablution and wiped his leather socks / khuffain /. №13

414) It is reported that Qatada told from the words of his father that the Prophet ﷺ forbade a person to touch his genitals with his right hand. №15

415) It is reported that 'Abdurrahman ibn Yazid said: «Salman (al-Farisi) was told: «Your Prophet ﷺ teaches

you everything, and even how to relieve yourself?»
Salman said, «Yes. He forbade us to turn towards the
qibla when defecation and urination, to wash with the
right hand, or to use less than three stones for cleansing (after defecation), or to cleanse ourselves with
dung or bones». №16

416) It is reported that 'Aisha (may Allah be pleased with
her) said: «Tell your husbands to wash with water, and
I am truly embarrassed (to explain this) to them. And
indeed, the Messenger of Allah ﷺ did so». №19

417) It is reported that Abu Hurairah said: «The Messenger
of Allah ﷺ said: «If I were not afraid of burdening the
members of my ummah, I would have ordered them to
use a toothpick before each prayer». №22

418) It is narrated from the words of Rabah ibn 'Abdurrahman ibn Abu Sufyan ibn Khuwaytib that his grandmother, according to the words of her father (Sa'id ibn
Zeyd ibn 'Amr ibn Nufail) said: «I heard the Messenger of Allah ﷺ say: «There is no ablution at whoever
did not mention the name of Allah (when approaching) it». №25

419) It is narrated from the words of Ibn 'Abbas that the
Messenger of Allah ﷺ said: «When you perform
ablution, wash the places between the fingers and
toes».№39

420) It is narrated from the words of 'Ali, may Allah be
pleased with him: «The Prophet ﷺ performed ablution, washing parts of the body three times.» Abu 'Isa
(at-Tirmidhi) said: «Regarding this topic, there are
also hadiths from 'Uthman, 'Aisha, ar-Rubayyi'a, Ibn
'Umar, Abu Umama, Abu Rafi'a, 'Abdullah ibn 'Amr,
Mu' Aviya, Abu Hurayrah, Jabir, 'Abdullah ibn Zayd
and Ubayyah (ibn Ka'ba). Abu 'Isa (at-Tirmidhi) said:
«Hadith 'Ali is the most reliable and the best of the hadiths related to this chapter, as it is transmitted along
other paths. Most scholars believe that one should act
under this (hadith) and that doing ablution by washing
the parts of the body once is enough, twice is even

better, and it is best to do it three times, and one should not do it more than three once. Ibn al-Mubarak said: «I do not consider that one who, when performing ablution (washes parts of the body) more than three times, commits a sin.» Ahmad and Ishaq said: «Only a person who is in doubt (when performing ablution, washes parts of the body) more than three times». №44

421) Abu Hayyah is reported to have said, «I saw 'Ali perform ablution. He washed his hands until they were clean, then rinsed his mouth three times, then cleared his nose with water three times and washed his face three times, washed his hands together with his elbows three times, rubbed his head once, then washed his feet with ankles, after which rising from his seat, he took the rest of the water and drank it while standing, and then said: «I wanted to show you how the ablution of the Messenger of Allah ﷺ». №48

422) It is reported that 'Aisha said: «The Messenger of Allah ﷺ had a piece of cloth with which he wiped himself after performing ablution». №53

423) Abu Hurayrah reported that a man asked the Messenger of Allah ﷺ: «O Messenger of Allah when we go out to sea, we take some water with us. If we begin to perform ablution with it, we will experience intense thirst. Is it possible to perform ablution with sea water? The Messenger of Allah ﷺ replied: «Sea water is suitable for purification, and animals that die in it are allowed to be eaten». № 69

424) It is reported from the words of Ibn 'Abbas that one day, passing by two graves, the Messenger of Allah ﷺ said: «Truly, (the inhabitants of these two graves) are tormented, but this did not happen because of great sins. As for this, he did not hide from his urine, and as for (the second), he spread gossip /namima/». №70

425) It is reported from the words of Humaida bint 'Ubayd ibn Rifa‘a that Kabsha bint Ka‘b ibn Malik, who was the wife of the son of Abu Qatada, (told) that (somehow) Abu Qatada came to her. She said, «And I poured

water for him to bathe in. Suddenly a cat came up and began to drink, and he tilted the vessel for her (and held it there) until she had finished. Kabsha said: «He saw that I was watching her and said: «Are you surprised, O daughter of my brother?» I said yes». And he said: «Verily, the Messenger of Allah ﷺ (once) said: «Verily, she is not an impurity/najas/, and, verily, she is from among those who always surround you». №92

426) It is narrated from the words of Khuzayma ibn Thabit, may Allah be pleased with him, that (somehow) the Prophet ﷺ was asked about wiping leather socks and he said: «(The term for wiping leather socks) for a traveller (is) three (days and three nights), and for those who stay at the place of permanent residence - one day (and one night)». №95

427) It is reported that al-Mughira ibn Shu'ba (may Allah be pleased with him) said: «(Once) the Prophet ﷺ performed ablution and wiped over socks and sandals (shoes)». №99

428) It is reported that Umm Salama (may Allah be pleased with her) said: «(Once) I asked:« O Messenger of Allah, I am a woman who braids her hair on her head. So should I let them loose for bathing from sexual defilement?» He replied: «No. It will be enough for you to pour three handfuls of water on your head. Then pour water on the rest of the body and you will be cleansed (or he said: and then you will be already cleansed)». №105

429) It was narrated from Abu Hurairah (narrated) that the Prophet ﷺ said: «Sexual defilement / janaba / lies under every hair, so wash your hair and cleanse your skin (body)». №106

430) It is reported that Abu Qatada (may Allah be pleased with him) said: «(One day people) asked the Prophet ﷺ about missing prayer due to sleep, and he said: «Sleep is not an omission (negligence), but an omission (occurs) while awake. Therefore, if one of you forgets to perform a prayer or oversleep it, let him perform it

when he remembers it». №177

431) It is reported that Abu Hurayrah said: «The Messenger of Allah ﷺ said: «The Imam is the guarantor, and the muazzin is the one who is trusted. O Allah, guide the Imams to the straight path and forgive (the sins of) the Mu'azzins!» №207

432) Narrated 'Uthman ibn al-'As: «Indeed, the last thing that the Messenger of Allah ﷺ bequeathed to me: «Choose a muazzin who does not charge for adhan». №207

433) It is narrated from the words of Abu Hurairah, may Allah be pleased with him, that the Messenger of Allah ﷺ said: «Five (daily) prayers and (participation in each subsequent) Friday prayer (after the previous one serve) atonement for the sins committed between (these prayers) unless there were no (among them) grave sins». №214

434) It is reported from the words of Ibn 'Umar, may Allah be pleased with them both, that the Messenger of Allah ﷺ said: «Collective prayer is twenty-seven times greater than individual prayer». №215

435) It is reported that Abu Mas'ud said: «Let the mature and intelligent (men) of you follow me, then those who follow them, and then those who follow them. And do not break uniformity, otherwise, there will be no agreement between your hearts. And in no case (do not act like you are) in the market!» №228

436) Abu Hurayra (may Allah be pleased with him) reported that the Prophet ﷺ said: «Let the one who leads the people in prayer facilitate it, for verily among them there may be old, sick, weak, and those who have what -something. And when one of you prays alone, let him pray (for as long) as he pleases.». №236

437) It was narrated by Ibn Abbas that the Prophet ﷺ said: «We are ordered to prostrate on seven bones, not to roll up our clothes and not to braid our hair». №273

438) It is reported that Abu Hurayrah, may Allah be pleased

with him, said: «The Messenger of Allah ﷺ said: «After the start of the prayer is announced, do not run to her, but come to her (normal) step, and remain calm. Pray (starting with the rak'at that) you find, and make up for what you missed». №327

439) It is reported that Abu 'Atiyah said: «Usually Malik ibn Khuwayris came to us at this place where we prayed, and (once) when (the mu'azzin) announced the iqam, we said to him: «Come forward and lead the prayer.» And he said to us, «Let one of you come forward and pray with you, and I will tell you why I don't want to lead you in prayer. I heard the Messenger of Allah ﷺ say: ‹Let the one who visits some people not lead them (in prayer), and let a person from among them lead them». №356

440) It is reported that Ibn 'Umar, may Allah be pleased with both of them, said: - I watched the Prophet ﷺ (a whole) month, (and all this time) performing two rak'ats before the (obligatory) morning prayer, the Prophet ﷺ read: « Say: «O disbelievers!», and also: «Say: «He, Allah, is the One ...». №417

441) It was narrated from Sahl ibn Mu'adh ibn Anas al-Juhani, who narrated from the words of his father, who said: «The Messenger of Allah ﷺ said: «He who moves forward through the ranks on Friday (in the mosque, pushing and stepping over people) paves himself bridge to hell!» №513

442) It is narrated from the words of Salim ibn 'Amir, who said: - I heard Abu Umama (Suday ibn 'Ajlan al-Bahili), may Allah be pleased with him, said: «I heard how during the farewell pilgrimage, the Messenger of Allah ﷺ said sermon and said: «Fear Allah, your Lord! Perform your five prayers, fast during your month (Ramadan), pay zakat on your property, obey your rulers and you will enter the Paradise of your Lord.» I asked Abu Umama: «How long ago did you hear this hadith from the Messenger of Allah ﷺ?» He replied: «I heard it when I was thirty years old». №616

443) It is reported that Anas, may Allah be pleased with him, said: «The Messenger of Allah ﷺ said: «Verily, charity extinguishes the wrath of the Lord and saves from a bad death». №664

444) 'Abdullah ibn Busr reported from the words of his sister, may Allah be pleased with her, that the Messenger of Allah ﷺ said: «Do not fast on Shabbat, except for fasting, which is obligatory, and if you find nothing but grape skins or branches from a tree, then chew them». №744

445) It is reported that Zayd ibn Khalid al-Juhani (may Allah be pleased with him) said: «The Messenger of Allah ﷺ said: «The one who feeds the fasting (when breaking the fast) will receive the same reward as he, but the reward (of the fasting) will not decrease not one iota». №807

446) It is reported that Ibn 'Abbas said: «The Messenger of Allah ﷺ said: «A black stone was sent down from Paradise and it was whiter than milk, and the sins of the sons of Adam made it black». №877

447) It is reported from the words of Suwayr ibn Abu Fahit that his father (Sa'id ibn 'Ilaqa al-Hashimi) said: «(One day) 'Ali, may Allah be pleased with him, took my hand and said: «Come with us Let's visit al-Hasan.» (When we got there) we found Abu Musa (al-Ash'ari) with him, and 'Ali said: «O Abu Musa, did you come to visit (the sick) or (just) visit (him)?» (Abu Musa) said: «No, visiting (the sick).» And 'Ali, may Allah be pleased with him, said: «I heard the Messenger of Allah ﷺ say:« There is no Muslim who visited a (sick) Muslim in the early morning, for whom seventy thousand angels would not pray until the evening, and if he visited him in the evening, seventy thousand angels pray for him until morning, and a garden in Paradise is prepared for him». №969

448) It is narrated from the words of Abu Hurairah (may Allah be pleased with him) that the Prophet ﷺ said: «Carry the deceased quickly, because if he was right-

eous, then you bring him closer to good, but if he was unrighteous, you (can quickly) remove (evil) with their necks». №1015

449) It is reported that 'Aisha (may Allah be pleased with her) said: «When the Messenger of Allah 🕮 died, (the people) differed (in opinion) regarding his burial, and Abu Bakr, may Allah be pleased with him, said:» I heard from the Messenger Allah 🕮 something that I have not forgotten. He said: «Allah did not kill any prophet except in the place where he wanted to be buried.» (Therefore) bury him where (where) his bed is». №1018

450) It is reported from Abu Hurairah, may Allah be pleased with him, that the Messenger of Allah 🕮 said: «When a dead person is buried (or he said: «one of you»), two black angels with blue (eyes) come to him, one of which name is Munkar and the other is Nakir. They ask him, «What did you say about this man?» He will say what he said before: «This is the servant of Allah and His messenger. I testify that there is no deity worthy of worship except Allah and that Muhammad is His servant and messenger.» They will say to him: «We knew you would answer like that.» Then his tomb will be widened for him seventy cubits in length and breadth, after which it will be illuminated. Then he will be told: «Sleep!» But he will answer: «I will return to my family and inform them.» But they will say to him: «Sleep like a bride who will not be awakened by anyone except the most beloved person from her family until Allah raises him from this bed.» And if he is a hypocrite, he will say: «I heard what people said and, not knowing, I said the same as what they said.» They'll say, «We knew you'd say that.» And the earth will be ordered: «Close up!». And the earth will close over him so that his ribs will enter into each other, and he will be punished in it until Allah raises him from this bed». №1071

451) It was narrated from 'Abdullah (ibn Mas'ud, may Allah be pleased with him) that the Prophet 🕮 said:

«Whoever comforts a person in trouble, (destined) the same reward as (and this person)». №1073

452) Abu Hurayrah (may Allah be pleased with him) reported that the Messenger of Allah ﷺ said: «The soul of a believer (remains) bound to his debt until it is paid». №1078

453) Передается от 'Аиши, что Посланник Аллаха ﷺ сказал: «Объявляйте об этом бракосочетании, проводите его в мечети и бейте при этом в бубны». №1089

454) It is reported that Abul-'Ajfa as-Sulami said: «(Once, during a sermon) 'Umar ibn al-Khattab, may Allah be pleased with him, said: «Do not increase the wedding gift to women. If it were honour in this life and piety before Allah, then the Prophet ﷺ would have outstripped you in this. I did not see the Messenger of Allah ﷺ marrying his wives or marrying his daughters, paying or taking more than twelve». №1114

455) Abu Hurayrah (may Allah be pleased with him) reported that the Prophet ﷺ said: «If a man has two wives, and he does not treat them equally, then on the Day of Judgment he will appear (before Allah) with half dragging behind him (body)». №1141

456) 'Abdullah ibn Mas'ud, may Allah be pleased with him, narrated that the Prophet ﷺ said: «A woman is 'awra, and when she leaves her house, the shaitan begins to look at her and tempt her». №1173

457) Narrated by Muhammad ibn Sirin that Yunus ibn Jubair said: «(Once) I asked Ibn 'Umar about a man who divorced his wife while she was menstruating, and he said: «You know 'Abdullah ibn 'Umar? Indeed, (somehow) he divorced his wife at the time when she was menstruating, and 'Umar asked (about this) the Prophet ﷺ and he ordered him to return her. (Yunus ibn Jubayr) said: «I asked: «Was this divorce counted?» (Ibn 'Umar) replied: «Tell me, what if he was not counted since he showed weakness and stupidity?!»

458) It is narrated from Isma'il ibn 'Ubayd ibn Rifa'a, who narrated from his father, who transmitted from his grandfather that one day he went with the Prophet 🕌 to a place of prayer, and when he saw trading people, he said: «O merchants!» They, responding (to the call) of the Messenger of Allah 🕌, raised their heads and fixed their eyes on him, and then he said: «Verily, on the Day of Resurrection, the merchants will be resurrected by the wicked, except for those who feared Allah, kept their promises and were truthful». №1210

459) It is reported that Hakim ibn Khizam said: «Once I came to the Messenger of Allah 🕌 and said: «A man comes to me and asks me to sell what I do not have, and I buy it for him from the market, after which I sell it to him», - (to which the Messenger of Allah 🕌) replied: «Do not sell what you do not have». №1232

460) It is reported that Abu Ayyub al-Ansari (may Allah be pleased with him) said: «I heard the Messenger of Allah 🕌 say: «Whoever separates a mother from her child, Allah will separate him from his beloved on the Day of Resurrection». №1283

461) It is reported that Anas ibn Malik said: «The Messenger of Allah 🕌 cursed ten people associated with wine: the one who squeezes the fruits for its production and the one for whom they are squeezed; the one who drinks it; the one who carries it, and the one to whom it is carried; the one who feeds them; the one who sells it; the one who makes a profit for it; the one who buys it and the one to whom they buy it». №1295

462) It is narrated from the words of Anas that the Prophet 🕌 said: «Whoever seeks and asks (to appoint him to a position) a judge, seeking the petition of others, will be left to himself, and whoever is forced to do this, Allah will send an angel with the one to show him the right way». №1324

463) It is reported that 'Abdurrahman ibn Abu Bakr said:

«Once my father wrote to 'Ubaydullah ibn Abu Bakr when he was a judge: «Do not decide between two being in anger, for I heard the Messenger of Allah ﷺ say:» judge to judge two when he is angry». №1334

464) It is reported from Anas ibn Malik that the Messenger of Allah ﷺ said: «If a (lamb) leg was presented to me as a gift, then I would accept (this gift). If I were invited to taste it, then I would certainly accept the invitations». №1338

465) It is reported from the words of Abu Sa'eed al-Khudri and Abu Hurairah, may Allah be pleased with them, that the Messenger of Allah ﷺ said: «If the inhabitants of heaven and earth were all (guilty of shedding) the blood of (one) believer, Allah would certainly plunge would them (all) in the Fire». №1398

466) Salim reported from the words of his father ('Abdullah ibn 'Umar, may Allah be pleased with both of them) that the Messenger of Allah ﷺ said: «A Muslim is a brother to a Muslim, and he (should not) neither oppress nor betray him. Whoever (helps) his brother in his need, Allah (will help) in his own need, whoever delivers a Muslim from sorrow, the Great and Almighty Allah will deliver from one of the sorrows of the Day of Resurrection, and (sins) of the one who covers (sins) of a Muslim, Allah will cover on the Day of Resurrection». №1426

467) It is reported from Abu Umama and some other companions of the Prophet ﷺ that the Prophet ﷺ said: «If any Muslim frees from slavery (a slave who is) a Muslim, then (the reward for him will be) liberation from the Fire, and every part of the body (the slave) deliver (from Fire) parts of the body (liberator). If any Muslim frees two Muslim women from slavery, then (the reward for him will be) liberation from the Fire, and each part of their body will deliver (from the Fire) parts of the body (liberator). If any Muslim woman frees from slavery a woman (who is) a Muslim woman, then (the reward for her will be) liberation from

the Fire, and each part of the body (of the slave) will deliver (from the Fire) parts of the body (of the woman who freed her)». №1547

468) It is reported that Sauban said: «The Messenger of Allah ﷺ said: «He who died without being involved in three (things): arrogance, theft of trophies/ghouls / and debt, will enter Paradise!» This chapter also contains hadiths from Abu Hurairah and Zayd ibn Khalid al-Juhani. №1572

469) It is reported that 'Abdullah ibn Mas'ud said: «The Messenger of Allah ﷺ said: «Bad omens / tiyara / are shirk!» And each of us ... But Allah removes it if you trust in Him». №1614

470) It is narrated from the words of Anas ibn Malik that when the Prophet ﷺ went out on some [his] business, he liked to hear (words): «O walking on the right path! O one to whom success accompanies! Abu 'Isa (at-Tirmidhi) said: «This hadith is good, rare and reliable». №1616

471) Abu Musa, may Allah be pleased with him, said: «Once the Messenger of Allah ﷺ was asked about a man who fights because of (his) courage, other fights (under the influence of) rage, and a third fights for show. Which of these is (struggle) in the way of Allah? He said: «Whoever fights so that the word of Allah is above all, he is in the path of Allah». №1646

472) It is reported that 'Abdullah ibn 'Amr, may Allah be pleased with both of them, said: «(Once) a man came to the Prophet ﷺ and asked him for permission to take part in jihad. (The Prophet ﷺ) asked: «Do you have parents?» (The man) said, «Yes.» (Then the Prophet ﷺ) said: «So give all your strength / jahid / to them!» №1671

473) It is narrated from the words of Ibn 'Umar, may Allah be pleased with them both, that the Messenger of Allah ﷺ said: «If people knew about loneliness what I know, not a single horseman would set off on a jour-

ney at night,» meaning alone. №1673

474) It is reported that 'Ubeydullah ibn 'Abdillah ibn 'Utba
said that once he visited Abu Talha al-Ansari during
his illness and found Sahl ibn Hunayf with him. Abu
Talha asked one of those present to pull out from under him a mat (on which he was lying). Sahl asked
him, «Why did you (decide) to pull her out?» (Abu
Talhah) replied: «There are images (of living beings)
on it, and you know what the Prophet ﷺ said about
this.» Then Sahl said: «Didn't he say: «Except for the
pattern on the clothes!»?» (Abu Talhah) replied: «Yes,
but this way I will be calmer!» №1750

475) It is reported that 'Umar ibn al-Khattab (may Allah
be pleased with him) said: «The Messenger of Allah
ﷺ said: «Eat olive oil and anoint yourself with it, for
verily, it (is derived) from a blessed tree». №1851

476) Abu Hurayrah (may Allah be pleased with him) reported that the Prophet ﷺ said: «If a servant of any
of you (cooks food) after saving (his master) from the
heat (coming from this food) and his smoke, let him
take him for hand and sit down with him (so that he
eats), and if he refuses, let him take (at least) a piece (of
food) and feed him». №1853

477) It is reported that 'Abdullah ibn 'Amr (may Allah
be pleased with them both) said: «The Messenger of
Allah ﷺ said: «Worship the Merciful, feed (people),
spread salam, and you will enter Paradise in peace».
№1855

478) It was narrated from Anas ibn Malik, may Allah be pleased with him, that the Prophet ﷺ said:
«Eat at least a handful of low-grade dates, for verily, leaving supper (leads to) decrepitude». №1856
479)   It is narrated from the words of 'Umar ibn
Abu Salam (may Allah be pleased with them both)
that (once) he went to the Messenger of Allah ﷺ in
front of whom there was food, (and the Messenger of
Allah ﷺ) said: «Come, O boy! Say: «In the name of
Allah!» / Bismi-Llahi! /, - eat with your right hand and

take what is next to you!» №1857

480) It was narrated from Abu Hurayrah (may Allah be pleased with him) that the Messenger of Allah ﷺ said: «Verily, Satan is sensitive, licking, so take care of yourself from him. He who spent the night with (traces of) fat and the smell of meat on his hands, and something befell him, let him not blame anyone but himself». №1859

481) It was narrated from Abu Hurayrah (may Allah be pleased with him) that the Messenger of Allah ﷺ said: «A Muslim is a brother of a Muslim. He (must) neither betray him, nor lie to him, nor leave him without support. For every Muslim (should be) inviolable honour, property and life of another Muslim, and piety is hidden here. To cause harm (to oneself), it is enough for a person to show contempt towards his brother in Islam!» №1927

482) It is reported from the words of Sa'eed ibn al-'As (may Allah be pleased with him) that the Messenger of Allah ﷺ said: «No father gave his son a gift that would be better than a good upbringing». №1952

483) It is narrated from the words of Abu Dharr (may Allah be pleased with him) that the Messenger of Allah ﷺ said: «Your smile in the face of your brother (in faith) is alms/sadaqah / for you. Commanding what you approve and forbidding what you dislike is almsgiving. Showing the right path to a person who is lost on earth is almsgiving for you. Helping a person who sees badly (or the blind) sees what he cannot see is the charity for you. Removing a stone, thorn or bone from the road (which hinders people) is the charity for you, and pouring water from your bucket into your brother's bucket (in Islam) is the charity for you». №1956

484) It is narrated from the words of Safwan ibn Sulaym (may Allah be pleased with him) that the Prophet ﷺ said: «The one who takes care of the widow and the poor is like the one who fights in the path of Allah or the one who (constantly) fasts during the day and

prays (all) nights away». №1969

485) Abu Hurayrah (may Allah be pleased with him) reported that the Prophet ﷺ said: «Study your genealogy, through which you will maintain family ties. Indeed, maintaining family ties is the cause of love between relatives, helps to increase property and prolong (term) life». №1979

486) Abdullah ibn Mas'ud, may Allah be pleased with him, narrates that the Messenger of Allah ﷺ said: «Reproaching a Muslim (indicates) wickedness, and fighting with him is (a manifestation of) unbelief». №1983

487) Abu Hurayrah (may Allah be pleased with him) narrated that the Messenger of Allah ﷺ said: «Indeed, the worst of people with Allah on the Day of Resurrection is the two-faced». №2025

488) It is reported that Mahmoud ibn Labid reported from the words of Qatada ibn an-Nu'man (may Allah be pleased with him) that the Messenger of Allah ﷺ said: «If Allah loves (some of His) slave, He protects him in this world, as any of you protect your patient from water». №2036

489) It is reported that Umm al-Mundhir (may Allah be pleased with her) said: «(Once) the Messenger of Allah ﷺ came to me with 'Ali, and we (at that time) had bunches of unripe dates hanging.» (Umm al-Mundhir, may Allah be pleased with her) said: «And the Messenger of Allah ﷺ began to eat (them) and together with him (it began to do) 'Ali, but the Messenger of Allah ﷺ said to 'Ali: «Stop! Stop, O Ali! After all, you are (still) recovering!» Then 'Ali sat down, and the Prophet ﷺ (continued) to eat. (Umm al-Mundhir, may Allah be pleased with her) said: «I prepared beets and barley for them, and then the Prophet ﷺ said:« O 'Ali, try this, for verily, this will suit you. Another version says: «... it is more useful for you». №2037

490) It is reported that Usama ibn Shariyyk (may Allah be pleased with him) said: «(Once) the Bedouins said:« O

Messenger of Allah, should we be treated? He replied: «Yes, O slaves of Allah, get treated, for verily, Allah did not create a single disease without creating a cure for it (or he said: medicines), except for one.» They asked: «O Messenger of Allah, what is this?» He said: «(This is) old age». №2038

491) It is reported from 'Uqba ibn 'Amir al-Juhani (may Allah be pleased with him) that the Messenger of Allah ﷺ said: «Do not force your sick to eat, for Allah feeds and waters them». №2040

492) It is reported that Abu Salama narrated from the words of Abu Hurairah (may Allah be pleased with him) that the Messenger of Allah ﷺ said: «You should use this black cumin, for, verily, in it is a cure for every disease, except for «samma», and «samm» - (is) death». №2041

493) It is narrated from the words of Abu Hurairah (may Allah be pleased with him) that the Messenger of Allah ﷺ) said: «Whoever kills himself with a piece of iron will hold this piece of iron in his hands and hit himself in the stomach with it in hellfire forever. And the one who kills himself (by drinking or swallowing) poison will hold this poison in his hand, which he will drink forever in hellfire. And the one who (deliberately) throws himself down from the mountain and destroys himself, will fly down all the time in hellfire, (where he abides) forever». №2044

494) It is narrated from the words of Simak that he heard how 'Alqama ibn Wail, according to the words of his father, said that (once) he witnessed how Suwayd ibn Tariq (or: Tariq ibn Suwayd) asked the Prophet ﷺ about wine, and he forbade it to him, and (Suwayd (or: Tariq)) said: «But we (use it as) medicine!» - (to which the Prophet ﷺ) said: «Truly, this is not a medicine, but a disease!» №2046

495) It was narrated from Ibn 'Abbas (may Allah be pleased with him) that the Messenger of Allah ﷺ said: «Indeed, the best means of treatment for you are sa'ut /

putting medicine in the nose /, lyudud, bloodletting and laxative (for the stomach)». And when the Messenger of Allah ﷺ fell ill, his companions put medicine in the corner of his mouth, and when they finished, (the Prophet ﷺ) said: «Give them the medicine by force!» (Ibn 'Abbas) said: «And everyone (who was present in the house) was forcibly forced to take medicine, except for al-'Abbas.» 'Abd said: «An-Nadr said: «Al-Ladud» is a dose of medicine (given to the patient through the mouth)». №2047

496) It is reported from the words of 'Imran ibn Husayn (may Allah be pleased with him) that the Messenger of Allah ﷺ forbade (doing) cauterization. ('Imran) said: «And we were put to the test and made cauterization, but we did not achieve either success or result». №2049

497) It is reported that Ibn Mas'ud (may Allah be pleased with him) said: «The Messenger of Allah ﷺ spoke about the night in which he was taken up (to heaven) and that he did not pass by any community of angels so that they did not order him: «Order the members of your community to do bloodletting!» №2052

498) It is reported from the words of 'Ali ibn 'Ubaydullah that his grandmother (Umm Rafi') Salma (may Allah be pleased with her), who served the Prophet ﷺ said: «Every time the Messenger of Allah ﷺ had an injury or (some other) wound, he ordered me to put henna on it». №2054

499) It is narrated from Anas (may Allah be pleased with him) that the Messenger of Allah ﷺ allowed (to read) spells from the bite (poisonous creatures), the evil eye and acne. №2056

500) It is reported that (once) Asma bint 'Umays (may Allah be pleased with her) said: «O Messenger of Allah, the children of Ja'far are very easily succumbed (to) the evil eye, so should I (find one who) read for spells /rukya/?» He said: «Yes, for, verily, if anything were ahead of predestination (of Allah), then the evil eye

would be ahead of him / al-'ayn /». №2059

501) It was narrated from Ibn 'Abbas (may Allah be pleased with them both) that the Messenger of Allah ﷺ said: «If anything could get ahead of predestination, then it would be an evil eye, and therefore if you are asked to make a complete ablution, make it». №2062

502) Narrated from Abu Khizama, (narrated) from his father, (who) said: «(Once) I asked a question to the Messenger of Allah ﷺ and said:« O Messenger of Allah, tell me, the spells that we read, the medicines with which we are treated, or the precautions that we take - does (all this) repel from us anything from the pre-destination of Allah? (The Prophet ﷺ) replied: «This (everything) is from the predestination of Allah!» №2065

503) 'Utba ibn 'Abdullah told me from the words of Asma bint 'Umays, (who told) that (once) the Messenger of Allah ﷺ asked her: «What laxatives (means) do you use?» She replied, «Shubroom.» (The Prophet ﷺ) said: «A strong laxative!» (Asma) said: «Then I used hay as a laxative, and then the Prophet ﷺ said:« If there was a cure for death in anything, then it would be in senna». №2081

504) It is narrated from the words of Ibn 'Abbas (may Allah be pleased with them both) that the Prophet ﷺ said: «If any slave professing Islam visits a sick person whose life has not yet expired, and says seven times:« I ask Allah the Great, Lord of the great throne so that He heals you / Asalu-Llaha-l-'azyma, Rabba-l-'arshi-l-'azimi, an yashfiyaka /», he will be healed». №2083

505) It is narrated from the words of Abu Hurairah (may Allah be pleased with him) that (once) the Prophet ﷺ, who visited a man who was suffering from a fever, said: «Rejoice! Verily, Allah says: «This (fever) is My fire, into the power of which I give My sinful servant (in this world) so that it becomes a deliverance for him from (hell) fire (in the next world)». №2088

506) Abu Waqid al-Laysi said that when the Messenger of Allah ﷺ went on a military campaign to Khaybar, he passed by a tree of the polytheists, which they called «Zatu anvat», and on which they hung their weapons. And they said: «O Messenger of Allah, make us the same Zatu Anwat as theirs.» To which the Prophet ﷺ exclaimed: «Holy Allah / Subhanallah /! This is similar to what the people of Musa said: «Make us a god-like theirs» (Surah al-A'raf 7:138). I swear by Him in whose hand my soul is, you follow the ways of those who were before you!» №2180

507) It is reported that Sauban, may Allah be pleased with him, said: «The Messenger of Allah ﷺ said:« If a sword falls in my community, then it will not rise until the Day of Resurrection!» №2202

508) It was narrated from Abu Hurayrah (may Allah be pleased with him) that the Messenger of Allah ﷺ said: «When booty goes to the rich, the property entrusted with storage will be perceived as a trophy, and zakat as damage, when knowledge will be acquired not for the sake of religion when a man will obey his wife and disobey his mother, will bring his friend closer to him and alienate his father when voices rise in the mosques, the tribe will be headed by a wicked one from among them, the leader of the people will be the lowest of them, and the person will be honoured for fear of evil emanating from it when singers and musical instruments spread, the wine will be drunk, and the last of this Ummah will curse the first, then expect a red wind, an earthquake, failures, ugliness and rockfall (from the sky), and signs will follow one after another, like a necklace whose thread has broken and one bead, falls after another». №2211

509) It is reported that Ziyad ibn Kusayb al-'Adawi said: «Once I was with Abu Bakra (Nufay' ibn al-Harith), may Allah be pleased with him, under the minbar of Ibn 'Amir, who read the khutba and was wearing clothes made of thin fabrics. And Abu Bilal said: «Look at our amir who puts on the clothes of the wick-

ed!» Then Abu Bakra said: «Shut up! For I heard the Messenger of Allah ﷺ say: «Whoever humiliates the power of Allah on earth, Allah will humiliate him». №2224

510) It is reported from Ubay ibn Ka'b that the Messenger of Allah ﷺ said: «Do not scold the wind! If you see (in it) something that you do not like, then say: «O Allah! We ask You for the good of this wind, as well as the good of what it carries in itself, and the good of what it is commanded to. We seek Your protection from the evil of this wind, as well as the evil of what it carries in itself, and the evil of what it is ordered to». №2252

511) Hudhayfa (may Allah be pleased with him) reported that the Messenger of Allah ﷺ said: «A believer should not humiliate himself!» (People) asked: «How can he humiliate himself?!» He replied: «By taking on such difficulties that he cannot bear». №2254

512) It is reported from Anas ibn Malik (may Allah be pleased with him) that the Messenger of Allah ﷺ said: «There will come a time for people when among them patient (adhering) to their religion will be like holding (in hand) hot coals». №2260

513) It was reported from Ibn 'Umar (may Allah be pleased with them both) that the Messenger of Allah ﷺ said: «When the members of my community begin to walk proudly and their servants become the children of kings, the children of Persians and Romans, then the worst of them will be given power over their best». №2261

514) It was narrated from Abu Hurayrah (may Allah be pleased with him) that the Messenger of Allah ﷺ said: «If your rulers are the best of you, your rich people are generous of you, and your affairs (are decided) in council among themselves, then the top the earth is better for you than its bottom. But if your rulers are the worst of you, your rich are greedy among you, and your affairs (will be in charge) of your women, then the bottom of the earth is better for you than its top».

515) It is reported from Anas ibn Malik that the Messenger of Allah ﷺ said: «Indeed, the mission of the messenger and the prophecy have ceased, and after me, there will be neither a messenger nor a prophet.» These (words) seemed heavy to the people, and (then the Prophet ﷺ) said: «But (there will be) good news!» (People) asked: «O Messenger of Allah! What is meant by good news? (The Prophet ﷺ) replied: «Dreams of a Muslim! They are part of the prophecy». №2272

516) It is reported that 'Ubada ibn as-Samit, may Allah be pleased with him, said: «(Once) I asked the Messenger of Allah ﷺ about the words (of Allah Almighty): «The good news in this world is destined for them» (Surah «Yunus» 10: 64), and he said: «This is a good dream, which the believer sees himself or which others see about him». №2275

517) It is reported from Ibn 'Abbas (may Allah be pleased with them both) that the Messenger of Allah ﷺ said: «Many people are deprived of two favours: health and free time». №2304

518) It was narrated from Abu Hurayrah, may Allah be pleased with him, that the Messenger of Allah ﷺ said: «If you knew what I know, then, of course, you would laugh a little and cry a lot!» №2313

519) It was reported from Abu Hurayrah, may Allah be pleased with him, that the Messenger of Allah ﷺ said: «Verily, a person can say just one word, not seeing anything bad in it, because of which he will fall into the Fire for seventy years». №2314

520) It is reported that Abu Hurairah (may Allah be pleased with him) said: «I heard the Messenger of Allah ﷺ say: «Cursed is this world and cursed (everything) that is in it, except for the remembrance of Allah Almighty/ dhikr/, and what is close to it, and knowing and learning!» №2322

521) It is reported from Abu Kabsha al-Anmari that the

Messenger of Allah ﷺ said: «I will swear on three things and tell you a hadith, and you remember it: alms do not reduce the property (distributing it) of a slave, and if an injustice is caused to a slave, and he shows patience, then Allah will certainly add greatness to him, and if a slave opens (for himself) the gates of requests (from people), then Allah will certainly open before him the gates of poverty - or words like these. I will tell you also (another) hadith, and you memorize it! There are four groups of people in this world: (Firstly) a servant (of Allah), endowed by Allah with wealth and knowledge, and he is wary (punishment) of his Lord in these things, maintains family ties, and recognizes the right of Allah to this (wealth and knowledge). Such a (slave) will occupy the best degree. (Secondly), a slave (of Allah), endowed with knowledge by Allah, but not endowed with wealth by Him. However, he truthfully says: «If I had wealth, then I would certainly act in the same way as (the first) does.» Under his (truthful) intention, the reward for these two is the same. (Thirdly), a servant (of Allah), endowed by Allah with wealth, but not endowed with knowledge by Him, and he spends his wealth without any knowledge: he does not beware (punishment) of his Lord in (his) wealth, does not maintain family ties and does not recognize the right of Allah to this (wealth). Such a (slave) will occupy the worst degree. (Fourthly), a servant (of Allah), not endowed by Allah with either wealth or knowledge, but at the same time he says: «If I had wealth, then I would certainly act in the same way as such and such does.» By his intention, the sin of these two is the same». №2325

522) It is reported from Ibn Mas'ud, may Allah be pleased with him, that the Messenger of Allah ﷺ said: «Never get rid of the need of the one who, experiencing it, will turn to people for help, the same one who turns to Allah with this, He will sooner or later send (his) inheritance». №2326

523) It is reported from Anas ibn Malik that the Messenger

of Allah ﷺ said: «This is the descendant of Adam, and this is his life span», and he put his hand on the back of his head, after which he extended it (far forward) and said: «And there are his dreams (plans)! And then there are his dreams!» №2334

524) It is reported that Ka'b ibn 'Iyad, may Allah be pleased with him, said: «I heard the Prophet ﷺ say:« Verily, each community has its temptation, but the temptation of my community (will be) wealth». №2336

525) It is reported that Mutarrif narrated from his father that once he came to the Prophet ﷺ when he was reading «The passion for multiplication carries you away ...». He said, «The son of Adam says, «My wealth! My wealth!» But after all, you get from your wealth only what you donated and left (for the future life), or what you ate and ruined, or what you put on and wore out.». №2342

526) It is reported that Anas ibn Malik said: «During the time of the Prophet ﷺ, there lived two brothers, one of whom visited the Prophet ﷺ, and the other was engaged in his craft. One day, the one who was engaged in a craft complained to the Prophet ﷺ about his brother, to which (the Prophet ﷺ) said: «(How do you know), perhaps your food is given to you (only) because of your brother?!». №2345

527) It is reported by 'Ubaydullah ibn Mihsan al-Ansari al-Khatmi, may Allah be pleased with him, who was a companion, that the Messenger of Allah ﷺ said: «It can be said that the whole world went to one of you who met the morning with a calm heart being in good health and having enough food to last him a day». №2346

528) It is reported from 'Abdullah ibn 'Amr that the Messenger of Allah ﷺ said: «The one who converted to Islam and was endowed with food sufficient to (maintain) life, succeeded, and Allah made him pleased with what He gave him». №2348

529) Abu Hurairah reported that the Messenger of Allah ﷺ said: «O Allah! Give the family of Muhammad a provision that will be enough (to sustain life)!». №2361

530) It is narrated from the words of Ka'b ibn Malik, may Allah be pleased with him, that the Messenger of Allah ﷺ said: «A pair of hungry wolves launched into (herd) sheep cannot do more damage to them than a person's desire for wealth and honour causes his religion». №2376

531) It is reported that al-Miqdam ibn Ma'dikarib (may Allah be pleased with him) said: «I heard the Messenger of Allah ﷺ say: «(Never) did a person fill a vessel worse than (his own) womb! It is enough for the son of Adam (a few) pieces of food, thanks to which he will be able to straighten his back, and if it is inevitable (for him there is more, let) a third (of his stomach be) for eating, a third for drinking, and another third for (lightness) respiration». №2380

532) It is reported from al-Walid ibn Abul-Walid Abu 'Uthman al-Madini that 'Uqba ibn Muslim told him that Shufayy al-Asbahi told him that one day when he came to Medina he met people who gathered around one person and he asked, «Who is this man?» (People) said: «Abu Hurairah.» (Shufayy) said: «I approached him and sat opposite him, and he told the people. When Abu Hurairah finished speaking and fell silent, I asked him: «I ask you for the true truth, tell me the hadith that you heard from the Messenger of Allah ﷺ understood and memorized it!» Then Abu Hurayrah said: «I will do it, I will tell you the hadith that the Messenger of Allah ﷺ told me, which I understood and learned.» Then Abu Hurairah began to wheeze and fainted. We waited a bit, and then he came to his senses and then said: «I will definitely tell you the hadith that the Messenger of Allah ﷺ told me and then there was no one with us in this house except me and him.» Again Abu Hurairah began to wheeze and fainted. Then, waking up again, he rubbed his face (with his hands) and said, «I will do it! I will tell you the hadith that the Messen-

ger of Allah ﷺ told me and then there was no one with us in this house except me and him. But Abu Hurairah (again) began to wheeze strongly and then fell on his face, and I propped him up with myself for a long time and then waking up, he said: «The Messenger of Allah ﷺ told me that on the Day of Resurrection, the Almighty and Almighty Allah will descend to His servants to pass judgment upon them, and at that time all the congregations will be on their knees. The first to be called to account (on this day) will be the person who memorized the Quran, the person who fought in the way of Allah, and the owner of a large property. The Great and Almighty Allah will say to the reader of the Quran: «Did I not teach you what I sent down to My Messenger ?!» He will answer: «Of course, my Lord!» Then He will ask: «What did you do according to what you were taught?» He will answer: «All I did was stand up prayers, reading it day and night.» Then the Great and Almighty Allah will say to him: «You lied.» And the angels will also say to him: «You lied.» And Allah Almighty and Almighty will say: «On the contrary, you only wished for (people) to say: «Such and such a reader,» and they said this. Then a rich man will be brought and the Great and Almighty Allah will ask him: «Did I not continue to multiply your property until you no longer need anyone ?!» He will answer: «Yes, my Lord!» Then He will ask: «What did you do with what I gave you?» He will say: «I maintained family ties and distributed sadaqah/alms/». Then Allah will say: «You lied!» And the angels will repeat: «You lied!» And Allah Almighty and Almighty will say: «On the contrary, you wanted only that (people) say:« He is a generous person, »and they said it. Then they will bring the fallen in the path of Allah and He will ask him: «For what were you killed?» He will reply: «O my Lord, I was ordered to do jihad in Your way and I fought until I was killed!» But Allah will say to him: «You lied!» And the angels will repeat: «You lied.» And Allah will say: «On the contrary, you wanted only that (people) say: «So-and-so brave!»,

And they said it. Then the Messenger of Allah ﷺ hit me on the thigh and said: «O Abu Hurairah, it is these three creatures of Allah that will first kindle hellfire on the Day of Resurrection!» №2382

533) It is narrated from the words of Abu Sa'id (al-Khudri) that he heard the Prophet ﷺ say: «Do not associate with anyone except a believer and let no one eat your food except the God-fearing». №2395

534) It is reported that Sa'd ibn Abi Waqqas said: «Once I asked: «O Messenger of Allah! Who among the people undergoes the most difficult trials? (The Prophet ﷺ) replied: «The Prophets, and then those who are closest to them, and then those who are closest to them. The servant (of Allah) is tested according to his religion: if he confesses it firmly, then his tests are difficult, but if he confesses it weakly, then he is tested according to his religion. Trials do not cease to befall a slave until he walks the earth without a single sin». №2398

535) Abu Hurairah and Abu Sa'eed reported that the Messenger of Allah ﷺ said: «On the Day of Resurrection, (one of) the slaves will be brought, and Allah will say to him:» Did I not give you hearing, sight, wealth and children, and did not subjugated livestock and arable land to you, and did not leave you to lead (people), and did not (allow you) to receive a quarter of the spoils of war?! Did you know that you will meet Me on this day?!» He will answer: «No», and then (Allah) will say: «Today I will consign you to oblivion just as you forgot about Me!». №2428

536) It is reported that 'Abdullah ibn Salam, may Allah be pleased with him, said: «When the Messenger of Allah ﷺ arrived in Medina, people rushed to him and said: «The Messenger of Allah ﷺ has arrived! The Messenger of Allah ﷺ has arrived! The Messenger of Allah ﷺ has arrived! Among the people, I also came to look at him. When I saw the face of the Messenger of Allah ﷺ, I realized that this was not the face of a liar, and the first thing I heard from him was the words:

«O people, spread greetings/salam/, feed food (other people), maintain family ties, pray when (other) people will sleep and you will enter Paradise in peace». №2485

537) It was narrated from the words of Abu Hurairah, may Allah be pleased with him, that the Prophet ﷺ said: «The one who eats and gives thanks (for this to Allah), in the degree of the one who fasts and shows patience». №2486

538) It is reported from the words of 'Abdullah ibn Mas'ud that the Messenger of Allah ﷺ said: «Shall I not inform you about who will become forbidden for fire (or: ... about who will become forbidden for fire)? Forbidden (for fire) will be everyone close (to people), soft and simple». №2488

539) It is reported that 'Amr ibn Shu'ayb reported from the words of his father, who transmitted from his grandfather ('Abdullah ibn 'Amr, may Allah be pleased with him) that the Prophet ﷺ said: «On the Day of Resurrection, the arrogant will be resurrected with the size of ants in the form of people who will be surrounded by humiliation on all sides. They will be dragged to the dungeon located in Gehenna, which is called «Bulyas». And the (hellish) fires will cover them, and they will be watered by the secretions of the inhabitants of Hell, (who are called) «tynatul-khabal». №2495

540) It is narrated from Abu Hurairah that the Prophet ﷺ said: «Beware of spoiling relations (with each other), as this shaves off (religion)». №2508

541) It is reported that Abu ad-Darda said: «The Messenger of Allah ﷺ said:« Shall I tell you what is better (higher) in degree than fasting, prayer and alms/sadaqah/? They said, «Of course!» He said: «Settlement of relationships, for the breakdown of relationships is shaving off (religion).» Abu 'Isa (at-Tirmidhi) said: «This hadith is authentic. It was narrated from the Prophet ﷺ that he said: «This (hatred) is shaving. I'm not saying she shaves her hair, but she shaves her religion!»

542) It is narrated from the words of Ya'ish ibn al-Walid
that the freedman az-Zubayr told him that Az-Zubair
ibn al-'Awwam told him that the Prophet ﷺ said: «A
disease is approaching you that was inherent in communities who lived before you: envy and hatred. This
(hatred) is shaving. I'm not saying she shaves her hair,
but she shaves her religion! I swear by Him in Whose
hand is my soul, you will not enter Paradise until you
believe, and you will not believe until you love one
another. So why don't I point out to you what will
strengthen all this in you? Spread salam/greetings /
among yourselves!» №2510

543) It is reported that Ibn 'Abbas, may Allah be pleased
with them both, said: «Once when I was sitting on
horseback behind the Messenger of Allah ﷺ, he said:»
O boy, I will teach you a few words: remember Allah,
and He will keep you, remember Allah and you will
find Him before you. If (you want) to ask (for something), ask Allah, if (you want) to ask for help, ask Allah for it, and know that if all people come together to
do something useful for you, they will bring you only
benefit from what Allah has ordained for you, and if
they gather together to harm you, they will harm you
only what Allah has ordained for you, for the feathers
have already been raised and the pages have dried up».
№2516

544) Al-Mughira ibn Abu Qurra as-Sadusiy told us, who
said: - I heard Anas ibn Malik say: «Once a man said
(to the Prophet ﷺ): «O Messenger of Allah, I tie (a
camel) and trust (in Allah), or unbind and trust?»
(The Prophet ﷺ) replied: «Bind and trust!». №2517

545) It is reported that Abul-Hawra as-Saadi said: «Once
I asked al-Hasan ibn Ali: «Which of the words of the
Messenger of Allah ﷺdid you remember?» He replied:
«I memorized from the Messenger of Allah ﷺ (the fol-
lowing words): «Leave that which inspires you with
doubts, and turn to that which does not cause doubts,

for truthfulness is calmness, and falsehood is doubts». №2518

546) It is narrated from the words of Mu'adh ibn Jabal (may Allah be pleased with him) that the Messenger of Allah ﷺ said: of this hadith said: «I do not know whether he mentioned zakat or not» - has the right (hope that) Allah will forgive him, regardless of whether he migrated in the way of Allah or remained in (that) land, on which he was born. Mu'az asked: «Should I tell people about this?» (To this) the Messenger of Allah ﷺ said: «Leave people, (let) do deeds, for, truly, in paradise, there are a hundred degrees, and between every two degrees (the same distance) as between heaven and earth, and Firdaus is located on in the middle of paradise and on its very peak, above which is (only) the Throne of the Merciful, the rivers of paradise originate from there. And if you ask Allah, ask Him for Firdaus!» №2530

547) It is narrated from the words of Mu'adh ibn Jabal (may Allah be pleased with him) that the Prophet ﷺ said: «Its inhabitants will enter Paradise without hair on the body, without a beard, with eyes tinted with antimony, at the age of thirty (or: thirty-three) years!» №2545

548) It was reported from Jabir, may Allah be pleased with him, that the Messenger of Allah ﷺ said: «People (from among) adherents of monotheism will be punished in the Fire until they turn into coal there. Then they will be seized by the mercy (of Allah) and they will be taken out (from there) and thrown at the gates of Paradise. (The Prophet ﷺ also) said: «And the inhabitants of Paradise will sprinkle water on them and they will grow like rubbish that brings with it a stream, after which they will enter Paradise». №2597

549) Abu Hurairah, may Allah be pleased with him, reported that the Messenger of Allah ﷺ said: «I was ordered to fight (these) people until they testify that there is no deity worthy of worship except Allah. If they say this, then they will protect their blood and property from

me, except, as by right, and (then) an account from them (only Allah will have the right to demand)». №2606

550) 'Abdullah ibn Mas'ud (may Allah be pleased with him) narrated that the Messenger of Allah ﷺ said: «A Muslim fighting with his brother is (a manifestation of) unbelief, and reviling him (testifies to) impiety». №2634

551) It is reported from the words of Ibn 'Abbas, may Allah be pleased with both of them, that the Messenger of Allah ﷺ said: «Allah leads to an understanding of the religion of the one whom He wishes good». №2645

552) It is reported that Anas ibn Malik said: «(Once) a man came to the Prophet ﷺ with a request to give him a riding animal, but he did not find from him what to give him and pointed him to another who gave him one. Then he came to the Prophet ﷺ and informed him about it and then he said: «Verily, he who points to the good is like the one who does it». №2670

553) It is reported from the words of Abu Tamima al-Khujaimi that a man from his tribe said: «Once I began to look for the Prophet ﷺ, but I could not find him and sat down. And when (I saw him) he was among a group of people, but I (yet) did not know him (then), he reconciled them, and when he finished, some of them stood up with him and said: «O Messenger of Allah.» And when I saw this, I said: «Peace be upon you, O Messenger of Allah! Peace be upon you, O Messenger of Allah! Peace be upon you, O Messenger of Allah! / 'Aleyka-s-salaam ya rasulu-Allah! 'Aleyka-s-salaam ya rasulu-Allah! 'Aleyka-s-salaam ya rasulu-Allah! (The Prophet ﷺ) said: «Indeed, (with the words)« Peace be upon you »greet the dead!», repeating this three times, after which he turned to me and said: «If a person meets his Muslim brother, let him say: «As-Salamu 'Alaykum wa rahmatu-llah!», after which the Prophet ﷺ answered me, saying: «And the mercy of Allah to you! And God bless you! And God bless

you! / Wa 'alaika wa rahmatu-llah! Wa 'alaika wa rah-matu-llah! Wa 'alaika wa rahmatu-llah!» №2721

554) It is reported from Ibn Abbas that the Prophet ﷺ trimmed and shaved his moustache, just like Ibrahim Khalil-ur-Rahman. №2760

555) It is reported that Zaid ibn Arkam said: «The Prophet ﷺ said: «Those who do not shave off his moustache is not one of us». №2761

556) It is reported from Amr ibn Shuayb, from his father, from his grandfather it was narrated: «The Messenger of Allah ﷺ shortened his beard in length and width» №2762

557) Narrated Ibn Abbas that the Messenger of Allah ﷺ cursed women who imitate men and cursed men who imitate women. №2784

558) It is reported that Ibn 'Umar, may Allah be pleased with both of them, said: «The Messenger of Allah ﷺ said: «Three (things) are not refused: pillows, oil and milk.» (At-Tirmidhi said): «By» oil «he meant incense». №2790

559) It is reported from Abu 'Uthman al-Nahdi, who said: «The Messenger of Allah ﷺ said: «If any of you are given basil / Rayhan /, let him not refuse it, for, verily, he came out of paradise». №2791

560) It is reported from the words of 'Abdurrahman ibn Abu Sa'id al-Khudri that his father (Abu Sa'id al-Khudri), may Allah be pleased with him, said: «The Messenger of Allah ﷺ said:» Let a man not look at the 'awrah of a man and a woman does not look at the 'awrah of a woman, and let not a man lie under the same veil with a man, and a woman does not lie under the same veil with a woman». №2793

561) It is narrated from the words of Samur ibn Jundab: «The Messenger of Allah ﷺ said: «Dress in clothes of white colour, indeed, they are clean and beautiful, and wrap dead in them». №2810

562) Narrated Anas ibn Malik that the Prophet ﷺ forbade men to use saffron. №2815

563) Narrated Ismail ibn Abi Khalid: «Abu Juhayfa said that he saw the Prophet ﷺ, al-Hasan ibn Ali was the most like him. №2827

564) It is reported that Ibn Umar said that the Prophet ﷺ said: «The most beloved names of Allah are Abdullah and Abdurahman» №2833

565) It is reported that al-Harith al-Ash'ari narrated that the Prophet ﷺ said: - Verily, Allah ordered (the prophet) Yahya, the son of Zakariya, to observe the five commandments and command the sons of Israel to observe them, but Yahya began to delay in fulfilling this decree. Then (the prophet) Isa said (to him): «Allah ordered you to keep the five commandments and command the children of Israel to keep them. Either you turn to them with this command, or I (will do it for you).» Yahya replied: «I am afraid that if you get ahead of me in this, then I will be swallowed up (by the earth) or I will be tormented.» After that, he gathered people in Jerusalem so that the temple was filled (with people), and even the balconies were occupied. He said (to them): «Indeed, Allah commanded me to keep the five commandments and commanded me to command the same for you. First, (Allah commanded) that you worship (only) Him and do not associate anyone with Him. The one who associates partners with Allah is like a bought slave, for whom the buyer gave his property in the form of gold or silver. He said (to this slave): «This is my house, and this is my work, so work and give me wages.» This slave set to work, but began to give out his earnings, not to his master. Who among you would want his slave to be like that?! Secondly, Allah ordered you to pray. When you perform it, do not look around, because, during prayer, the face of Allah is in front of the face of His slave until he begins to look around. Thirdly, Allah has commanded you to fast. A fasting person is like a person walking with people and carrying a bag of musk with him, and

all these people like this fragrance. Indeed, the smell from the mouth of a fasting person is more pleasing to Allah than the smell of musk. Fourthly, Allah ordered you to give alms. The giver of alms is like a man who was captured by enemies, his hands were tied at the neck and brought forward to be executed, but he said: «I ransom myself from you, regardless of whether this ransom is small or large.» (After that) he redeemed himself from them. Fifthly, Allah ordered you to remember Him, because the one who remembers Allah is like a man, after whom enemies set off, but he protected himself from them by entering an impregnable fortress. Similarly, a person is not able to protect himself from the shaitan, except by the remembrance of Allah. Then the Prophet ﷺ said: «I also command you five commandments that were commanded to me by Allah: listen and obey (the ruler), strive in the way of Allah, migrate and keep the community (Muslims). Whoever left the community even for a span, threw off the noose of Islam from his neck (and will remain in this position) until he repents. The one who calls with the call of pre-Islamic ignorance will be among the kneeling in Gehenna. A man asked: «O Messenger of Allah, even if he prayed and fasted?» (The Prophet ﷺ) replied: «Even if he prayed and fasted, and therefore call on the call of Allah, who called you Muslims, believers and servants of Allah». №2863

566) From the words of Numan ibn Bashir, may Allah be pleased with him, it is reported that the Messenger of Allah ﷺ said: «Indeed, Allah wrote the Book two thousand years before He created the heavens and the earth, and He sent down two verses from it, which ends Surah al-Baqarah. And to the house in which they will be read for three nights, the shaitan will not come». №2882

567) Ibn Masud (may Allah be pleased with him) said: «Allah did not create in heaven or earth anything that would be greater than the verse «al-Kursi». Having transmitted these words, the transmitter Sufyan ibn

'Uyaina said: «The fact is that the verse «al-Kursi» are the words of Allah, and the words of Allah exceed any of His creations in heaven and on earth». №2884

568) It was narrated from 'Ali ibn Abu Talib (may Allah be pleased with him) that the Messenger of Allah ﷺ said: «Whoever recited the Quran and memorized it, considered what was permitted by him as lawful and forbidden by him as forbidden, Allah will lead through him to Paradise, and accept his intercession for ten people from among the members of his family, each of whom must have fallen into the Fire». №2905

569) It is reported from the words of 'Abdurrahman ibn Ishaq, (reported) from an-Numan ibn Sa'd, (reported) that 'Ali ibn Abu Talib (may Allah be pleased with him) said: «The Messenger of Allah ﷺ said: «The best of you is the one who studies the Quran and teaches it (to others)». №2909

570) It is reported from Ibn Mas'ud (may Allah be pleased with him) that the Messenger of Allah ﷺ said: «Whoever reads (at least one) letter from the Book of Allah (one) good deed will be written, and for (every) good deed (will be rewarded) tenfold, and I do not say that «Alif, Lam, Mim» is one letter, no, «Alif» is a letter, «Lam» is a letter and «Mim» is a letter». №2910

571) It was narrated from Ibn 'Abbas (may Allah be pleased with them both) that the Messenger of Allah ﷺ said: «Verily, that (man) in whom there is nothing from the Quran is like a ruined house». №2913

572) It is reported from the words of al-Hasan (al-Basri) that (once) 'Imran Ibn Husayn (may Allah be pleased with him) passed by a narrator who read (the Quran) and then asked (something from the people). And ('Imran) said (the words): «Verily, we belong to Allah and we will return to Him! /Inna lillahi wa inna ileihi raji'una/», after which he said: «I heard the Messenger of Allah ﷺ say:» Let the one who reads the Quran ask Allah through it, for there will be people who will read the Quran and ask people through it!» №2917

573) It is reported that Jabir (may Allah be pleased with him) said: «In the season of Hajj, the Prophet ﷺ introduced himself (to people and addressed them), he said:« Is there (among you) a person who will take me to his people? Verily, the Quraish hinder me from conveying (to the people) the words of my Lord!» №2925

574) It is reported that Umm Salama (may Allah be pleased with him) said: «Usually when reading (the Quran), the Messenger of Allah ﷺ separated it, reading: «Praise be to Allah, the Lord of the worlds ...», after which he stopped. (Then he continued): «To the Merciful, Merciful...», and then (again) stopped. And he read (verse from this surah in this way): «To the Lord of the Day of Retribution /Maliki yaumi-d-din/!». №2927

575) It is narrated from the words of 'Abdullah (ibn Mas'ud, may Allah be pleased with him) that the Prophet ﷺ said: «It is bad when one of you says:« I forgot such and such a verse, »(for not he forgot,) but made him forget (Allah), so continue to memorize the Quran, for, by the One in Whose hand is my soul, he leaves the hearts of people faster than camels (with tangled legs, are freed) from their fetters». №2942

576) It was narrated by Ibn 'Abbas, (may Allah be pleased with them both), who) said: «(Once) a man asked:« O Messenger of Allah! Which deed does Allah love the most? (The Prophet ﷺ) replied: «Stopping the traveller and sending him on his way again.» (He again) asked: «And what is the stopping of the traveller and sending him on his way again?» (The Prophet ﷺ) said: «(He is) the one who reads the Quran from beginning to end, and every time he stops (having completed it), he goes on, (reading it from the beginning)». №2948

577) It is narrated from the words of 'Abdullah ibn 'Amr (ibn al-'As, may Allah be pleased with both of them) that the Prophet ﷺ said: «The one who reads it in less than three (days) does not understand the Quran». №2949

578) It is reported that 'Abdullah ibn 'Amir ibn Rabi'a re-

ported from the words of his father, (may Allah be pleased with him) said: «(Once) on a dark night we were on a journey with the Prophet ﷺ and could not determine exactly (the direction) of the qibla, and each of us prayed in his direction. When morning came, we told the Prophet ﷺ about it and then it was sent down (verse, which says): «Wherever you turn, there will be the Face of Allah» (Surah al-Baqarah, verse 115)». №2957

579) It is narrated from the words of an-Numan ibn Bashir (may Allah be pleased with both of them) that regarding the words of the Almighty (Allah) «Your Lord said: «Call on Me, and I will answer you» (surah «al-Ghafir», verse 60), the Prophet ﷺ said: «Supplication to Allah / du'a / is (this) worship», after which he read (verse, which says): «Call on Me, and I will answer you» and to the words: «... humiliated». №2969

580) It is reported that Abu Ghalib said: «(Once) Abu Umama saw the (severed) heads (of the Kharijites) placed on the stairs of the Damascus mosque and said: «The dogs (of the inhabitants) of the Fire are the worst that have ever been killed under the firmament, and the best the slain are those whom they killed», and then he recited (the verse which says): «On the day when the faces will turn white and the faces will turn black!» (Surah Ali 'Imran, verse 106) - (until the end of the verse). I then asked Abu Umama: «Did you hear this from the Messenger of Allah ﷺ?» He replied: «If I had only heard it from him once, twice, three, or four times,» he counted to seven times, «I would not tell you about it». №3000

581) It is reported that Umm Salamah narrated that she once said: «O Messenger of Allah! I have never heard Allah, Mighty and Exalted, mention the migration of women.» And then Allah Almighty sent down: «I will not destroy the deeds committed by any of you, be it a man or a woman. Some of you are descended from others.» (Surah Ali 'Imran, verse 195). №3023

582) It is reported that Anas ibn Malik said: «Once the Prophet 🌑 sent (surah) Renunciation (Baraa) along with Abu Bakr, but then called him (back) and said: «This surah (to people) should not be conveyed to anyone except a member of my families!» After that, he called 'Ali and handed (a scroll) with a surah to him». №3090

583) Waqi' ibn Hudus reported that his uncle from his father's side, Abu Razin, said: «Once I said: «O Messenger of Allah! Where was our Lord before He created His creations?» He said: «He was in the void /'ama/. What is above He is emptiness, and what is below Him is emptiness. Then He created His Throne on the water.» Ahmad ibn Muni' said: – Yazid ibn Harun said: «Emptiness» /'ama / - that is, there was nothing with Him». №3109

584) It is reported that Abu Yasar said: «Once one of the women came to me, wanting to buy dates from me. (When I saw her) I said, «There are better quality dates in the house.» Then she entered the house with me, and I reached out to her and kissed her. After that, I went to Abu Bakr and told him about what had happened, to which he told me: «Hide this offence of yours, repent and do not tell anyone about it.» (I did so), but then I could not stand it and went to 'Umar. I told him about what had happened, to which he replied: «Hide this offence of yours, repent and do not tell anyone about it.» (I did so), but then I could not stand it and went to the Messenger of Allah 🌑. I told him about what had happened, to which he replied: «Have you replaced a warrior who went on a campaign in the path of Allah with his family in this way ?!» (These words seemed so heavy to me) that I wanted to be converted to Islam only at that moment, and I thought that I was one of the inhabitants of the Fire. After that, the Messenger of Allah 🌑 sat for a long time with his head down, until the Almighty sent down to him: «Pray at the beginning and end of the day, and also at some hours of the night. Verily, good deeds take away evil deeds.

This is a Reminder for those who remember» (Surah «Hud», verse 114). Then I came to the Messenger of Allah ﷺ and he recited this verse to me. (Hearing this), his companions asked: «O Messenger of Allah! Does this only apply to him, or does it apply to all people?» The Messenger of Allah ﷺ replied: «No, on the contrary, this applies to all people». №3115

585) It was reported from Abu Umama that the Messenger of Allah ﷺ said: «People fell into error after being on the straight path, only because of disputes.» Then the Messenger of Allah ﷺ recited the verse (which says): «They use him as an example for you only to argue. They are people who quarrel.» (Surah Az-Zuhruf, verse 58)». №3253

586) 'Ata narrated from Ibn 'Abbas that regarding (verse): «They avoid great sins and abominations, except for minor and few offences» (Surah an-Najm, 53:32), the Prophet ﷺ said: «When You forgive, O Allah, You forgive with great generosity, and who among Your servants does not commit sins?» №3284

587) It is reported that 'Abdullah ibn Salam said: «Once we were sitting with a group of companions of the Messenger of Allah ﷺ and discussed (religious knowledge). We said: «If we knew which deed is the most beloved of Allah, then we would certainly do it.» After that, the Almighty sent down (the following verses): «All that is in heaven and all that is on earth praises Allah, and He is Great, Wise. O those who believe! Why do you say things you don't do?!» And the Messenger of Allah ﷺ recited to us these (verses)». №3309

588) It is reported that Abdullah ibn ash-Shihkhir transmitted from his father that one day he came to the Prophet ﷺ when he was reading the surah «The passion for multiplication carries you away ...». He said, «The son of Adam says, My wealth! My wealth!» But after all, you get from your wealth only what you donated and left (for the future life), or what you ate and ruined, or what you put on and wore out». №3354

589) It is reported that Abu Hurayrah, may Allah be pleased with him, said: «The Messenger of Allah ﷺ said: «Allah is angry with the one who does not ask Him!» №3373

590) It is reported from Jabir ibn 'Abdullah that the Messenger of Allah ﷺ said: «The best remembrance (of Allah) is the words «La ilaha illa-Allah / there is no deity worthy of worship except Allah /», and the best prayer is the words «al-hamdu li -Llah / all praise be to Allah /». №3383

591) It was reported from Abu Hurayrah, may Allah be pleased with him, that the Messenger of Allah ﷺ said: «If someone sees a person suffering (from this or that disease) and says:« Praise be to Allah, Who delivered me from what tested you, and gave me preference over many of those whom He created! /Al-hamdu li-Llahi-l-lezi 'afani mim-ma-btalyaka bihi wa faddalani 'ala kasirin mim-man halaka tafdylyan!/» - this disaster will not touch him». №3432

592) It is narrated from the words of Abu Sa'eed al-Khudri, may Allah be pleased with him, that he heard the Messenger of Allah ﷺ say: «If any of you sees a dream that he likes, (this means that) he is only from Allah, so let him praise Allah for him and tell what he saw (to others), but if he sees something else that he does not like, then this is from the shaitan, let him turn to Allah for protection from his evil and does not tell anyone, and then he will not harm him». №3453

593) It is narrated from the words of Jabir, may Allah be pleased with them, that the Prophet ﷺ said: «For the one who says:« Allah is holy and praise be to Him » / Subhana-Lahil-'Azimi wa bi-hamdihi /, a palm tree will be planted in paradise». №3464

594) It is reported from Sa'd that the Messenger of Allah ﷺ said: «The prayer of Zun-Nun, which he uttered while in the belly of a whale: «La ilaha illa Anta, subhanak-ya, inni kuntu mina-zzalimin / There is no true God but You! Blessed are You (from shortcomings)! Veri-

ly, I have been one of the unjust/». Whatever Muslim calls (to Allah) with this prayer, in whatever situation he is, Allah will certainly answer him». №3505

595) It is reported that 'Amr ibn Shu'ayb narrated from his father, and his grandfather, that the Messenger of Allah ﷺ said: «If any of you is frightened in a dream, let him say: «I resort to the perfect words of Allah from anger Him, and His punishment, and the evil of His servants, and from the instigations of the devils, and from the fact that they come to me. And 'Abdullah ibn 'Amr taught this to his children who reached the age of majority, and for those who did not reach this age, he wrote down these words on paper and hung them around his neck. №3528

596) It is reported that Anas, may Allah be pleased with him, said: «I heard the Messenger of Allah ﷺ say:« Allah said: «O son of Adam, verily, I will forgive you, not paying attention (to what sins you committed), until you stop crying out to Me and relying on Me! O son of Adam, if (you commit so many) sins that they reach the clouds of heaven, and then you ask Me for forgiveness, then I will forgive you! O son of Adam, truly, if you come to Me with (so many) sins (that they fill with themselves) almost the whole earth, but meet Me without worshipping anything else along with Me, I will surely grant you forgiveness, which (will cover all these sins)!» №3540

597) It was narrated from Ibn 'Umar, may Allah be pleased with him, that the Messenger of Allah ﷺ said: «To one of you to whom the gates of supplication were opened, the gates of mercy were opened. And there is nothing that is asked of Allah, which He grants, is more beloved to Him than a petition for well-being. And the Messenger of Allah ﷺ said: «Indeed, supplication is beneficial in what has befallen and in what it can comprehend. So turn with a prayer (to Allah), O servants of Allah!» №3548

598) According to 'Abdullah ibn Khubaib (may Allah be

pleased with him), it is reported that once the Messenger of Allah ﷺ said to him: «Read «Say:« He, Allah is One ...»» and two Surahs «Protective» three times in the morning and the evening, and it will protect you from all the bad». №3575

599) It is narrated from the words of Ziyad ibn 'Ilyak that his uncle from the side of his father (Kutba ibn Malik), may Allah be pleased with him, said: I resort to Your protection from vile moral qualities, deeds and aspirations!» /Allahumma, inni a'uzu bika min munkarati-l-ahlaki, wal-a'mali, wal-ahwa/» №3591

600) It is reported that Abu Hurayrah, may Allah be pleased with him, said: «The Messenger of Allah ﷺ said: «O Allah, help me benefit from what You have taught me; teach me what will be useful for me and increase my knowledge / Allahumma, infa 'ni bi-ma 'allyamtani, wa ' allimni bi-ma yanfa 'uni, vazidni 'ilman /. Praise be to Allah, whatever happens, and I resort to the protection of Allah from the state of the inhabitants of Hell». №3599

601) It is reported that Abu Hurayrah, may Allah be pleased with him, said: «(Once) the Messenger of Allah ﷺ said to me:« Say the words «No one has power and strength except Allah / La hawla wa la quwwata illa bi- Llah/», for they are among the treasures of paradise.» Makhul said: «And from the one who says «No one has power and strength except Allah, and there is no salvation from Allah, except turning to Him ileihi /», He will remove seventy kinds of losses, the smallest of which is poverty». №3601

602) It is reported that Abu Hurairah said: «(Once upon a time people) said: «O Messenger of Allah, when were you approved as a prophet?» He replied: «(When) Adam was (still) between the spirit and the body». №3609

603) It is reported that 'Abdullah ibn al-Harith ibn Jazz (may Allah be pleased with him) said: «I did not see anyone who smiled more than the Messenger of Allah

604) It is reported that 'Imran ibn Husain (may Allah be pleased with him) said: «(Once) the Prophet 🏺 sent an army and appointed them commander 'Ali ibn Abu Talib (may Allah be pleased with him). He went out with this detachment and (in this campaign 'Ali) entered into sexual intercourse with a slave girl (he got as a trophy, among other things), and (some) reprimanded him for this. Four people from among the companions of the Messenger of Allah 🏺 agreed (among themselves) and said: «When we meet the Messenger of Allah 🏺 we will inform him of what 'Ali did.» When Muslims returned from a trip, they usually started by (visiting) the Messenger of Allah, greeting him, and then only went home. When this detachment returned (to Medina), they greeted the Prophet 🏺 and one of these four stood up and said: «O Messenger of Allah! Look what 'Ali ibn Abi Talib did! He did such and such!», but the Messenger of Allah 🏺 turned away from him. Then the second one got up and said the same thing, but he turned away from him. Then a third one came up to him and said the same thing, but he turned away from him too. Then the fourth stood up and said the same thing that they said, and then the Messenger of Allah 🏺, whose face showed that he was angry, said: «What do you want from 'Ali? What do you want from 'Ali? What do you want from 'Ali? Indeed, 'Ali is from me, and I am from him, and he is the patron/wali / of every believer after me!» №3712

605) It is reported that Abu Tufail said that Abu Sariha or Zayd ibn Arkam transmitted the words of the Prophet 🏺: «'Ali is the patron (maulya) of the one whose patron I am». №3713

606) Ribi bin Hirash narrated: «In Ar-Rahba, Ali told us: «On the Day (of the Pledge) of Hudaibiya, people from the polytheists came out to us. Among them was Suhayl ibn Amr. They said: «O Messenger of Allah! People from our fathers, brothers and slaves came to you, and they do not know religion, but they

came fleeing from our wealth and property, so return them to us. If they don't know religion, we will teach them.» The Prophet (ﷺ) said: «O Quraish, you will refrain or Allah will send on you someone who will cut your necks with a sword, Allah tested their hearts regarding faith.» They said: «Who is he, O Messenger of Allah?» Abu Bakr said to him: «Who is he, O Messenger of Allah?» Umar said to him: «Who is he, O Messenger of Allah?» Allah? He said, «He is the one who mends the sandals.» - And he gave Ali his sandals to mend them. - He said: «Then ʿAli turned to us and said: The Messenger of Allah (ﷺ) said: «Whoever lies against me willfully, let him take his place in the Fire». №3715

607) Narrated al-Barra al-Azeeb that the Prophet ﷺ said to Ali ibn Abu Talib: «I am from you, and you are from me» №3716

608) Abu Sa'eed Khudri (may Allah be pleased with him) reported: «Indeed, we, the community of the Ansar, recognized the hypocrites by their hatred of 'Ali ibn Abi Talib». №3717

609) Buraidah narrated that the Messenger of Allah ﷺ said: «Indeed, Allah ordered me to love four, and announced that He loves them!» He was asked who they were. He replied: «Ali among them» and repeated these words three times. «And Abu Darr, al Miqdad and Salman. And He commanded me to love them and told me that He loves them» №3718

610) Khubshi ibn Junada narrated that the Prophet ﷺ said: «I am from Ali and Ali is from me. And no one can represent me but myself and Ali» №3719

611) It is reported that Ibn Umar said that the companions of the Prophet ﷺ became twin brothers among themselves. Then Ali came and asked: «O Messenger of Allah! You have made your companions brothers among yourselves, and who will be my brother? Then the Messenger of Allah ﷺ answered him: «I am your brother in this life and the next!» №3720

612) Narrated Anas ibn Malik: «The Prophet ﷺ was served a bird for dinner and he prayed: «O Allah, send this bird to dine with me, Your most beloved creation!». Then Ali came in and dined with him. №3721

613) Narrated Ali that the Messenger of Allah ﷺ said: «I am the house of wisdom, and Ali is his gate» №3723

614) Narrated Amir bin Sa'd bin Abi Waqqas: from his father, saying: «Mu'awiya bin Abu Sufyan ordered Sa'd, saying, 'What prevented you from offending Abu Turab?' He said: «Three things that I remember from the Messenger of Allah (ﷺ) keep me from reviling him. The fact that I have at least one of these things is more beloved to me than red camels. I heard the Messenger of Allah (ﷺ) talking to Ali and he left him behind in one of his battles. Then Ali said to him: «O Messenger of Allah! Are you leaving me with women and children?» Then the Messenger of Allah (ﷺ) said to him: «Are you not pleased that you should be with me in the position in which Harun was with Musa? Besides, there are no prophets after me?» And on the Day (of the battle) of Khaibar, I heard him say: «I will give a banner to a man who loves Allah and His Messenger, and Allah and His Messenger love him.» We were all waiting for this, then he said: «Call Ali for me», spat in his eye and gave him a banner, and Allah granted him victory. And when this verse was revealed: «Let us call our sons and your sons, our women and your women ...» (3:61) The Messenger of Allah (ﷺ) called Ali, Fatimah, Hasan and Hussein and said: «O Allah, this is my family» №3724

615) Narrated Al-Bara: «The Prophet (ﷺ) sent two armies and put Ali bin Abi Talib at the head of one of them, and Khalid bin al-Walid at the head of the other. He said: «When there is a fight, then (the leader) Ali.» He said, «So Ali conquered the fortress and took the slave girl. So Khalid sent me a letter to the Prophet (ﷺ) complaining about him. So I came to the Prophet (ﷺ) and he read the letter and its colour changed, then he said: «What is your opinion about the one who loves Allah

and His Messenger, and Allah and His Messenger love him?» He said: «I said: 'I seek the protection of Allah from the wrath of Allah and the wrath of His Messenger, and I am only a broadcaster» So he shut up. №3725

616) Jabir narrated: «The Messenger of Allah (ﷺ) called Ali on the Day (of the battle) of At-Taif and talked with him for a very long time in private, so the people said:« His conversation with his cousin became long. Therefore, the Messenger of Allah (ﷺ) said: «I did not speak to him in private, but Allah spoke to him in private». №3726

617) Abu Saeed reported that the Messenger of Allah ﷺ said to Ali: «O Ali! No one is allowed to enter the mosque in a state of sexual defilement except me and you» №3727

618) Narrated Anas bin Malik: «The first message of the Prophet (ﷺ) was on Monday, and Ali prayed already on Tuesday». №3728

619) Ali bin Hussein narrated: from his father, from his grandfather Ali ibn Abi Talib: «The Prophet (ﷺ) took Hasan and Hussein by the hand and said: «Whoever loves me and loves these two, as well as their father and mother, he will me». At my level on doomsday». №3733

620) Ibn Abbas narrated: «The first person to pray was Ali». №3734

621) Ali narrated: «The Prophet (ﷺ) - the Illiterate Prophet - admonished me (saying): «No one loves you except a believer, and no one hates you except a hypocrite.» 'Adi bin Thabit (narrator) said: «I am from the generation for whom the Prophet (ﷺ) prayed». №3736

622) It is reported that Abu Hurayrah (may Allah be pleased with him) said: «The Messenger of Allah ﷺ said: «I saw Ja'far flying in Paradise with angels». №3763

623) Abu Said narrated: that the Messenger of Allah (ﷺ)

said: «Al-Hasan and Al-Hussein are the leaders of the youths of Paradise». №3768

624) Narrated Usama bin Zayd: «One night I came to the Prophet (ﷺ) about some need, so the Prophet (ﷺ) came out when he was hiding something, and I did not know what it was. As soon as I took care of my need, I said, «What were you hiding? He opened it and I found that it was Hassan and Hussein [peace be upon them] on his thighs. Then he said: «These are my two sons and the sons of my daughter. O Allah! Truly I love them, so love them and love those who love them». №3769

625) Narrated Abdur-Rahman bin Abu Num: that a man from the people of Al-> Iraq asked Ibn ‹Umar about the blood of a mosquito that got on his clothes. Ibn Umar said: «Look at this, he asks about the blood of a mosquito when they killed the son of the Messenger of Allah (ﷺ)! And I heard the Messenger of Allah (ﷺ) say: «Verily, Al-Hasan and Al-Hussein are my two sweet basilicas in the world». №3770

626) Salma says: «I went to Umm Salamah when she was crying, so I said: «What makes you cry?» She said: «I saw the Messenger of Allah, that is, in a dream, and there was dirt on his head and beard, so I said:« What is the matter with you, O Messenger of Allah? He said, «I just witnessed the assassination of Al-Hussein». №3771

627) Narrated Yala bin Murra: that the Messenger of Allah (ﷺ) said: «Hussein is from me, and I am from Hussein. Allah loves the one who loves Hussein. Hussein is a sibt among the asbats. [Asbat, plural of Sibt: great tribe. This means that Al-Husayn will have many descendants, so they will become a great tribe. And it happened. №3775

628) Narrated Anas bin Malik: «I was with Ibn Ziyad, and they brought me the head of Al-Hussein. He began to poke her in the nose with the stick he had, saying, «I don't think it's beautiful like this, why is it mentioned as such?» He said: «I said: «Here, he was the closest of

them in resemblance to the Messenger of Allah (ﷺ)». №3778

629) Narrated Umar bin Umayr: «When the heads of Ubaydullah bin Ziyad and his companions were brought, they were stacked in the mosque in Ar-Rahba. I went up to them and they said, «It's here, it's here.» And so, the snake passed between the heads until it entered the nostrils of Ubaydullah ibn Ziyad, and remained there for a moment, then left and left until it disappeared. Then they said: «It has come, it has come.» It happened two or three times». №3780

630) Hudhayfah is reported to have said: «Once my mother asked me, 'When did you last see him? me. I replied to her: «Let me go to the Prophet ﷺ to perform the sunset prayer/maghrib / with him and ask him to ask forgiveness (from Allah) for me and you.» After that, I went to the Prophet ﷺ and performed the sunset prayer /maghrib/ with him, after which he (began) to perform (additional) prayers, and then performed the evening prayer /isha/ and left, and I followed him. He heard my voice and asked: «Who is this? Hudhaif?» I answered yes. He asked: «What is the matter, may Allah forgive you and your mother ?!», and then continued: «Truly, until this night, this angel had never descended to earth before, (but on this night) he asked permission from his Lord greet me with peace/salam / and make me glad that (my daughter) Fatimah will be the mistress of the women of Paradise, and (my grandchildren) al-Hasan and al-Hussein will be the masters of the youths of Paradise». №3781

631) It is reported that Jabir ibn 'Abdullah (may Allah be pleased with him) said: «I saw the Messenger of Allah ﷺ on the day of 'Arafat, (when) he performed Hajj, and he (at that time) was sitting on his camel, (which was called) Kasva, addressing people with a sermon. And I heard him say: «O people! Verily, I leave among you that by which you will not go astray if you adhere to them: (this is) the Book of Allah and the members of my family». №3786

632) Narrated 'Umar bin Abi Salamah, the stepson of the Prophet (ﷺ): «When these verses were sent down to the Prophet (ﷺ): «Allah only wants to remove filth from you, O members of the family, and cleanse you with thorough cleansing ...» (33:33) in Umm Salama's house, he called Fatimah, Hasan, Husayn and wrapped them in a cloak and Ali was behind him so he wrapped him in a cloak, then he said, «O Allah! I ask you to remove the filth from them and cleanse them with a thorough cleansing. Then Umm Salamah said: «Am I with them, O Messenger of Allah?» He said, «You are in your place and you are in good». №3787

633) Narrated Zaid bin Arqam, may Allah be pleased with them both: that the Messenger of Allah (ﷺ) said: «Verily, I leave among you that if you hold fast to them, you will not go astray after me. One of them is bigger than the other: The Book of Allah is a rope that stretches from heaven to earth, and my family is the people of my house - and they will not disperse until they meet at Hauz, so see how you will deal with them after me». №3788

634) Narrated Ibn Abbas: that the Messenger of Allah (ﷺ) said: «Love Allah for what He feeds you from His blessings, love me because of the love of Allah and love the people of my house (Ahl al-Bayt) because of the love of me». №3789

635) Narrated Anas bin Malik: that the Messenger of Allah (ﷺ) said: «Verily, Paradise is thirsty for three: Ali, Ammar and Salman». №3797

636) Ali narrated: that Ammar ibn Yasser came for permission to enter the Prophet (ﷺ), so he said: «Let him, welcome the pure, purified». №3798

637) Abu Hurairah narrated: that the Messenger of Allah (ﷺ) said: «Rejoice, Ammar, the criminal party will kill you». №3800

638) Hudhaifah narrated: what they said: «O Messenger of Allah if you would appoint someone as your succes-

sor.» He said, «If I appointed you a successor and you disobeyed him, you would be punished. But whatever Hudhaifa tells you, then believe him, and what Abdullah teaches you, read». №3812

639) Narrated Al-Miswar bin Mahram: «When he was in Minbar, I heard the Prophet (ﷺ) say: «Indeed, Banu Hisham bin Al-Mughira asked me if they could marry their daughter to Ali bin Abi Talib. But I don't allow it, I won't allow it, I won't allow it unless Ali ibn Abi Talib wants to divorce my daughter and marry their daughter because she is part of me. I'm unhappy with what she doesn't like and I'm hurt by what hurts her». №3867

640) Buraidah narrated: «The most beloved of the women of the Messenger of Allah (ﷺ) was Fatimah, and of the men was Ali». №3868

641) Narrated Zayd bin Arkam: what the Messenger of Allah (ﷺ) said to Ali, Fatimah, al-Hasan and al-Husayn: «I am at war with the one who is at war with you, and peace is with him who makes peace with you». №3870

642) Aisha narrated: «I did not see anyone closer in behaviour, manners and manners to the Messenger of Allah in terms of standing and sitting than Fatimah, the daughter of the Messenger of Allah (ﷺ).» She said, «Whenever she came to the Prophet (ﷺ), he would get up and kiss her and he would put her in her seat. Whenever the Prophet (ﷺ) entered her, she got up from her seat and kissed him. When the Prophet (ﷺ) fell ill and Fatimah came in, she leaned over and kissed him, then raised her head and wept, then bent over him, raised her head and laughed. Then I said: «I used to think that this is the smartest of our women, but she is just one of the women.» Therefore, when the Prophet (ﷺ) died, I said to her: «Do you remember how you bowed over the Prophet (ﷺ), raised your head and cried, then you leaned over him, then raised your head and laughed. What made you do it? She said, «Then I will be the one to spread the secrets. He (ﷺ)

told me that he must die from his illness, so I cried. He then told me that I would be the very first of his family to meet him. That's when I laughed». №3872

643) Umm Salama narrates: that the Messenger of Allah (ﷺ) called Fatimah on the Day of Conquest (of Mecca) and spoke to her so that she wept. Then he spoke to her and she laughed. She said: «Therefore when the Messenger of Allah (ﷺ) died, I asked her about her crying and laughter. She said: «The Messenger of Allah (ﷺ) told me that he would die, so I cried, then he told me that I would be mistress over all the women of the inhabitants of Paradise, except for Mariam, the daughter of Imran, so I laughed». №3873

644) Narrated Jumay bin Umayr at-Taimi: «I went in with my uncle to Aisha, and she was asked:« Which of the people was the most beloved to the Messenger of Allah (ﷺ)? She said, «Fatima.» So it was said, «From men?» She said: «Her husband, as far as I knew, fasts a lot and stands a lot in prayer». №3874

645) Aisha said: «I was not jealous of any wife of the Prophet (ﷺ), as I was jealous of Khadija, and it was not because I did not see her. It was only because the Messenger of Allah (ﷺ) mentioned her so often, and because whenever he slaughtered a sheep, he looked for Khadija's friends to give them a piece of it». №3875

646) Narrated Anas (may Allah be pleased with him): that the Prophet (ﷺ) said: «The best for you among the women of mankind are Maryam bint Imran, Khadija bint Khuwaylid, Fatimah bint Muhammad and Asiya, the wife of Faron». №3878

«Sunah» Abu Dawud

His full name is al-Imam al-Sabt Sayyid al-Huffaz Suleiman ibn al-Ash'ath ibn Ishaq al-Azdi al-Sijistani. Abu Dawud was born in 817 in the city of Sistan, in southeastern Iran and southwestern Afghanistan. An ancestor of Abu Dawud, Imran died at the Battle of Siffin, fighting on the side of Caliph Ali.

Lived in Basra. To collect hadiths, Abu Dawud visited Khorasan, Iraq, Egypt, Syria, Hijaz and other corners of the Caliphate. When he made his first journey, he was less than twenty years old. He studied hadith from more than 300 muhaddiths, among whom were such famous muhaddiths as Abu Salama, Ahmad ibn Hanbal, Ibn Abu Shayba, Yahya ibn Main and many others.

Abu Dawud paid the main attention to the hadiths of legal subjects. Considered the use of any «weak» hadith in legal matters better than the following judgment by analogy.

The hadiths from Sunan are strong evidence for many Sharia issues. Often in Sunan, you can find hadiths that are not in the collections of al-Bukhari and Muslims. Many scholars highly appreciated the work of Abu Dawud, because he very carefully selected the hadiths and included in his collection about 4800 hadiths from the 500,000 hadiths he studied.

The collection is known under the name «Sunan» of Abu Dawud. So the author himself called it. «Sunan» is the plural of the word «Sunnah». The Sunnah of the Messenger of Allah ﷺ includes his hadiths. However, Imam Abu Daud, calling his book that way, meant not just hadiths, but hadiths containing Sharia norms, since books called «Sunan» consist of chapters corresponding to various sections of fiqh: «Faith», «Purification», «Prayer », «Zakat» and so on. Imam Abu Dawud explained in his message to the people of Mecca: «In the collection «Sunan» I included only hadiths containing Sharia norms, and did not include hadiths about moderation in the use of worldly goods (zuhd) and the merits of various deeds ...».

647) It is reported that Zayd ibn Arkam said: «The Messenger of Allah ﷺ said: «Verily, these places of defecation are visited (by the devils). And (therefore) when one of you comes there, let him say: «I resort to the protection of Allah from male and female shaitans.». №6

648) It is reported that Salman (al-Farisi) said that (once) he was asked: «Is it true that your Prophet taught you everything, and even how to relieve yourself?» (Salman) said, «Yes. He forbade us to turn in the direction of the qibla when we relieve ourselves of great or small need, to wash with our right hand, to use less than three stones for cleansing (after relieving ourselves), and to cleanse ourselves with manure and bones». №7

649) It is reported that Hilal ibn 'Iyad said: - Abu Sa'id (al-Khudri) told me, who said: «I heard the Messenger of Allah ﷺ say:» Let not two of you retire (to relieve themselves), exposing their awrah, and talking to each other. Verily, Allah the Great and Almighty hates this». №15

650) It is reported that once al-Muhajir ibn Kunfuz came to

the Prophet ﷺ when he was urinating and greeted him, but the Prophet ﷺ did not answer him until he performed ablution. Then he apologized to him and said: «Verily, I do not like to remember Allah except when I am clean», or he said: «In a state of (ritual) purity». №17

651) It is reported that 'Abdurrahman ibn Hasana said: «(Once) I and 'Amr ibn al-'As went to the Prophet ﷺ and he came out holding (in his hand) a leather shield. Then he covered himself with it and urinated. We said, «Look at him, he relieves himself like a woman.» (The Prophet ﷺ) heard this and said, «Don't you know what happened to a man from among the children of Israel? When urine fell on them, they cut out the place where the urine fell, and he forbade them to do so, for which he was punished in his grave». №22

652) It is reported that Harisa ibn Wahb al-Khuza'iy said: «Hafsa, the wife of the Prophet ﷺ, told me that the Prophet ﷺ used his right hand when he ate, drank and dressed, and left - in all other cases». №32

653) It is reported that 'Aisha said: «(One day) the Messenger of Allah ﷺ was urinating, and 'Umar stood behind him with a jug of water. He said, «What is this, O 'Umar?» He replied: «It is water for you to bathe with it.» He said, «I am not commanded to perform ablution every time I urinate. If I did it, it would become Sunnah». №42

654) It is narrated from the words of Hudhayfa: «When the Messenger of Allah ﷺ woke up at night, he cleaned his mouth with a toothpick». №54

655) It is reported that Daoud ibn Salih ibn Dinar at-Tammar reported from the words of his mother that one day her mistress sent her with some harissa to 'Aisha, may Allah be pleased with her, and she found her praying. She gestured for me to put (what I brought). Suddenly a cat came up and began to eat it. When she finished her prayer, she ate from the place where the cat ate and (then) said: «Verily, the Messenger of Allah

ﷺ said: «Verily, she is not unclean, and they are from those who revolve around you.» And I saw how the Messenger of Allah ﷺ performed ablution (with water), which remained after her». №76

656) Muhammad ibn 'Isa narrated to us: - Ibn 'Ayyash told us from Habib ibn Salih, who narrated from Yazid ibn Shurayh al-Hadrami, who narrated from Abu Hayy al-Muazzin, who reported that Sauban said: «The Messenger of Allah ﷺ said:» There are three (a type of things) that no one is allowed to do: the collective prayer of people will not be led by the person who, invoking Allah, distinguishes himself, excluding the rest, and if he did so, then he betrayed them; no one looks into the depths of the house before asking permission, and if he does this, then it is considered that he has already entered it; no one will pray while holding back a need until he frees himself». №90

657) It is narrated from the words of 'Abdullah ibn 'Amr that once, seeing people whose heels were not washed, the Messenger of Allah ﷺ said: «Woe to the heels from the (hellish) Fire! Perform wudu carefully!» №97

658) It is reported that 'Abdu Khair said: «(Once) 'Ali came to us, may Allah be pleased with him, having already performed a prayer, and he asked for water for ablution. We said: «Why does he need water for ablution because he has already prayed?» But he only wanted to teach us, and when he was given water in a vessel and a basin, he poured the water on his right hand and washed his hands three times. Then he rinsed his mouth and nose three times each and did so with the hand with which he had drawn water. After that, he washed his face three times, then washed his right hand three times (including the elbow) and washed his left hand three times, after which he put his hand into a vessel and (wetting it or drawing water with it) wiped his head once. Then he washed his right foot three times and washed his left foot three times, and then he said: «Who will be glad to know (how he performed) ablution the Messenger of Allah ﷺ then here

it is». №111

659) It is reported that Ibn 'Abbas said: «The Messenger of Allah ﷺ said: «Pull water into your nose and blow your nose well, (and do this) two or three times». №141

660) It is reported that Sauban said: «Once the Messenger of Allah ﷺ sent (on a campaign) a detachment that was overtaken by cold, and when they returned to the Messenger of Allah ﷺ he ordered them to wipe the turbans and tasahins. №146

661) Ash-Sha'bi is reported to have said: «I heard 'Urwa ibn al-Mughira ibn Shu'ba narrate that his father said: 'We were in the caravan of the Messenger of Allah ﷺ and I had a vessel of skin. He went out to relieve himself, and when he returned, I met him with a vessel (with water) and began to pour water for him. He washed his hands and face, and then he wanted to take his hands out, and he was dressed in a Byzantine Jubba made of wool, which had narrow sleeves and pulled his hands out from under the Jubba. Then I stretched out my hands to take off his leather socks /khuffain/, but he said to me: «Leave them, indeed, I put them on clean feet», and he (simply) wiped them». №151

662) It is narrated from the words of Al-Mughira ibn Shu'ba: «The Messenger of Allah ﷺ performed ablution and wiped over socks / jaurabain / and shoes / na 'layn /». №159

663) Al-A'mash narrates the same hadith, which reports that ('Ali ibn Abu Talib, may Allah be pleased with him) said: «If religion were based on judgment, then wiping the lower part of the legs would be more correct than the top, but the Prophet ﷺ wiped his leather socks from above. Waqi' narrated with isnad the same hadith from al-A'mash which reports that ('Ali ibn Abu Talib, may Allah be pleased with him) said: «I thought that the soles of the feet deserved to be wiped more than the upper part of the legs until he saw that the Messenger of Allah ﷺ was wiping his legs from above. Vaki' said: «That is, leather socks / khuffain /».

664) It is narrated from the words of Suleiman ibn Buraida that his father said: «On the day of the conquest of Mecca, the Messenger of Allah ﷺ performed five prayers with one ablution and wiped his leather socks. 'Umar said to him: «Indeed, today I saw that you have done something that you have not done before!» He replied: «I did it on purpose». №172

665) It is reported that 'Urwa (ibn az-Zubayr) reported from the words of 'Aisha that «The Prophet ﷺ kissed one of his wives, and then went out to prayer without performing ablution.» 'Urva said: «I said to her: «Who is this but you?» And she smiled». №179

666) It is reported that al-Bara ibn 'Azeeb said: «The Messenger of Allah ﷺ was asked about performing ablution after eating the meat of a camel and he replied: «Do ablution from it.» He was asked about the mutton and he replied: «Do not perform wudu after it.» He was asked about praying in the camel pen, and he replied: «Do not pray in the camel pen, for verily, they (are like) shaitans.» He was asked about praying in the sheep pen and he said, «Pray there, for they are blessed». №184

667) It is narrated from the words of Abu Sa'id (al-Khudri) that «once the Prophet ﷺ passed by a boy who was skinning a sheep and the Messenger of Allah ﷺ said to him: «Go away! I'll show you». And (the Prophet ﷺ) put his hand between the skin and the meat so that it disappeared up to the armpit. Then he left and prayed with the people without taking ablution.» Abu Dawud said: «In the narration of this hadith narrated from the words of 'Amr, it is added that «he did not touch the water». №185

668) It is reported from the words of 'Ali, may Allah be pleased with him, that the Messenger of Allah ﷺ said: «Whoever leaves without washing at least something of his hair while bathing, then Allah will subject him to such and such a punishment in the fire.» 'Ali said:

«Because of this, I became enmity with my head,» repeating this three times. And he shaved off his hair. №249

669)	It is reported that Shuraikh ibn 'Ubayd said: «Jubayr ibn Nufair decided for me regarding bathing because of defilement, because Sauban told that they asked the Prophet ﷺ about this and he said:» As for the man, then let him dissolve his hair and washes it until (the water) reaches its roots. As for the woman, she is not obliged to dissolve them, (and it will be enough for her if) she pours three handfuls (of water) on her head with her hands». №255

670)	It is narrated from the words of Anas ibn Malik: «The Jews, when their women began to menstruate, took them out of the house, did not sit down with them to eat and drink, and did not communicate with them in the house. And (people) asked the Messenger of Allah ﷺ about this and Allah Almighty revealed the verse: «They ask you about menstruation. Say: «They cause suffering. Therefore, avoid sexual intercourse with women during menstruation ... «and so on until the end of this verse. And then the Messenger of Allah ﷺ said: «Stay with them in the same house and do everything except copulation.» The Jews said, «No matter what we do, this man doesn't want to be like us in it.» And Usaid ibn Hudair and 'Abbad ibn Bishr came to the Prophet ﷺ and said: «O Messenger of Allah, verily, the Jews say such and such, so can we not have sexual intercourse with women at a time when they with menstruation? And the complexion of the face of the Messenger of Allah ﷺ changed so that they thought that he was angry with them. When they left him, they brought milk as a gift to the Messenger of Allah ﷺ. He immediately sent after them and got them drunk, and it became clear to us that he was not angry with them.». №258

671)	It is reported that 'Aisha said: «(Once) the Messenger of Allah ﷺ said to me: «Pass me a carpet from the mosque. I said, «I'm menstruating.» And the Messenger of Allah ﷺ said: «Your menstruation is not on your hand». №261

672) Shaqiq is reported to have said: «Once I was sitting between 'Abdullah (ibn Mas'ud) and Abu Musa (al-Ash'ari) and Abu Musa said, 'O Abu 'Abdu-r-Rahman, what can you say about a man who defiled and did not find water for a month, can he perform tayammum? He said, «No, even if he doesn't find water for a month.» Abu Musa said: «What about this verse from Surah al-Maida: «And if you do not find water, then cleanse yourself with clean sand»? 'Abdullah said: «If they were allowed to do this, then they may begin to cleanse with sand even because of the cold water.» Abu Musa said to him: «Do you consider it forbidden for them?» He said yes. Abu Musa said to him: «Have you not heard what 'Ammar (ibn Yasir) said to 'Umar? ('Ammar said): «Once the Messenger of Allah ﷺ sent me on an assignment, during which I became defiled. I could not find water, and because of this, I began to wallow in the sand like an animal. Then, when I returned to the Prophet ﷺ, I told him about it and he said: «Verily, it was enough for you to do this,» and he struck the ground with his hand and shook it off his hands. Then he hit his left hand on his right hand and his right hand on his left hand, after which he wiped his face. 'Abdullah said to him: «Do you know that 'Umar was not satisfied with what 'Ammar said?» №321

673) Jabir is reported to have said, «One day while we were on a trip, one of our numbers hit his head on a rock and broke his head. In a dream, he had a wet dream, and he asked his companions: «Can I cleanse myself with sand?» They said, «We think that you should not cleanse yourself with sand if you can bathe in water.» He bathed and died. When they returned, they told the Prophet ﷺ about it and he said: «They killed him! May Allah destroy them! Why didn't they ask about what they didn't know?! Indeed, the cure for ignorance is a question. It was enough for him to cleanse himself

with sand, and wipe (the bandage) »- or (he said):« bandage (the wound) - (here) Musa doubted, - bandage the wound, then wipe it and wash the rest of the body». №336

674) It is reported from the words of Abu Sa'eed al-Khudri that the Messenger of Allah ﷺ said: «Friday bathing is an obligation/wajib / of every adult». №341

675) It is narrated from the words of al-Awza'i, who said: «Hasan ibn 'Atiyya informed me, who said:» Abu-l-Ash'as as-San'ani told me: «Aws ibn Aus as-Thaqafi told me, who said: «I heard the Messenger of Allah ﷺ say: «He who on Friday will wash (his head) and bathe (himself), will go early (to Friday prayer) on foot, and not on horseback, will take a place near the imam, will listen to a sermon attentively and without being distracted, then he will receive for each of his steps (from home to the mosque) a reward equal to (the reward) for observing fasting and night prayers during the year». №345

676) It is reported that Lubaba bint al-Harith said: «Once, when al-Husayn ibn 'Ali, may Allah be pleased with him, (sitting) on the lap of the Messenger of Allah ﷺ, he urinated on him. I said: «Put on (other) clothes and give me your Izar so that I can wash them.» He said: «The girl's urine should be washed off, and the boy's urine (enough) be sprinkled with water». №375

677) It is narrated from the words of Abu Hurairah: «Once, some Bedouin entered the mosque, and at that time the Messenger of Allah ﷺ was sitting and praying.» Ibn 'Abda said: «In two rak'ats.» Then he (Bedouin) said: «O Allah, have mercy on me and Muhammad and do not forgive anyone with us!» The Prophet ﷺ said: «You deprive (the people of the mercy of Allah, which is) vast.» Then he (Bedouin) went to the side of the mosque and began to urinate, and people rushed to stop him, but the Prophet ﷺ forbade them (to interfere with him) and said: «Verily, you were sent to facilitate, and not to complicate. Pour a bucket of water over this

place.» Or did he say, «Big bucket of water»? №380

678) It is narrated from the words of Abu Hurairah that the Messenger of Allah ﷺ said: «If one of you steps with the sole (shoe) on something unclean, then the earth will serve as a means of purification for his shoes». №385

679) It is reported that Muhammad ibn 'Amr - and this is ibn Hasan ibn 'Ali ibn Abu Talib - said: «Once we asked Jabir about the prayer times of the Prophet ﷺ and he said:« He performed the noon prayer at noon, the afternoon when the sun was still bright, sunset - when it was already setting, and evening - (at different times). (If he saw) that there were already a lot of people, then he began (prayer) early, and if (he saw) that there were few of them, then he put it off. (As for) the morning prayer, he performed it in the predawn twilight». №397

680) It is reported from the words of Malik that al-'Alayi ibn 'Abdurrahman said: «Once we went to Anas ibn Malik after the midday prayer, and he stood and performed the afternoon /'asr/ prayer. When he finished the prayer, we mentioned (in his presence) the quick performance of this prayer or (simply) mentioned it, and he said: «I heard the Messenger of Allah ﷺ say:« This is the prayer of a hypocrite, this is the prayer of a hypocrite, this is the prayer of a hypocrite! One of them sits until the sun turns yellow. And when it stands between the horns of the shaitan or: on the horns of the shaitan, he gets up and makes four pecks, while remembering Allah only a little». №413

681) It is reported that Abu Dharr said: «(Once) the Messenger of Allah ﷺ said to me: «O Abu Dharr, what will it be like for you when the rulers standing over you kill prayer?» or did he say, «Will they postpone prayer?» I said: «O Messenger of Allah, and how do you order me (to act in such a case)?» He said: «Perform a prayer at the time set for it, and if you find them during the performance (prayer), then pray (together

with them), and verily, it will be additional / nafila / for you.». №431

682) It is reported that 'Ubadah ibn as-Samit said: «The Messenger of Allah ﷺ said: «Indeed, you will have rulers after me, whom some things will prevent from performing prayer until their time runs out. And you pray at its appointed time. A man said, «O Messenger of Allah, should I pray with them?» He replied, «Yes if you wish.» Sufyan (in his riwayah) said: «And if I find them in prayer, should I pray with them?» He replied: «Yes if you wish». №433

683) It is reported that Ibn 'Abbas said: «The Messenger of Allah ﷺ said: «I was not ordered to build too decorated mosques.» Ibn 'Abbas said: «You will certainly decorate them, as Jews and Christians do (in their temples)». №448

684) It is narrated from the words of Anas (ibn Malik) that the Prophet ﷺ said: «The Hour will not come until people begin to brag about mosques to each other». №449

685) It is reported that 'Aisha said: «The Messenger of Allah ﷺ ordered the construction of mosques in the quarters, keep them clean and smear with incense». №455

686) It is reported that Abu Sa'id (al-Khudri) said: «The Messenger of Allah ﷺ said:» The whole earth is a mosque, except for baths and cemeteries». №492

687) It is reported that 'Amr ibn Shu'ayb narrated the words of his father, who reported that his grandfather said: «The Messenger of Allah ﷺ said: «Tell your children to pray from the age of seven, and beat them for it, from the age of ten, and put them to bed separately». №495

688) It is reported that Abu Sa'id al-Khudri said: «The Messenger of Allah ﷺ said:» Prayer in the Jama'at is equal (by reward) to twenty-five prayers, and if (a person) performs it in the desert, properly bowing and bowing to the ground, then (according to the degree of reward)

she will reach fifty prayers». №560

689) It is narrated from the words of Abu Hurairah that the Messenger of Allah ﷺ said: «Do not forbid the slave girls of Allah to visit the mosques of Allah but do not let them go out perfumed with incense». №565

690) It is reported that Mujahid said: «(Once) 'Abdullah ibn 'Umar said: «The Prophet ﷺ said:« Allow women to visit mosques at night. His son said to him: «By Allah, we will not allow them, because they will use it for evil. I swear by Allah, we will not let them.» (Mujahid) said: «And he cursed him and, being angry, said: «I tell you that the Messenger of Allah ﷺ said: «Allow them, »and you say:« We will not allow them?!». №568

691) It is reported that 'Amr ibn Salima said: «(When) we were in the settlement, people passed by us who were heading to the Prophet ﷺ, and when they returned, they again passed us and informed us that the Messenger of Allah ﷺ said, so-and-so. I was (at that time) a boy with good memory and memorized from what (they told) many (verses from) the Quran. And when my father went with a delegation to the Messenger of Allah ﷺ with a group from among his tribe, and he taught them to pray, he said: «Let the one who knows the Quran better than all of you be an imam for you.» And I knew the Quran more than all of them because I memorized it and they put me in front (as imam). Leading them (in prayer), I was wearing a short yellow cloak, and when I bowed to the ground, she rode up, and one of the women said: «Cover your reader's awrah (so that we don't see him)!», after which (people) bought me an Omani shirt, and I did not rejoice at anything (then so much), after Islam, like this (shirt). And I led them in prayer when I was seven or eight». №585

692) It is reported that Ibn 'Umar said: «When the first settlers (muhajirs) arrived, they stopped at al-'Asba until the arrival of the Prophet ﷺ and at that time their

imam (in prayer) was Salim, the freedman of Abu Hudhaifah, who is the most the Quran knew them. Al-Haytham added: «And among them were 'Umar ibn al-Khattab and Abu Salama ibn 'Abdul-Asad». №588

693) It is reported that Abu Hurairah said: «The Messenger of Allah ﷺ said: «Isn't he afraid» - or (he said:) «Isn't he afraid of you who raises his head while the imam is still in prostration, that Allah will turn his head into a donkey's. Or (he said): «Will he likens his appearance to a donkey?!». №623

694) It is reported that Salama ibn al-Akua 'said: «(Once) I said:« O Messenger of Allah, verily, I am a person engaged in hunting (asid), so can I pray in one shirt? (The Messenger of Allah ﷺ), said: «Yes, and fasten it at least with a thorn». №632

695) It is reported that Ibn 'Umar said: «The Messenger of Allah ﷺ said: - or he said:» 'Umar, may Allah be pleased with him, said: «If one of you has two clothes, let him pray in it, and if he has only one garment, let him wrap it (around the waist). And don't wrap your-self up as the Jews do». №635

696) It is narrated from the words of 'Aisha that the Prophet ﷺ said: «Allah will not accept prayer from a woman who has reached the age of majority, except in a head-scarf». №641

697) It is reported from the words of 'Amr ibn al-Harith that Bukayr told him that Qurayb, a freedman of Ibn 'Abbas, informed him that (once) 'Abdullah ibn 'Ab-bas saw how 'Abdullah ibn al-Harith prayed, whose hair was braided at the back. He stood behind him and began to untie them, but he did not budge. When he finished the prayer, he approached Ibn 'Abbas and asked him: «What did you want from my head?». He replied: «Indeed, I heard the Messenger of Allah ﷺ say: «Surely such (a person) is like one who prays with his hands tied behind». №647

698)   It is reported that Abu Sa'eed al-Khudri said: «Once when the Messenger of Allah 🙰 was praying with his companions, he took off his sandals and placed them on his left. When the people (who were standing behind him) saw this, they also took off their sandals. After finishing the prayer, the Messenger of Allah 🙰 asked: «Why did you take off your sandals?» They said, «We saw that you took off your sandals, so we took off ours.» The Messenger of Allah 🙰 said: «Indeed, Jibril 🙰 came to me and said that there were impurities on them.» (Also) he said: «When one of you comes to the mosque, let him examine (the soles of) his sandals, and if he finds any impurity or dirt on them, let him wipe them (on the ground) and then pray in them». №650

699)   Ya'la ibn Shaddad ibn Aus narrated that his father said: «The Messenger of Allah 🙰 said:» Be different from the Jews, for verily, they do not pray in their sandals or leather socks». №652

700)   It is narrated from the words of 'Amr ibn Shu'ayb that his father reported that his grandfather said: «I saw the Messenger of Allah 🙰 pray in sandals and without them». №653

701)   It is narrated from the words of Abu Hurairah that the Messenger of Allah 🙰 said: «When one of you (wants) to pray, taking off his sandals, let him in no case interfere with anyone with them, but put them between his legs, or (let) pray for them». №655

702)   It is reported from the words of 'Abdullah ibn Shaddad that Maymuna bint al-Harith said: «The Messenger of Allah 🙰 often prayed, and I was at his feet when I had my period. And sometimes his clothes touched me when he prostrated, and also he often prayed on the khumra (rug)». №656

703)   It is reported that Simak ibn Harb said: «I heard an-Numan ibn Bashir say:» The Prophet 🙰 always aligned our ranks as carefully as if he was going to check the straightness of the arrows on them, and he

did this until he made sure that we understood what he (was trying to achieve from us). One day he turned to face the people and saw that the chest of one of those present was protruding forward, he said: «You should align your ranks, or Allah will surely change your faces». №663

704) It is reported that Talhah ibn 'Ubaydullah said: «The Messenger of Allah ﷺ said:« If you set something (height) in front of you with the back of a saddle (camel), then someone who passes in front of you will not interfere». №685

705) It is reported that Muhammad ibn Ka'b al-Qurazi said: «(Once) I said to him - meaning 'Umar ibn 'Abdul-'Aziz:» I was informed by Ibn 'Abbas that the Prophet ﷺ said: «Do not pray behind one who sleeps or talks». №694

706) It is narrated from the words of Abu Juhayfa that 'Ali, may Allah be pleased with him, said: «During prayer, under the Sunnah, you should lay the hand of one hand on the hand (other) under the navel». №756

707) It is transmitted from Jabir, may Allah be pleased with him and his father: «Usually Mu'az prayed with the Prophet ﷺ, and then returned and prayed with us (or: with his fellow tribesmen). Once the Prophet ﷺ made a prayer (or: evening prayer / 'isha /) late, and Mu'az prayed with the Prophet ﷺ, and then he came to lead the prayer of his fellow tribesmen and began to read Surah al-Baqarah, and some person left the row praying and prayed separately. They said to him: «You have fallen into hypocrisy, O so-and-so!» He said in response: «I did not fall into hypocrisy!» He came to the Prophet ﷺ and said: «Verily, Mu'az prays with you, and then returns and leads our prayer, O Messenger of Allah ﷺ. Indeed, we are the owners of camels used for irrigation, and we work with our own hands ... And he came to pray with us and recited Surah al-Baqarah! The Prophet ﷺ said: «O Mu'az, are you not a tempter?! Are you an adept?! Read this and that!» Abu az-

Zubayr said that the Messenger of Allah ﷺ ordered him to recite the suras «Praise your Lord, the Highest» and «I swear by the night when it covers.» (The transmitter) said: «And we asked 'Amr, and he said: «It seems that he said this». №791

708) It was narrated from Abu Sa'id, may Allah be pleased with him: «We were ordered to read al-Fatiha and what is easy for us from the Quran». №818

709) It was narrated from Abu Hurayrah, may Allah be pleased with him, that one day the Messenger of Allah ﷺ ended the prayer during which he recited the verses aloud, and said: «Did any of you read with me now?» One person said, «Yes, O Messenger of Allah.» He said: «So I said to myself: something is interrupting my reading.» Hearing this from the Messenger of Allah ﷺ, people stopped reciting verses along with the Prophet ﷺ in prayers in which the Prophet ﷺ recited verses aloud. №826

710) It is transmitted from Mutarrif: «Imran ibn Husayn and I prayed under the guidance of 'Ali ibn Abu Talib. He said the Takbir before bowing to the ground, before bowing from the waist, and before standing up after performing two rak'ats. When we finished, 'Imran took my hand and said: «Just now he prayed with us the way Muhammad ﷺ did it.». №835

711) Tawus said: «We told Ibn 'Abbas about sitting on the heels during prostration, and he said:« This is Sunnah. We said, «But we don't think it's proper for men.» Ibn 'Abbas said: «This is the Sunnah of your Prophet ﷺ!» №845

712) It is narrated from Al-Bar, may Allah be pleased with him, that making bows from the waist and the ground, as well as sitting between two bows to the earth, took the Messenger of Allah ﷺ about the same time. №852

713) It is transmitted from 'Abdu-r-Rahman ibn Shibli: «The Messenger of Allah ﷺ forbade making prostrations like a pecking crow and prostrating like a beast,

and he forbade constantly praying in the same place in the mosque like a camel who has chosen a place». №862

714) Al-Hasan reports from Anas ibn Hakim ad-Dabbi that he, fearing (the governor) Ziyad or Ibn Ziyad, arrived in Medina and met with Abu Hurairah. He said: «He asked me about my origin, and I told him, and then he said: «O young man! Shall I retell the hadith to you?» I replied: «Of course, may Allah have mercy on you!» The transmitter Yunus said: «And, as far as I know, he raised these words to the Prophet ﷺ: «The first of the deeds that people will be asked about on the Day of Judgment is prayer. Our Almighty and Great Lord say to the angels, although He knows everything: «Look at the prayer of My servant: is it perfect or has flaws?» If it is perfect, then it will be recorded as perfect. If there were flaws in it, then Almighty Allah says: «Look, if My servant performed additional prayers.» If he had them, Allah Almighty says: «Supplement the obligatory prayers of My slave with additional ones.» And then all the rest of his deeds will be evaluated in the same way.». №864

715) It is narrated from Abu Hurairah, may Allah be pleased with him, that during the performance of earthly prostrations, the Prophet ﷺ used to turn to Allah with such a prayer: «O Allah, forgive me all my sins: small and large, first and last.» And in the version of Ibn al-Sarj there is an addition: «... explicit and secret (Allahumma, gfir li zanbi kulla-hu: dikka-hu wa jilla-hu, wa av-vala-hu wa akhira-hu, va alyaniyata-hu va sirra-hu)!» №878

716) It was narrated from Musa ibn Abu 'Aish that a man was praying on the roof of his house and when he re-cited the verse «Is He not able to revive the dead?» (Surah «al-Qiyama» verse 40), exclaimed: «Glory to You, of course (yes) (Subhana-ka fa-Bala)!», - and when he was asked about this, he said: «I heard this from the Messenger of Allah «. Abu Dawud narrates that Ahmad says: «I like to turn to Allah with sup-

plications from the Quran in the obligatory prayers».
№884

717) It was narrated from Isma'il ibn Abu Umayya: «I heard a Bedouin say that he heard Abu Hurairah, may Allah be pleased with him, say that the Messenger of Allah ﷺ said: «Which of you recited the Surah «I swear by the fig tree and the olive tree » and read it to the end, that is, to the words «Is not Allah the Wisest Judge?», let him say: «Of course, and I am one of those who testify to this.» And who read the surah «No, I swear on the Day of Resurrection!» and read until the words «Is He not able to raise the dead?», let him say: «Of course.» And whoever read the surah «By the Messengers» and read up to the words «In what story after this will you believe?», let him say: «We have believed in Allah.» Ismail said: «And I began to repeat to this Bedouin to see if he remembered well, and he said:« O son of my brother! You rightly think that I did not remember this hadith ... So, I performed sixty hajj's, and I remember on which camel I performed each of them!» №887

718) It was narrated from Ibn 'Abbas, may Allah be pleased with him and his father, that the Prophet ﷺ said: «I (or: your Prophet) was ordered to prostrate to seven (parts of the body) and not to remove neither hair nor clothes». №890

719) It was narrated from Anas, may Allah be pleased with him, that the Prophet ﷺ said: «Moderately (raise your hands) in prostration and let none of you put your forearms on the ground as a dog puts». №897

720) It was narrated from 'Aisha, may Allah be pleased with her: «I asked the Messenger of Allah ﷺ about a person who looks around during prayer, and he said:« This is what the shaitan steals from the prayer of the servant of Allah». №910

721) It was narrated from Anas ibn Malik, may Allah be pleased with him, that the Messenger of Allah ﷺ said: «What do people think when they raise their eyes to

the sky during prayer?» And he spoke out harshly about it, saying, «Either they stop doing it or they lose their sight!» №913

722) 'Abdullah, may Allah be pleased with him, said: «During prayer, we greeted and gave the necessary orders. And so I came to the Messenger of Allah ﷺ when he was praying, and greeted him, but he did not answer my greeting. I began to think about what I could have done, long ago and recently. Having completed the prayer, the Messenger of Allah ﷺ said: «Verily, the Almighty and Great Allah commands what He wills, and, verily, Allah Almighty has commanded that during prayer you should not talk.» After that, he answered my greeting». №924

723) It is transmitted from 'Abdullah ibn 'Amr, may Allah be pleased with him and his father: «It became known to me that the Messenger of Allah ﷺ said:« The prayer of the one who prays while sitting is half a prayer, »and one day I came to him and I saw him performing the (additional) prayer while seated. I grabbed my head, and (the Messenger of Allah ﷺ) asked: «What is the matter with you, O 'Abdullah ibn 'Amr?» I replied: «O Messenger of Allah! I have come to know that you have said: «The prayer of one who prays sitting down is half a prayer.» And you pray while sitting. (The Messenger of Allah ﷺ) said: «Yes, everything is so ... However, I am not like you». №950

724) It is transmitted from 'Abdullah ibn Shakyk: «I asked 'Aisha if the Messenger of Allah ﷺ recited a whole surah in one rak'at, and she said: «Short suras (mufassal).» I asked, «And he prayed while sitting?» She replied, «When the people overpowered him». №956

725) 'Abdullah ibn 'Umar, may Allah be pleased with him and his father, said: «The vertical setting of the right foot and the prostration of the left foot (during tashahhud) belong to the sunnah of prayer». №958

726) 'Abdullah ibn Mas'ud, may Allah be pleased with him, said: «When praying with the Messenger of Al-

lah 🕌, we used to say while sitting:» Peace be to Allah before His servants, peace to such and such, «but once the Messenger of Allah 🕌 said: «Do not say: «Peace / as-salaam / Allah», because Allah is As-Salam, but when one of you sits down, let him say: «Greetings, prayers and all good things to Allah, peace be upon you, O Prophet, mercy Allah and His blessings, peace be upon us and all the righteous servants of Allah barakatu-hu, as-salamu 'alay-na wa 'ala 'ibadi-Lla-hi-s-salihin /. Truly, if you utter these words, they will touch every righteous slave in heaven and on earth (or: between heaven and earth). And say: «I testify that there is no god [worthy of worship] except Allah, and I testify that Muhammad is His slave and Messenger / Ashkhadu alla ilaha illa-Llahu wa ashhadu anna Mu-hammadan 'abdu-hu wa rasulu-hu /, after why let each of you choose the words of prayer that he likes the most and turn to Allah with them». №968

727) It is narrated from 'Abdullah ibn al-Zubair, may Allah be pleased with him and his father, that the Messenger of Allah 🕌, sitting down in prayer, placed his left foot under his right thigh and shin and extended his right foot. At the same time, he placed his left hand on his left thigh, and his right hand on his right, and extended his finger. (The transmitter) said: «And (the transmit-ter) 'Abdul-Wahid showed us by extending his index finger». №988

728) It is narrated from 'Imran ibn Husayn, may Allah be pleased with him and his father, that one day the Mes-senger of Allah 🕌, performing the afternoon prayer, said the words of taslim after the third rak'ah, after which he went into the house of one of his wives, and one man with long arms, nicknamed Khirbak, asked: «Has the prayer been shortened, O Messenger of Al-lah?» And (the Messenger of Allah 🕌) came out angry, dragging his cloak, and said: «Is he telling the truth?» The people answered, «Yes.» Then he made the re-maining rak'at, said the words of taslim, made two bows to the earth and again said the words of taslim.

729) It was narrated from 'Abdullah, may Allah be pleased with him, that one day the Messenger of Allah ﷺ offered a prayer. (Transmitter) Ibrahim said: «And I don't know if he added or subtracted something.» It further says: «... and the people asked:« O Messenger of Allah! Has anything new been introduced into prayer?» He replied: «Why did you decide that?» The people said, «But you prayed so-and-so.» Then the Messenger of Allah ﷺ turned towards the qibla, made two earthly bows with them, said the words of taslim and said, turning to the people: «If any changes were made to the prayer, I would inform you about it ... The fact is, that I am a man and I forget like you, and if I forget anything, remind me.» (The Messenger of Allah ﷺ) also said: «If any of you doubts in his prayer, let him choose what seems to him the most probable, and continue based on this, and after taslim, he will make two bows to the earth». №1020

730) It is transmitted from Ibn 'Abbas, may Allah be pleased with him and his father, that the Prophet ﷺ called two prostrations to the earth, performed to atone for an oversight, performed in defiance of Shaitan. №1025

731) 'Ata al-Khorasani narrates from the words of his wife's freedman Umm 'Uthman: «I heard 'Ali, may Allah be pleased with him, say on the minbar of Kufa:» When Friday comes, the devils go with their banners to the market and try to detain people and prevent them from going to Friday prayers. And the angels come and sit at the door of the mosque and write down those who come earlier and those who come later until the imam appears, and if a person sat down so that he could hear and see well, listened silently and did not idle talk, two kifles of reward will be written to him. If he sat far away, where he could not hear well, but listened and did not idle talk, one kifl of reward is recorded for him. If a person sat down so that he could see and hear, but did not listen and talked idle, one kifle of sin is recorded for him. Who, during Friday prayers, will

say to his comrade: «Shh!» - he is already talking idle, and whoever has talked idly will not receive any benefit from this Friday prayer. And at the end, he said: «I heard the Messenger of Allah ﷺ say this». №1051

732) Abu al-Malih narrates from his father that on the day of Hunayn it rained, and the Prophet (peace be upon him) ordered the herald to announce that prayer should be performed in places. №1057

733) Abu al-Malih narrates from his father that he saw the Prophet ﷺ on Friday in Hudaybiyyah and ordered people to pray in places when it began to rain, from which the soles of their sandals did not even get wet. №1059

734) It is narrated from Nafi'a that Ibn 'Umar, may Allah be pleased with him and his father, stopped at Dajnan on a cold night and ordered the herald to announce that people should pray in their places. Ibn 'Umar narrates that on cold or rainy nights, the Messenger of Allah ﷺ ordered the herald to announce to the people that they should pray in their places. №1060

735) Abdullah ibn al-Harith, the son of Muhammad ibn Sirin, narrates that Ibn 'Abbas, may Allah be pleased with him and his father, said to his muezzin on a rainy day: «When you say:« I bear witness that Muhammad is the Messenger of Allah, do not say: «Hurry to prayer,» but say: «Pray in your homes.» And as if people thought it was reprehensible. Then Ibn 'Abbas said: «The one who is better than me did this ... Verily, it is necessary to perform the Friday prayer, but, verily, I did not want to create difficulties for you and force you to walk on clay in the rain». №1066

736) It was narrated from Tariq ibn Shihab that the Prophet ﷺ said: «Friday prayer is the right (of Allah) and the duty of every Muslim in the community, except for four. This is a slave, woman, child and sick». №1067

737) It is transmitted from 'Ata ibn Abu Rabah: «Ibn al-Zubayr prayed with us on a holiday that fell on Friday, at the beginning of the day, after which we gathered

to perform Friday prayers, but he did not come out to us and we prayed without him. And Ibn 'Abbas was in Taif and when he returned, we told him about it and he said: «He acted under the Sunnah». №1071

738) It was narrated from 'Abdullah ibn 'Umar, may Allah be pleased with him and his father, that one day 'Umar ibn al-Khattab, may Allah be pleased with him, saw a striped garment made of silk-based fabric being sold at the gate of the mosque and said: «O Messenger Allah! It would be nice if you bought these clothes, put them on Fridays and met delegations arriving at you in them. The Messenger of Allah ﷺ said: «The one who has no share in eternal life wears such clothes!» Later, the Messenger of Allah ﷺ brought such clothes, and he gave one to 'Umar ibn al-Khattab. 'Umar said: «O Messenger of Allah! Are you dressing me in this after you said what you said about the clothes of 'Utarida?!» The Messenger of Allah ﷺ said: «I did not give it to you so that you would wear it.» Then 'Umar gave it to his pagan brother who lived in Mecca. №1076

739) 'Amr ibn Shu'ayb relates from the words of his father the story of his grandfather, may Allah be pleased with him and his father, that the Messenger of Allah ﷺ forbade buying and selling in the mosque, asking about the missing thing there, reciting verses and gathering in mugs before Friday prayer. №1079

740) Narrated Sahl ibn Sa'd, may Allah be pleased with him, narrates: «We rested and dined after the Friday prayer». №1086

741) It is reported from As-Saib ibn Yazid that during the time of the Prophet ﷺ Abu Bakr and 'Umar, the first adhan was distributed when the imam sat down at the minbar on Friday. And in the time of 'Uthman, when there were many people, 'Uthman ordered to pronounce the third call, which was pronounced in Az-Zaur, and so it continued in the future. №1087

742) It is narrated from As-Sahib that the Messenger of Allah ﷺ had only one muazzin, namely Bilal. Then he

narrated a hadith similar to the previous one.. №1089

743)   It was narrated from Jabir ibn Samur, may Allah be pleased with him and his father: «The Messenger of Allah ﷺ delivered a sermon while standing, then sat down, then again delivered a sermon while standing, and whoever tells you that he delivered a sermon while sitting, he is lying.» And he said: «And by Allah, I have performed with him more than two thousand prayers». №1093

744)   Al-Hakam ibn Khazn al-Kulafi, may Allah be pleased with him, one of the companions of the Messenger of Allah ﷺ reports: «I arrived at the Messenger of Allah ﷺ as part of a delegation of seven or nine people. We went into him and said: «O Messenger of Allah! We have come to visit you, so turn to Allah with good prayers for us.» And he ordered to give us some dates, and the situation then was difficult for everyone. We stayed there for several days and performed the Friday prayer together with the Messenger of Allah ﷺ. He stood up, leaning on a stick or a bow, and praised Allah with few, but good and blessed words, after which he said: «O people! You will never be able to do everything that you are commanded, but try and rejoice (good news).» Abu 'Ali said: «I heard Abu Dawud say: «One of our comrades confirmed me in some part of this hadith, which disappeared from my records». №1096

745)   It is narrated from 'Adi ibn Hatim, may Allah be pleased with him, that once in the presence of the Prophet ﷺ, one person delivered a sermon and said: «... the one who obeys Allah and His Messenger ... and the one who disobeys them...» (Messenger of Allah ﷺ) said: «Get up (or: go)! You are a bad speaker». №1099

746)   Sahl ibn Mu'az ibn Anas reported from the words of his father: «The Messenger of Allah ﷺ forbade sitting on the buttocks, raising his knees and clasping them with his hands, on Friday, at the time when the imam pronounces the khutba». №1110

747) It was narrated from Umm 'Atiyah, may Allah be pleased with her: «The Messenger of Allah ﷺ ordered us to take with us girls who usually did not go out on the day of the holiday, and he was asked: «And even those who have menstruation?» He said: «Let them see the good together with other Muslims and participate in their assembly.» One woman asked: «O Messenger of Allah! And what about the one of us who does not have the right clothes to go out? (The Messenger of Allah ﷺ) said: «Let her friend share her clothes with her if she has extra». №1136

748) Narrated from Yahya ibn Yazid al-Hunai: «I asked Anas ibn Malik, may Allah be pleased with him, about shortening the prayer. And Anas said: «When the Messenger of Allah ﷺ set off, then after travelling three miles or three farsahs, he already made two rak'ahs (instead of four)». №1201

749) Narrated from Sa'eed ibn Jubair: «Ibn 'Abbas, may Allah be pleased with him and his father, said that the Messenger of Allah ﷺ combined the midday prayer / zuhr / with the afternoon / 'asr / and the sunset prayer/ maghrib / with the evening / 'isha / in Medina, although it was not in danger and it was not raining. He was asked: «Why did he do this?» He replied, «He wanted his community to have no trouble». №1211

750) It is narrated from Ibn 'Abbas, may Allah be pleased with him and his father, that the Messenger of Allah ﷺ lived in Mecca for seventeen days and all this time shortened the prayer, and the one who stayed in some place for seventeen days shortens the prayer, and the one who whoever stays anywhere for a longer time should perform prayers in full. №1230

751) Narrated from Ibn 'Abbas, may Allah be pleased with him and his father: «Almighty Allah, through the mouth of your Prophet ﷺ, charged you with the obligation to pray four rak'ats at rest, two rak'ats on the way and one rak'at when you are in danger». №1247

752) It is narrated from 'Aisha, may Allah be pleased with

her, that the Messenger of Allah ﷺ did not perform any additional prayer as steadily as two rak'ats before the obligatory morning prayer. №1254

753) It is narrated from Abu Hurairah, may Allah be pleased with him, that the Prophet ﷺ read when performing two rak'ats before the morning prayer of the surah «Say: O you disbelievers» and «Say: He is Allah the Only». №1256

754) It was narrated from Abu Hurayrah, may Allah be pleased with him, that the Messenger of Allah ﷺ said: «When one of you prays two rak'ahs before the obligatory morning prayer, let him lie on his right side after that.» Marwan ibn al-Hakam said to him: «Is it not enough for any of us that he goes to the mosque? Why else would he lie on his right side?» In the version of 'Ubaydullah, he replied: «No.» When Ibn 'Umar found out about this, he said: «Abu Hurayrah takes on a lot.» Ibn 'Umar was told: «Are you denying something of what he says?» Ibn 'Umar said: «No. It's just that he boldly speaks out, but we don't.» Abu Hurayrah, learning about this, said: «Am I to blame for what I remembered, and they forgot?!» №1261

755) It is narrated from 'Ali that the Messenger of Allah ﷺ performed two rak'ats after all the obligatory prayers, except for the morning/fajr / and afternoon / 'asr /. №1275

756) It was narrated from Abu Umamah, may Allah be pleased with him, that the Messenger of Allah ﷺ said: «Prayer after prayer without idle talk in the intervals between them is an entry in 'Illiyun». №1288

757) It was narrated from Abu Sa'eed and Abu Hurairah, may Allah be pleased with them both, that the Messenger of Allah ﷺ said: «If a person wakes up on his own and wakes his wife at night and they pray together in two rak'ats (additional prayer), then they will be written among the men and women who remember Allah.» (Transmitter) Ibn Kathir did not raise these words to the Prophet ﷺ and did not mention Abu

Hurairah, but transmitted it as the words of Abu Sa'id.
№1309

758) It was narrated from Abu Hurayrah, may Allah be pleased with him, that the Messenger of Allah ﷺ said: «If a person got up at night to pray and then felt that (because of drowsiness) he could not read the Quran properly and he did not understand, what he says, let him go to sleep». №1311

759) It was narrated from 'Aisha, may Allah be pleased with her, the wife of the Prophet ﷺ that the Messenger of Allah ﷺ said: «If a person regularly performs a night prayer, and one day (unintentionally) oversleeps her, a reward will be recorded for him, as if he had performed it, and his dream will be (given to him by Allah) alms». №1314

760) It was narrated from Rabi'i ibn Ka'ba al-Aslamy, may Allah be pleased with him: «I spent the night with the Messenger of Allah ﷺ and brought him water for ablution and everything he needed, and one day he said: «Ask me (O whatever you want). I said, «I want to be with you in Paradise.» (The Messenger of Allah ﷺ) said: «Anything else?» I replied, «Just that.» (The Messenger of Allah ﷺ) said: «Then help me against your soul by frequently prostrating». №1320

761) It is narrated from 'Aisha, may Allah be pleased with her, the wife of the Prophet ﷺ that the Prophet ﷺ prayed in the mosque and people joined him and also began to pray. The next night, the Prophet ﷺ also performed an additional prayer and many people gathered. On the third night, they gathered, but the Messenger of Allah ﷺ did not come out to them. In the morning he said to them: «I saw what you did, and I was prevented from going out to you only by the fear that it would be charged to you.» And it was Ramadan. №1373

762) It was narrated from Ibn 'Abbas, may Allah be pleased with him and his father, that the Prophet ﷺ said: «Look for the Night of Destiny among the last ten nights of Ramadan. Look for her when there are nine, seven or

five nights left.». №1381

763) It was narrated from 'Ali, may Allah be pleased with him, that the Messenger of Allah ﷺ said: «O followers of the Quran! Make witr, for verily Allah is One and He loves the odd». №1416

764) It is transmitted from 'Abdullah, may Allah be pleased with him: «The Prophet ﷺ ...» Then he retold a hadith similar to the one mentioned above, and said: «A Bedouin asked him:« What do you say (about us)? The Prophet ﷺ replied: «It is not for you and not for your companions». №1417

765) It was narrated by Abu Ayyub al-Ansari, may Allah be pleased with him, that the Messenger of Allah ﷺ said: «Witr is approved for every Muslim, and whoever wishes to perform five rak'ats, let him do it, and whoever wishes to perform three rak'ats, let him perform, and whoever wishes to perform one rak'at, let him perform». №1422

766) It is narrated from Ubayya ibn Ka'ba, may Allah be pleased with him, that the Messenger of Allah ﷺ, making witr, recited the surahs «Praise the name of your Lord the Highest ...», «Speak to those who disbelieved ...» and «He is Allah the Only ...». №1423

767) Al-Hasan ibn 'Ali, may Allah be pleased with him and his father, said that the Messenger of Allah ﷺ taught him to read during witr (or qunut during witr) as follows: «O Allah, guide me to the right path along with those whom You have guided to it, grant me well-being along with those to whom You have granted it, take care of me along with those whom You take care of, make grace for me what You have given, and protect me from the evil of what You have predestined, for You decide, but no decisions are made about You. Verily, the one whom You have supported will not be humbled, and the one with whom You are at enmity will not be exalted. Our Lord, You are the Blessed One, the Almighty /Allahumma hdini fiman hadaita, wa'afini fiman 'afaita, wa-tavallyani fiman tawallaita,

wa barik li fima a'taita, wa ki-ni sharra ma kadayta, fainnaka takdy walya yukda 'alayka, innahu la yazillu man walayta, tabarakta rabbana va ta'alaita/». №1425

768) It is reported from the words of 'Ali, may Allah be pleased with him, that at the end of the witr, the Messenger of Allah ﷺ said: «O Allah, verily, I resort to the protection of Your favour from Your indignation, and the protection of Your forgiveness from Your punishment, and I seek Your protection from You! I cannot count Your praises and glorify You as You Himself glorified Yourself, anta kama asnaita 'ala nafsika /». №1427

769) It was narrated from Abu Sa'id, may Allah be pleased with him, that the Messenger of Allah ﷺ said: «Whoever overslept witr or forgot about it, let him perform it when he remembers it». №1431

770) It is narrated from Zayd ibn Thabit, may Allah be pleased with him, that once the Messenger of Allah ﷺ fenced off a small space for himself in the mosque and began to pray there at night, and some people began to pray, following his example. They came every night, but one night he did not come out to them. They crowded at his door and began to throw stones at the door. And then the Messenger of Allah ﷺ came out to them angry and said: «O people! You did this until I began to think that this prayer would be charged to you! Pray in your homes, for truly, apart from the obligatory prayers, the best prayer is the one that a person performs at home!» №1447

771) It was narrated from Abu Sa'eed al-Khudri and Abu Hurairah, may Allah be pleased with them both, that the Messenger of Allah ﷺsaid: «If a person wakes up on his own and wakes his wife at night and they pray together in two rak'ats, they will be written down among men and women who remember Allah much». №1451

772) It was narrated from 'Uthman, may Allah be pleased with him, that the Prophet ﷺ said: «The best of you is

the one who learns the Quran and teaches it to others».
№1452

773) It was narrated from Sa'd ibn Abu Waqqas, may Allah be pleased with him, that the Messenger of Allah ﷺ said: «The one who does not recite the Quran in a singsong voice does not belong to us». №1469

774) It is narrated from an-Numan ibn Bashir, may Allah be pleased with him and his father, that the Prophet ﷺ said: «Supplication is worship:« And your Lord said: «Call on Me, and I will answer you ...» (Surah Ghafir, verse 60)». №1479

775) It is narrated from Fadali ibn 'Ubayd, may Allah be pleased with him, a companion of the Messenger of Allah ﷺ that one day the Messenger of Allah ﷺ heard a man cry out (to Allah) with prayers, without first praising Allah Almighty and without invoking a blessing on the Prophet ﷺ. The Messenger of Allah ﷺ said: «This one hastened.» Then he called him and said to him or someone else: «When one of you makes a prayer, let him first give praise to his Almighty and Great Lord, then call blessings on the Prophet ﷺ, and then ask Allah for whatever he wants». №1481

776) It was narrated from Abu Hurayrah, may Allah be pleased with him, that the Messenger of Allah ﷺ said: «Let none of you says: «O Allah, forgive me if you wish» or «O Allah, have mercy on me if you wish.» Let him ask decisively, for no one can force Allah to do anything». №1483

777) It was narrated from Abu Hurayrah, may Allah be pleased with him, that the Messenger of Allah ﷺ said: «An answer will come to the prayer of any of you, unless he rushes and says:« Behold, I called, but there was no answer!» №1484

778) It was narrated from 'Abdullah ibn 'Amr, may Allah be pleased with him and his father: «I saw how the Messenger of Allah ﷺcounted the words of remembrance of Allah with his fingers.» Ibn Kudama said in

his version: «... the right hand». №1502

779) It was narrated from 'Ali ibn Abu Talib (may Allah be pleased with him) that the Prophet ﷺ said after taslim: «O Allah, forgive me what I did before and what I put aside, what I did secretly and openly, what I overdid, and what You know better than me! You are the Pusher and You are the Pusher, there is no god but You! / Allahumma, gfir li ma kaddamtu, wa ma akhhartu, wa ma asrartu, va ma a'lyantu, wa ma asraftu wa ma Anta a'lamu bi-hi minni! Anta-l-Mukaddimu wa Anta-l-Muakhkhir, la ilaha illa Anta /». №1509

780) It is transmitted from 'Aisha, may Allah be pleased with her, that, having finished the prayer, the Prophet ﷺ said after taslim: «O Allah, You are the Perfect / As-Salam /, and from You is well-being/salam/, blessed are You, O Possessor of greatness and generosity! /Allahumma Anta-s-salamu wa min-ka-s-salamu, tabarakta, ya Za-l-jalali wa-l-ikram/». №1512

781) Abu Hurairah (may Allah be pleased with him) reported that the Prophet ﷺ said: «There is no doubt that three prayers will be heard: the prayer of the parent, the prayer of the traveller and the prayer of the oppressed». №1536

782) It was narrated from Anas ibn Malik, may Allah be pleased with him, that the Messenger of Allah ﷺ often said: «O Allah, verily, I seek protection from You from weakness, laziness, cowardice, stinginess and senility, and I seek protection from You from torment graves, and I seek protection from You from the trials of life and death! / Allahumma, inni a'uzu bi-ka min al-'ajzi, wa-l-kasali, wa-l-jubni, wa-l-bukhli wa-l-harami, wa a'uzu bi-ka min 'azabi- l-kabri, wa a'uzu bi-ka min fitnati-l-mahya wa-l-mamat/». №1540

783) It is reported that Abu Hurayrah, may Allah be pleased with him, said: - When the Messenger of Allah ﷺ died, Abu Bakr after him became (caliph), and some of the Arabs returned to disbelief, Umar ibn al-Khattab said to Abu Bakr: «How can you fight these people?! In-

deed, the Messenger of Allah ﷺ said: «I was ordered to fight with these people until they say:« There is no god worthy of worship but Allah, »and whoever says« There is no god worthy of worship except Allah »(, thereby) will protect his property and his life from me, unless (he does nothing for which it will be possible to deprive him of his property or life) by right, and then (only) the Great and Almighty Allah (will be able to demand) an account from him «! (In response to this) Abu Bakr, may Allah be pleased with him, said: «By Allah, I will certainly fight with those who separate prayer from zakat, because it is obligatory to take zakat from the property! And I swear by Allah if they refuse to give me even the (camel's) fetters that they gave to the Messenger of Allah ﷺ I will fight them because of this! Then Umar ibn al-Khattab said: «By Allah, Allah Himself opened the heart of Abu Bakr (who made the decision) to fight, and I realized that this is the right (decision)!» №1556

784) It is reported that 'Abdullah ibn Shaddad ibn al-Had said: «Once when we went to the wife of the Prophet ﷺ 'Aisha, she said: Once the Messenger of Allah ﷺ entered me and noticed that I had massive rings of silver. He asked, «'Aisha, what is this?» I replied, «O Messenger of Allah! I put them on to please you.» Then he asked: «Have you paid Zakat on them?» I answered: «No», or whatever was pleasing to Allah. To this, he said: «This is enough for you to fall into the Fire!». №1565

785) Salim reports from his father ('Abdullah ibn 'Umar, may Allah be pleased with him and his father) that the Messenger of Allah ﷺ wrote down the amount of zakat, but did not give it to his zakat collectors until his death. She lay with his sword. According to this charter, Abu Bakr acted until his very death and 'Umar until his very death. And it was written in it as follows: «One sheep should be charged from every five camels, and every ten two sheep, from fifteen three sheep and twenty-four sheep. If there are twen-

ty-five to thirty-five camels in the herd, one-year-old she-camel should be given to them. If their number is from thirty-six to forty-five, one two-year-old camel should be given to them. If their number is from forty-six to sixty, one mature three-year-old camel should be given to them.If their number is from sixty-one to seventy-five, one four-year-old camel should be given to them. If their number is from seventy-six to ninety, two two-year-old camels should be given for them. If their number is from ninety-one to one hundred and twenty, two mature three-year-old camels should be given for them. If their number exceeds one hundred and twenty, then for every fifty camels one three-year-old she-camel should be given, and for every forty-one two-year-old. As for the sheep, if there are between forty and a hundred and twenty, one sheep is taken from them. If there are between one hundred and twenty-one and two hundred, two sheep should be given for them. If they are between two hundred and one and three hundred, three sheep should be given for them. And if there are more than three hundred of them, then one sheep should be given from each hundred, and if there is not enough to the next hundred, then nothing is charged from this hundred. And people should not separate their flocks and, on the contrary, unite them for fear that they will have to pay zakat. If the herds of two people are united into one, zakat is taken from one, and then the second compensates him with his justice share. And one should not take as zakat neither old animals nor those that have any vices». №1568

786) 'Ali (ibn Abu Talib), may Allah be pleased with him, narrates from the Prophet ﷺ that he said: «Pay zakat in the amount of a quarter of a tenth, from every forty dirhams - a dirham. And you are not obliged to pay anything until there are two hundred dirhams. If there are two hundred of them, then you must give five dirhams. If there are more dirhams, then it should be calculated based on this. As for the sheep, one sheep is taken from every forty, and if there are thirty-nine,

then nothing needs to be given. And further, in this version, the zakat paid from the sheep is described in the same way as in the hadith al-Zuhri. And he said: «And for every thirty cows, a calf under one year old, and for every forty, a cow under two years of age. You don't have to pay anything for working cows. And from the camels ... «And he described the zakat taken from them, just like az-Zuhri, and said:» If there are twenty-five of them, then five sheep should be given, and if there are more of them, then a one-year-old camel is given, and if her no, then a two-year-old camel, a male. If there are more than thirty-five of them, then a two-year-old camel is given. If there are more than forty-five of them, then a three-year-old camel suitable for covering by a male is given, and so on up to sixty ...» Then he quoted the same part of the hadith like that of al-Zuhri, and then said: «And if there are more than ninety, then two three-year-old camels suitable for covering by a male should be given. And if there are more than one hundred and twenty camels, then for every fifty they give a three-year-old camel. And people should not separate their flocks and, on the contrary, unite them for fear that they will have to pay zakat. And one should not take as zakat either old animals, or those that have any vices, nor males - unless the one who pays the zakat wishes (to give the male). From plants that are watered by rivers (or: heaven), a tenth is charged, and from those that are watered by buckets, a twentieth. In the hadith of 'Asim and al-Harith, it is said: «Zakat is paid every year.» Zuhair said, «And I think he said, 'Once (a year)'.» And in the hadith 'Asimah it says: «If there is neither a one-year-old camel nor a two-year-old camel, then ten dirhams or two sheep should be given». №1572

787)   'Ali (ibn Abu Talib), may Allah be pleased with him, quoted the beginning of this hadith from the Prophet ﷺ saying: «If you have two hundred silver dirhams that you owned for a whole year, then you must pay five dirhams from them. And you are not obliged to pay zakat if you have less than twenty dinars of gold.

And if you have twenty dinars that you have owned for a whole year, then you must pay half a dinar from them. If there is more money, then the zakat should be calculated from the same calculation. However, Zakat is not paid on property that a person has not owned for a whole year». №1573

788) 'Abdullah ibn Mu'awiya al-Ghadiri from Gadirat Qais narrates that the Prophet ﷺ said: «He who performs three actions has known the true taste of faith. This is the one who worships only Allah, believes that there is no god [worthy of worship] except Allah, and every year pays zakat from the property of his own free will, so that his soul incites him to this, and does not give away any old neither the lousy, nor the sick, nor the worst animals, but gives the average of what he owns, for, verily, Allah does not ask you for the best of your property, nor does he command you to give the worst». №1583

789) ('Abdullah) ibn 'Abbas, may Allah be pleased with him and his father, reports that sending Mu'adh (ibn Jabal) to Yemen, the Messenger of Allah ﷺ said to him: «You will come to a people who belong to the people of the Book, and let the first thing you call them to be the testimony that there is no god [worthy of worship] but Allah. If they submit to you in this, then let them know that Allah has obligated them to perform five daily prayers. If they submit to you in this also, then let them know that Allah obligated their rich to make donations for their poor. If they submit to you in this, then do not dare to encroach on their best property and be afraid of the prayer of the oppressed, for there is no barrier between her and Allah». №1584

790) Abu Hurairah, may Allah be pleased with him, reported that the Prophet ﷺ said: «Zakat is not paid from horses and slaves, except for Zakat al-Fitr, which is also collected from slaves». №1594

791) Jabir ibn 'Abdullah, may Allah be pleased with him and his father, narrates that the Messenger of Allah

said: «A tenth is charged from what is irrigated by rivers and streams, and half a tenth is charged from what is irrigated with the help of camels.». №1597

792) It was narrated from Abu Huraira, may Allah be pleased with him, that once the Prophet ﷺ sent 'Umar ibn al-Khattab to collect zakat, and Ibn Jamil, Khalid ibn al-Walid and al-'Abbas ibn 'Abdulmuttalib refused to pay zakat. The Messenger of Allah ﷺ said: «As for Ibn Jamil, he has no excuse, except that he used to be a beggar, and then Allah gave him wealth ... As for Khalid, you do him unfairly, for he keeps his chain mail, weapons and equipment for battles in the way of Allah. As for al-'Abbas, I will pay zakat for him and the same amount,» then he said: «Don't you know that a man's uncle is like his father?» №1623

793) Ibrahim ibn 'Ata, a freedman of 'Imran ibn Husayn, reports from his father that Ziyad or another governor sent 'Imran ibn Husayn as a zakat collector. When 'Imran returned, he asked: «Where is the property?» 'Imran asked instead of answering: «Did you send me for the property? We took it from where we took it in the time of the Messenger of Allah ﷺ and gave it to where we gave it in the time of the Messenger of Allah ﷺ». №1625

794) Ziyad ibn al-Harith as-Sudai, may Allah be pleased with him, said: «I came to the Messenger of Allah ﷺ and swore allegiance to him.» And he brought a long hadith and said: «And then a man came to him and said to him:» Give me something from the zakat. The Messenger of Allah ﷺ said: «Indeed, Allah did not want the prophet or anyone else to decide on zakat. He passed judgment on it, dividing it into eight parts. If you are one of those eligible to receive one of these parts, I will give you what you are entitled to». №1630

795) Abu Hurairah, may Allah be pleased with him, reported that the Messenger of Allah ﷺ said: «He is not poor who goes around people, receiving one or two dates or a piece or two of food. The really poor person is the

one whose condition people do not guess and therefore do not give him, and he does not ask people». №1631

796) It is reported that 'Ubaydullah ibn 'Adi ibn al-Khiyar said: - Two people told me that they came to the Prophet ﷺ during the farewell Hajj, when he divided Sadak (to distribute them to people), and asked me to give them something: «The Prophet ﷺ looked up at us and then lowered it. He saw that we were strong and healthy, and said: «If you want, I will give you something, but there is no share in it either for the wealthy or for the one who is strong enough to earn». №1633

797) It was narrated from 'Abdullah ibn 'Amr, may Allah be pleased with him and his father, that the Prophet ﷺ said: «It is not allowed to take anything from the zakat, neither wealthy nor strong and healthy». №1634

798) Samura [ibn Jundub], may Allah be pleased with him, reports that the Prophet ﷺ said: «Appeals to people with requests are marked on a person's face, and whoever wishes can leave them on his face, and whoever wishes can remove them. The exception is when a person makes a request to someone in power or asks for something that he really cannot do without.». №1639

799) Anas ibn Malik, may Allah be pleased with him, reports: «Once a man from among the Ansar came to the Prophet ﷺ and asked him to give him something (from donations). He asked him, «Is there anything in your house?» He replied: «Yes. Clothes made of thick fabric - we put on part of it, and lay the other on the floor - and also a vessel from which we drink water. The Prophet ﷺ said: «Bring it to me,» and the man brought it. Then the Prophet ﷺ took these things in his hand and asked: «Who will buy this?» One person said: «I will buy them for a dirham.» The Prophet ﷺ said: «Who will give more dirham?» He asked this question twice or thrice. One man said: «I will buy them for two dirhams» - and he gave him things, took two dirhams and gave them to the Ansar, saying: «Buy food with one of them and take it to your family,

and buy an axe with the second one and bring it to me». And he brought him an axe, and the Messenger of Allah ﷺ fixed his axe handle and said: «Go, chop wood and sell. And do not come to me until fifteen days have passed.» And the Ansar did this and returned to him, earning ten dirhams, and bought some of their clothes and some of their food. The Messenger of Allah ﷺ also said: «It is better for you than asking, for making requests will be a mark on your face on the Day of Judgment. Indeed, asking is permitted only for three reasons. This is extreme poverty, unsustainable debt and spending to reconcile people». №1641

800) It was narrated from 'Awf ibn Malik (al-Ashja'i) that he said: «We were with the Messenger of Allah, peace and blessings of Allah be upon him. We were seven, eight or eight people. He asked us: «Will you swear allegiance to the Messenger of Allah?» And we just took the oath. We said: «We have already pledged allegiance to you, O Messenger of Allah.» They repeat three times. Then we stretched out our hands and someone said: «We swear allegiance to you, O Messenger of Allah. And what exactly should we swear to you? He replied: «In that, they worship Allah and do not associate Him with partners, perform five prayers, and obey.» And he added very quietly: «And do not ask people for anything.» He said: «And it happened that a whip fell from one of the people, but he did not ask anyone to take it». №1642

801) It is narrated from the words of Abu Sa'id al-Khudri that (once) some people from among the Ansar asked (something) from the Messenger of Allah ﷺ and he gave them (it), then they (again) asked him (something), and he gave it to them, and finally giving away everything he had, he said: «Whatever is in my hands, I will never hide it from you, (but remember that) whoever strives for abstinence, Allah will lead to abstinence, whoever tries to manage on his own, Allah will deliver (from the need to turn to others), and whoever begins to show patience, Allah will inspire

patience, and no one has ever received a more generous gift from Allah than patience». №1644

802) It is reported that Ibn Mas'ud, may Allah be pleased with him, said: «The Messenger of Allah ﷺ said: «If one who suffers poverty begins to seek help from people, he will never get rid of his poverty. Whoever turns to Allah for help with this, Allah will hasten to enrich him, either through early death or through an early enrichment». №1645

803) ['Abdullah] ibn 'Abbas, may Allah be pleased with him and his father, narrates: «When the verse was sent down: «Rejoice those who accumulate gold and silver and do not spend them in the path of Allah with painful suffering» (9:34), this proved to be a severe test for the Muslims, and 'Umar [ibn al-Khattab] said: «I will bring you deliverance.» And they went to the Messenger of Allah ﷺ and said: «O Prophet of Allah, this verse has become a severe test for your companions.» The Messenger of Allah ﷺ said: «Indeed, Allah has prescribed zakat only to make good the rest of your property, and he has prescribed inheritance so that the inheritance goes to those who outlive you.» 'Umar exclaimed: «Allah is Great!» Then the Messenger of Allah ﷺ said: «Shall I tell you about the best that a man can save for himself? This is a righteous wife: if he looks at her, it will bring him joy, if he tells her something, then she will obey him, and if he leaves her for a while, then she will keep his property and honour». №1664

804) Asma [bint Abu Bakr], may Allah be pleased with her and her father, said: «After the conclusion of the peace treaty between the Muslims and the Quraysh, my mother came to me, who desired something and at the same time was an unbeliever and abhorred Islam. I said, «O Messenger of Allah! My mother came to me with an aversion to Islam. Should I be in a relationship with her?» He replied, «Yes, keep in touch with your mother». №1668

805) It was narrated from 'Abdullah ibn 'Umar, may Allah be pleased with him and his father, that the Messenger of Allah ﷺ said: «Protect the one who asks for protection from Allah, give to the one who asks for the sake of Allah, answer the one who called you, and who has done good to you, do good to him in return. And if you have nothing to thank him with, then turn to Allah with prayers for him until you begin to think that you have thanked him enough». №1672

806) Abu Hurayra (may Allah be pleased with him) narrates that the Messenger of Allah ﷺ said: «The best charity is the one that leaves a person wealthy, or the one that a person gives when he is wealthy. And start with those who are on your payroll». №1676

807) It was narrated from Sa'd ibn 'Ubada, may Allah be pleased with him, that he said: «O Messenger of Allah, verily, the mother of Sa'd has passed away ... What is the best almsgiving?» (The Messenger of Allah ﷺ) said: «Water.» And he dug a well on behalf of his mother. №1681

808) When Abu Hurairah (may Allah be pleased with him) was asked about a woman who gives alms from her husband's property, he said: «She should not do this unless she gives from her maintenance. The reward will be divided between them. And she is not allowed to give alms from her husband's property, except with his permission». №1688

809) It was narrated from Abu Hurayrah, may Allah be pleased with him, that once the Prophet ﷺ ordered people to give alms. Then one person said: «I have a dinar.» The Prophet ﷺ said to him: «Spend it on yourself.» The man said, «I have another one.» He said, «Spend it on your children.» He said, «I have another one.» He said, «Spend it on your wife.» The man said, «I have another one.» He said, «Spend it on your servant.» The man said, «I have another one.» The Prophet ﷺ said: «You know better where to spend it». №1691

810) It is narrated from 'Abdullah ibn 'Amr, may Allah be

pleased with him and his father, that the Messenger of Allah ﷺ once addressed people with a speech and said: «Beware of stinginess, for it destroyed those who lived before you. She told them to be mean, and they became mean. She told them to break their family ties, and they began to break their family ties. She told them to do wickedness, and they began to do wickedness». №1698

811) It was narrated from Ibn 'Abbas, may Allah be pleased with him and his father, that al-Akra 'ibn Habis asked the Prophet ﷺ: «O Messenger of Allah! Should we perform Hajj every year or just once?» He replied: «No, only once, and if someone does more, then this will be an additional». №1721

812) It was narrated from Abu Waqid al-Laysi, may Allah be pleased with him, that he said: «I heard the Messenger of Allah ﷺ say to his wives during the farewell Hajj:« This (Hajj), and then - home mats». №1722

813) Nubaikh ibn Wahb said: «Umar ibn 'Ubaydullah ibn Ma'mar's eyes hurt, and he sent to Aban ibn 'Uthman. And he was the leader of the Hajj. He asked what he should do with them, and he said: «Let him put aloe on his eyes. I heard 'Uthman, may Allah be pleased with him, spoke about this from the words of the Messenger of Allah ﷺ». №1838

814) Salim narrates from his father (Abdullah ibn Umar, may Allah be pleased with him and his father) that the Prophet ﷺ was asked about which animals are allowed to be killed by a person wearing ihram, and he replied: «Killing five kinds of animals is not a sin ihram, nor in the normal state. This is a scorpion, a raven, a mouse, a kite and a dog attacking people». №1846

815) It is narrated from Ibn 'Abbas, may Allah be pleased with him and his father, that the Prophet ﷺ was asked on the day of Mina [about the mistakes made] and he invariably answered: «It's okay.» One man said, «I shaved my head before I slaughtered the sacrificial animal.» The Messenger of Allah ﷺ said: «Cut now, it's

okay.» And the other said, «I didn't throw the pebbles until the evening.» The Messenger of Allah ﷺ said: «Give it up now, it's okay». №1983

816) Usama ibn Shariq, may Allah be pleased with him, reports: «I went out with the Prophet ﷺ to perform Hajj, and people came to him. Someone said: «O Messenger of Allah! I made a run to the detour! And I did something earlier, and then something later ... «However, the Messenger of Allah ﷺ said:» It's okay, it's okay ... It's scary when a person unfairly offends the honour of another Muslim - this is scary and disastrous!» №2015

817) It was narrated from Abu Hurayrah, may Allah be pleased with him, that the Prophet ﷺ said: «You can go on a journey [for worship] for the sake of visiting only three mosques: the Sacred Mosque, this mosque of mine and the Farthest Mosque / Al-Aqsa /». №2033

818) 'Ali, may Allah be pleased with him, narrates: «We did not write down anything that the Messenger of Allah ﷺ said, except for the Quran and what is written in this scroll. The Messenger of Allah ﷺ said: «Medina is a protected area from 'Air to Thaur, and whoever makes any innovation (in religion) here or provides shelter to someone who introduces innovations in religion, the curse of Allah, the angels and all people will befall and on the Day of Resurrection, Allah will not accept anything additional or obligatory from him. The protection of Muslims is one, and it is valid even when it is provided by the lowest of them, the same who violates the protection provided by a Muslim will suffer the curse of Allah, angels and all people, and on the Day of Resurrection Allah will not accept from him either a replacement or an equal. And the one who calls his patrons without the permission of (real) patrons, the curse of Allah, the angels and all people will befall, and on the Day of Resurrection Allah will not accept from him either obligatory or additional». №2034

819) It was narrated from Abu Hurayrah, may Allah be

pleased with him, that the Messenger of Allah ﷺ said: «Do not turn your houses into graves and do not make my grave a place of regular meetings. And call upon me the blessings of the Highest, for verily your blessings reach me wherever you are». №2042

820) It was narrated from Abu Hurayrah, may Allah be pleased with him, that the Prophet ﷺ said: «Women are married because of four things: wealth, origin, beauty and religion. Try to get the owner of religion, may your hands be covered with dust!» №2047

821) Narrated from Jabir ibn 'Abdullah, may Allah be pleased with him and his father: «The Messenger of Allah ﷺ asked me: «Are you married?» I answered yes. He asked: «A virgin or a married woman?» I answered: «To the one who has been married.» He asked: «Why not on a virgin with whom you would play and who would play with you?» №2048

822) It was narrated from Makyl ibn Yasar, may Allah be pleased with him, that a man came to the Prophet ﷺ and said: «I found a woman from a noble family and also beautiful, but she cannot have children. Should I marry her?» The Prophet ﷺ said: No. Then he came to him a second time, and (the Prophet ﷺ again) forbade him. Then he came a third time, but the Prophet ﷺ said to him: «Marry those who are loving and fruitful, and verily, I will outnumber (other communities) by number.». №2050

823) 'Amr ibn Shu'ayb narrates from his father the story of his grandfather (may Allah be pleased with him and his father) that Marsad ibn Abu Marsad al-Ganawi was engaged in the sale of slaves in Mecca, and in Mecca, there was a harlot named 'Anak, with whom he was friends. Marsad said: «I came to the Prophet ﷺ and asked: «O Messenger of Allah, can I marry 'Anak?» He didn't answer me. And then it was sent down: «An adulterer marries only an adulteress or a polytheist ...» (Surah 24 «Light», verse 3). (The Messenger of Allah ﷺ) called me, recited this verse to me

and said: «Do not marry her». №2051

824) It is narrated from 'Ali ibn al-Husayn (grandson of the Messenger of Allah ﷺ) that he and his companions arrived in Medina from Yazid ibn Mu'awiya after the death of al-Husayn ibn 'Ali (who was killed in 61 AH), yes Allah be pleased with him and his father, and he met al-Miswar ibn Mahram, who asked: «Do you need anything from me?» He replied: «No.» Then he said: «Will you give me the sword of the Messenger of Allah ﷺ? Truly, I am afraid that people will take it from you. I swear by Allah, if you give it to me, I will not give it to anyone until my death! And I, who had already reached the age of majority, heard how the Messenger of Allah ﷺ addressed people with a speech on this issue from this minbar and said: «Truly, Fatima is a part of me, and I am afraid that this will reflect badly on her religion.» After that, he mentioned his son-in-law from Bani 'Abd Shams and praised him, saying: «When speaking to me, he was truthful, and promising me something, he kept his promise ... I do not forbid what is lawful and I do not allow what is forbidden, however, I swear The daughter of the Messenger of Allah ﷺ and the daughter of the enemy of Allah cannot be together!» №2069

825) It was narrated from al-Miswar ibn Mahram that he heard the Messenger of Allah ﷺ say while standing on the minbar: «The sons of Hisham ibn al-Mughira asked me for permission to marry their daughter to 'Ali ibn Abu Talib. And this is what: I do not allow them, and again I do not allow them, and I do not allow them again unless Ibn Abu Talib wants to divorce my daughter and marry their daughter. Verily, my daughter is a part of me, and I am troubled by the same thing as her, and I am offended by what offends her». №2071

826) It was narrated from Jabir ibn 'Abdullah that the Messenger of Allah ﷺ said: «If one of you is wooing a woman, then if he has the opportunity to look at what will induce him to marry her, let him do so.» He said:

«And I wooed a certain girl and looked at her slyly, and seeing what prompted me to marry her, married her». №2082

827) It was narrated from Abu Musa, may Allah be pleased with him, that the Prophet ﷺ said: «There can be no marriage without a patron /wali/». №2085

828) It was narrated from Abu Hurairah, may Allah be pleased with him, that the Prophet ﷺ once said: «You should not marry a woman who has been married without consulting her, and you should not marry a virgin without asking her permission.» People asked: «O Messenger of Allah, how do we know about her permission?» He replied: «According to her silence». №2092

829) It was narrated from Jabir ibn 'Abdullah, may Allah be pleased with him and his father, that the Prophet ﷺ said: «The gift of the one who gave a woman as a marriage gift a handful of saviq or dates is valid». №2110

830) It was narrated from Ibn 'Abbas, may Allah be pleased with him and his father: «When 'Ali married Fatimah, may Allah be pleased with them both, the Messenger of Allah ﷺ said to him: «Give her something.» He said, «But I don't have anything.» The Messenger of Allah ﷺ asked: «Where is your coat of mail from Khutam?» №2125

831) It is transmitted from Qays ibn Sa'd: «I arrived in Hira and saw that the locals were prostrating to the marzuban. And I thought that the Messenger of Allah ﷺ is more deserving to prostrate before him. I went to the Prophet ﷺ and said: «I was in Hira and saw people there prostrating to the marzuban. And you, O Messenger of Allah, deserve more to prostrate before you.» He asked, «If you walked past my grave, would you prostrate to it?» I answered: «No.» (The Messenger of Allah ﷺ) said: «Do not do this (and during my lifetime) ... If I could order one of the people to bow to the ground before another, I would order the wives to prostrate before their husbands because of the right to

them, which Allah gave them». №2140

832) It is transmitted from Bahz ibn Hakim: «My father told me from my grandfather:« I asked: «O Messenger of Allah, what are we allowed to do with our wives, and what is forbidden?» He replied: «Come to your arable land as you wish ... Feed your wife when you eat yourself, dress her when you dress, and do not insult her and do not beat». №2143

833) It was narrated from Iyas ibn 'Abdullah ibn Abu Zubab, may Allah be pleased with him, that the Messenger of Allah ﷺ said: «Do not beat the slave girls of Allah!» Then 'Umar came to the Messenger of Allah ﷺ and said: «Women have grown bolder and rebel against their husbands!» Then he allowed them to be hit. After that, many women came to the wives of the Messenger of Allah ﷺ, who complained about their husbands. Then the Prophet ﷺ said: «Indeed, many women came to the wives of Muhammad. They complained about their husbands, who are not the best of you!» №2146

834) Ibn 'Abbas, may Allah be pleased with him and his father, said: «I have never seen anything more like small transgressions than that reported by Abu Hurairah from the Prophet ﷺ: »Verily, Allah predestined for the son of Adam his share of adultery, and he will certainly receive it. The adultery of the eyes is the glance, but the adultery of the tongue is the words. The soul desires and strives, and the sexual organs confirm or do not confirm». №2152

835) Ibn 'Abbas, may Allah be pleased with him and his father, said: «Ibn 'Umar, may Allah forgive him, made a mistake. He argued that this tribe of the Ansar-pagans coexisted with the tribe of the Jews - the People of the Book, and the Ansar treated them with respect because the Jews had knowledge that they did not have, and imitated them in many ways. The People of the Scripture copulated with women in only one position when the woman was covered as much as possible.

And the Ansar adopted this custom from them. And in the quarter inhabited by the Quraysh, on the contrary, they opened the women completely and enjoyed them, coming to them from behind, and in front, and when they lay on their side. And so, when the Muhajirs arrived in Medina, one of them married a woman from among the Ansar and began to do this to her, and she began to condemn him for this. She told him: «We have always been entered in only one way. Do the same or don't come near me!» Soon, many people learned about their situation, and the news of this reached the Messenger of Allah ﷺ. Then the Almighty and Great Allah sent down: «Your wives are arable land for you. So come to your arable land when and how you wish» (Surah 2 «al-Baqarah», verse 223). In other words, come to them from the front and from behind and when they are lying on their back, but only to the genitals». №2164

836) It was narrated from Abu Hurayrah, may Allah be pleased with him, that the Messenger of Allah ﷺ said: «He who sets a woman against her husband or a slave against his master has nothing to do with us». №2175

837) It was narrated from Ibn 'Umar, may Allah be pleased with him and his father, that the Prophet ﷺ said: «The most hateful thing for the Almighty and Great Allah from what is permitted is divorce». №2178
838) It was narrated from Abu Hurayrah, may Allah be pleased with him, that the Messenger of Allah ﷺ said: «Three things are valid, regardless of whether they are serious or not. This is marriage, divorce and the return of the wife after the divorce.». №2194

839) Narrated by Hammad ibn Zayd: «I asked Ayyub: 'Do you know anyone who would share the opinion of al-Hasan regarding the words: 'Your destiny is in your hands?» He replied: «No, except for the fact that Qatada transmitted to us from Kasir, a freedman of Ibn Samura, from Abu Salama from Abu Hurairah, and he from the Prophet ﷺ something similar.» Ayyub said:

«Kasir came to us and I asked him about it. He said, «I never said anything like that.» And I told Qatada about it, and he said: «No, he said, he just forgot». №2204

840) It was narrated from 'Umar, may Allah be pleased with him, that the Prophet ﷺ gave Hafsa a divorce, and then returned her. №2283

841) It was narrated from 'Amr ibn al-'As, may Allah be pleased with him, that the Messenger of Allah ﷺ said: «Our fast is different from the fast of the People of the Book eating before dawn». №2343

842) It was narrated from Samur ibn Jundub, may Allah be pleased with him, that the Messenger of Allah ﷺ said: «Let neither the adhan of Bilal nor such a whiteness on the horizon, until it spreads, prevent you from performing suhoor». №2346

843) Narrated by Marwan ibn Salim al-Mukaffa': «I saw how Ibn 'Umar wrapped his hand around his beard and cut off everything below the grip. He said: «When the Messenger of Allah ﷺ broke his fast, he said: «The thirst is gone, and the vessels are filled, and the reward is established with the permission of Allah» №2357

844) 'Umar ibn al-Khattab, may Allah be pleased with him, said: «In joy, I kissed (my wife) during fasting and said: «O Messenger of Allah! Today I did something terrible: I kissed (my wife) while I was fasting!» He said: «If you rinsed your mouth with water while fasting, what would happen?» Hammad ibn Isa's version says: «I said: «I don't see anything wrong with that.» The Messenger of Allah ﷺsaid: «So it is». №2385

845) It was narrated from Anas, may Allah be pleased with him: «Once we set off with the Messenger of Allah ﷺ on a journey in Ramadan, and some of us fasted and some did not, and the fasting person did not reproach the one who did not fast, and the one who did not fast did not rebuke the fasting». №2405

846) It was narrated from Abu Sa'id al-Khudri, may Allah

be pleased with him, that the Messenger of Allah ﷺ forbade fasting on two days - on the feast of breaking the fast and on the feast of sacrifice. And he forbade two ways of wearing clothes - wrapping tightly in them, and also throwing on one clothes. And he forbade praying in two periods of time - after the morning prayer (until the sun rises) and after the afternoon prayer (until the sun sets). №2417

847) Abu Ayyub, may Allah be pleased with him, a companion of the Prophet ﷺ reports that the Prophet ﷺ said: «Whoever fasted the entire Ramadan, and then fasted for another six days in Shawwal, it is as if he is fasting continuously». №2433

848) It was narrated from the words of Abu Hurayrah, may Allah be pleased with him, that the Messenger of Allah ﷺ said: «Whoever died without fighting (in the path of Allah) and (never) saying to himself that (he should) fight, died (not getting rid) of one of the manifestations of hypocrisy». №2502

849) It is reported that 'Abdul-'Aziz ibn Marwan said: «I heard Abu Hurairah say: «I heard the Messenger of Allah ﷺ say: «The worst thing in a man is restless stinginess and strong cowardice». №2511

850) It is reported that Sahl ibn al-Khanzalia said: «Once the Messenger of Allah ﷺ passed by a camel, whose back was adjacent to his stomach (from hunger or fatigue), and said: «Beware (punishment) of Allah for (your attitude) towards these silent animals! Sit on them when they are suitable (for this), and eat them when they are suitable (for this)!». №2548

851) It is reported that Ibn 'Abbas said: «The Messenger of Allah ﷺ forbade the setting of animals against each other». №2562

852) Abu Hurayrah reported that the Messenger of Allah ﷺ said: «I was ordered to fight people until they testify that there is no god worthy of worship except Allah. And if they do this, they will protect their blood

and their property from me, unless (they do anything for which it will be possible to deprive them of their property or life) by right, and then (only) Allah (can demand) from them an account». №2640

853) 'Asim ibn Kuleib narrated from the words of his father that one man from among the Ansar said: «(Somehow, when) we went along with the Messenger of Allah ﷺ on a journey, people were beset by severe need and difficulties. When they captured the booty, they began to plunder it and our boilers (with meat) began to boil. And then the Messenger of Allah ﷺ came, walking (leaning) on his bow, and began to overturn our cauldrons with his bow and pour sand on the meat, after which he said: «Verily, the loot / nuhba / is no more permissible than carrion!» - or he said: «Indeed, carrion is no more lawful than loot!». №2705

854) It was narrated from Ibn 'Abbas, may Allah be pleased with him and his father, that the Prophet ﷺ said: «Whoever lives in the desert becomes rude and callous, whoever follows game becomes careless, and whoever enters the holders of power, he is subject to temptations«. Sufyan once said: «I know this hadith only as transmitted from the Prophet ﷺ». №2859

855) And in another version of the hadith from Abu Hurairah, may Allah be pleased with him, from the Prophet ﷺ says: «Whoever spends a lot of time with the ruler, he is subject to temptations,» and this version contains the addition: «The closer the servant of Allah is to the ruler, the farther he is from Allah». №2860

856) Narrated Abu Dharr, may Allah be pleased with him: «The Messenger of Allah ﷺ said to me: «O Abu Dharr, verily, I see that you are weak, and verily, I wish you the same as I wish myself. Do not become a ruler (even) for two and do not undertake to dispose of the property of an orphan». №2868

857) It was narrated from Abu Umamah, may Allah be pleased with him: «I heard the Messenger of Allah ﷺ say: «Indeed, Allah has ensured the observance of the

right of everyone who has the right, and there can be no testament to the heir». №2870

858) Narrated from 'Ali ibn Abu Talib, may Allah be pleased with him: «I remembered from the Messenger of Allah ﷺ: «There is no orphanhood after the appearance of wet dreams, and one should not be silent all day until evening». №2873

859) It was narrated from Abu Hurayrah, may Allah be pleased with him, that the Messenger of Allah ﷺ said: «When a person dies, all his deeds stop, except for three. This is continuous almsgiving, the knowledge that benefits people, and righteous children who turn to Allah with a prayer for him». №2880

860) It was narrated from Tamim ad-Dari, may Allah be pleased with him, that he said: «O Messenger of Allah, what if some person accepts Islam from some Muslim?» (The Messenger of Allah ﷺ) said: «Both in life and after death, he is closer to him than any of the people». №2918

861) Dawud ibn al-Husayn narrates: «I read the Quran in the presence of Umm Sa'd bint al-Rabi', who was an orphan and pupil of Abu Bakr, and I read: «Give those with whom you are bound by oaths their share.» She said: «Do not read: «Give those with whom you are bound by oaths their share» (Surah 4 «an-Nisa», verse 33) (with alif, but read without it). Verily, it was sent down concerning Abu Bakr and his son Abdu-r-Rahman. 'Abdu-r-Rahman refused to convert to Islam, and Abu Bakr swore that he would leave him without an inheritance. And then 'Abdu-r-Rahman converted to Islam, and the Prophet of Allah ﷺ ordered to give him his share. (Transmitter) Abdu-l-Aziz added: «And he did not accept Islam until he was forced to do so by the sword». №2923

862) It is transmitted from 'Abdu-r-Rahman ibn Samur, may Allah be pleased with him: «The Prophet ﷺ said to me:» O'Abd-r-Rahman ibn Samur, do not seek power, for if it is granted to you at your request, then you

will be left to yourself in it, and if it is given to you without requests from you, then you will be helped in (related to) it». №2929

863) It was narrated from 'Uqba ibn 'Amir, may Allah be pleased with him: «I heard the Messenger of Allah ﷺ say: «The collector of sunset will not enter Paradise». №2937

864) It was narrated by Ibn as-Saidit: «'Umar, may Allah be pleased with him, appointed me responsible for collecting zakat, and when I finished my work, he ordered me to be paid. I said: «Indeed, I have worked for the sake of Allah.» 'Umar said: «Take what they give you ... During the lifetime of the Messenger of Allah ﷺ, I was engaged in collecting zakat, and he gave me a payment». №2944

865) It is narrated from Abu Mutair that he went on Hajj and while they were in Suwayda, a man came. He seemed to be looking for medicines, in the particular hood. He said: «I was told by one who heard how the Messenger of Allah ﷺ during the farewell Hajj addressed people with instruction, ordering them to do one thing and forbidding another, that among other things he said: «O people! Take the content as long as it remains content (legalized by religion and not contrary to it), and when the Quraysh begin to fight for power and the content will be used to turn you away from religion, then do not take it». №2958

866) Sulaym ibn Mutair, a Shaykh from the people of Wadi al-Qur, narrates that his father told him: «I heard a man say: «I heard the Messenger of Allah ﷺ in his farewell hajj bring to the attention of the people commands and prohibitions and said: «Have I brought it?» People said: «O Allah, yes!» Then (the Messenger of Allah ﷺ) said: «When the Quraysh begin to fight with each other for power, and the content is like a bribe, leave it.» People asked, «Who was this man?» Others replied: «This is Abu al-Zawaid, a companion of the Messenger of Allah ﷺ». №2959

867) It was narrated from Abu at-Tufayl: «Fatimah, may Allah be pleased with her, came to Abu Bakr, may Allah be pleased with him, to ask him for her inheritance from the Prophet ﷺ and Abu Bakr, may Allah be pleased with him, said: «I heard the Messenger of Allah ﷺ say: «Everything that the Almighty and Great Allah bestowed on the prophet passes to the one who comes in his place». №2973

868) It is narrated from Yazid ibn Khurmuz that Najda al-Haruri, having gone on a hajj during the period of the turmoil of ibn az-Zubair, sent to Ibn 'Abbas to ask about the share of the relatives of the Messenger of Allah ﷺ: who is it due? Ibn 'Abbas replied: «This share is due to the relatives of the Messenger of Allah ﷺ - he allocated it to them. At one time, 'Umar offered us something from this share, but we considered that this was less than our right, and rejected his offer». №2982

869) Narrated from 'Abdullah ibn al-Harith ibn Nawfal al-Hashimi: «' Abdul-Muttalib ibn Rabi'a ibn al-Harith ibn 'Abdul-Muttalib said that his father Rabi'a ibn al-Harith and ' Abbas ibn 'Abdul-Muttalib said to 'Abdul-Muttalib ibn Rabi'a and al-Fadl ibn 'Abbas: «Go to the Messenger of Allah ﷺ and say to him: «O Messenger of Allah! You see what age we have reached and we want to get married. You, O Messenger of Allah, are the most pious of people and best of all maintain family ties, and our fathers do not have the means to pay the marriage gift to the brides on our behalf. O Messenger of Allah, appoint us as zakat collectors, and we will give you what the zakat collectors have to give you, and we will take advantage of the privileges that this position gives. 'Ali ibn Abu Talib came when we were in such a position and said that the Messenger of Allah ﷺ said: «I will never appoint any of you as a zakat collector.» Rabi'a said: «You are speaking from yourself. You became the son-in-law of the Messenger of Allah ﷺ and we do not envy you because of this ... «Then 'Ali, may Allah be pleased with him, threw his cloak on the ground, lay down on him and said:»

I am Abu al-Hasan, «karm» and by Allah, I will not budge until your sons return with what you sent them to the Prophet ﷺ!» Al-Fadl and I went to the door of the room of the Messenger of Allah ﷺ just in time for the noon prayer, which has already been announced. We prayed together with the people and then hurried to the door of one of the dwellings of the Prophet ﷺ. That day he was with Zeinab bint Jahsh. We stopped at the entrance. When the Messenger of Allah ﷺ came, he took each of us by the ear and said: «Well, lay out what you are hiding there.» Then he entered and allowed al-Fadl and me to enter. We went in and for some time-shifted the duty to state our request to each other, then I spoke (or: al-Fadl spoke) and said what our fathers told us. The Messenger of Allah ﷺ was silent for a while. He raised his eyes and stared up at the ceiling. We waited a long time and finally decided that he would not answer us at all. But then we noticed that Zeynab was making us a sign from behind the curtain to slow down and let us know that the Messenger of Allah ﷺ was still thinking about our business. Finally, the Messenger of Allah ﷺ lowered his head and said to us: «Verily, this alms/zakat / is human dirt, and neither Muhammad nor the members of Muhammad's family are allowed to take it ... Call Nawfal ibn al-Harith to me.» And Nawfal ibn al-Harith was called to him. The Messenger of Allah ﷺ said: «O Nawfal, marry 'Abdu-l-Muttalib, and Nawfal married me. Then the Prophet ﷺ said: «Call Mahmiya ibn Jazz to me.» And this was a man from Bani Zubayd, whom the Messenger of Allah ﷺ instructed to dispose of hummus. The Messenger of Allah ﷺ said to Mahmiya: «Jeni al-Fadl.» And he married him. Then the Messenger of Allah ﷺ said: «Get up and pay for them the marriage gift of hummus - so and so much.» The transmitter said: «'Abdullah ibn al-Harith did not tell me (the size of the marriage gift)». №2985

870) It is narrated from 'Urwa ibn al-Zubair that Hisham ibn Hakim ibn Khizam saw a man in Homs who forced several people from among the Nabataeans to

stand under the scorching sun because of non-payment of jizya, and exclaimed: «What is this?! I heard the Messenger of Allah ﷺ say: «Indeed, Allah will punish those who torment people in this world!» №3045

871) Safwan ibn Sulaym narrates from the words of several sons of the Companions from their fathers that the Messenger of Allah ﷺ said: «If someone does unfairly with a person who has agreed with Muslims / muahid /, or humiliates him (infringing on his rights), or imposes unbearable on him (as regards the payment of jizya and kharaj), or takes something from him against his will, I will litigate with him on the Day of Judgment». №3052

872) Muhammad ibn Khalid as-Sulami narrates the words of his father from his grandfather, who was a companion of the Messenger of Allah ﷺ: «I heard the Messenger of Allah ﷺ say: «Verily, if a slave does not reach the position allotted to him by Allah through his deeds, Allah exposes him trials that affect his body, property or children (Ibn Nawfal added: «and then inspires him with patience»), and this continues until he reaches the position that Allah Almighty has ordained for him». №3090

873) Abu Sa'eed al-Khudri (may Allah be pleased with him) narrated that the Messenger of Allah ﷺ said: «The best of your incense is musk». №3158

874) 'Amir reports that the body of the Messenger of Allah ﷺ was washed by 'Ali, al-Fadl and Usama ibn Zayd, and they also lowered his body into the grave. (The transmitter) said: «Murahhab (or Ibn Abu Murahhab) told me that they took 'Abdurrahman ibn 'Auf with them there, and 'Ali, having freed himself, said: «Verily, his relatives should deal with (burial) a person». №3209

875) It was narrated from 'Umar ibn al-Khattab, may Allah be pleased with him, that the Messenger of Allah ﷺ overtook him just at the moment when he swore by his father. (The Messenger of Allah ﷺ) said: «Indeed, Al-

lah forbade you to swear by your fathers, and whoever wants to swear, let him swear by Allah or be silent». №3249

876) It is narrated from Ibn 'Abbas, may Allah be pleased with him and his father, that the sister of 'Uqba ibn 'Amira vowed to perform the Hajj on foot, but the Prophet ﷺ, learning about this, said: «Verily, Allah does not need her vow. Tell her to ride». №3290

877) Jabir, may Allah be pleased with him, narrates: «The Messenger of Allah ﷺ did not perform the funeral prayer for a person who died leaving debts. And one day they brought the body of the deceased to him so that he would pray for him. He asked, «Does he have any debts left?» They told him: «We stayed. Two dinars. Then (the Messenger of Allah ﷺ) said: «Pray for your companion.» Abu Qatada al-Ansari said: «I will pay them, O Messenger of Allah.» And the Messenger of Allah ﷺ prayed for him. And when Allah granted the Messenger of Allah ﷺ more funds (than came to him before), he said: «I am closer to any believer than he, and if someone has a debt left, I will pay it, and when someone leaves the property, it should be given to heirs». №3343

878) 'Ubadah ibn as-Samit (may Allah be pleased with him) narrates: «I taught some people from among the people who lived under a canopy to write and the Quran, and one of them gave me a bow. I said to myself: «This is not money, and I will shoot from it in the way of the Almighty and Great Allah. But still, I will go to the Messenger of Allah ﷺ and ask him about it. I came to him and said: «O Messenger of Allah! One of those whom I taught writing and the Quran gave me a bow. It is not money, and I will shoot it in the way of Allah.» (The Messenger of Allah ﷺ) said: «If you want to put on a collar of Fire, accept this gift!» №3416

879) It was narrated from Anas, may Allah be pleased with him, that the people said: «O Messenger of Allah, the

prices are rising, so set the prices for us!» However, the Messenger of Allah ﷺ said: «Indeed, Allah is the Price-Setter, and He is the Sustainer and the Extender, and He is the Giver of sustenance. And verily, I hope to meet Allah without any of you litigating me with blood or property». №3451

880) It was narrated from Abu Hurayrah, may Allah be pleased with him, that the Prophet ﷺ said: «Whoever is appointed as a judge among the people, he is slaughtered without a knife». №3572

881) Ibn Buraida narrates from his father that the Prophet ﷺ said: «Judges are of three categories: one in Paradise and two in Fire. In Paradise, a person knew the truth and was judged by it. And the man who knew the truth, but did not judge by it, and the man who judged people, being ignorant, is in the Fire». №3573

882) It is transmitted from 'Abdullah ibn 'Amr, may Allah be pleased with him and his father: «The Messenger of Allah ﷺ cursed the giver and the taker of bribes». №3580

883) It was narrated from 'Ali, may Allah be pleased with him: «The Messenger of Allah ﷺ sent me to Yemen as a judge and I said: «O Messenger of Allah! You are sending me, and yet I am very young and have no knowledge of legal proceedings.» He said in response: «Indeed, Allah will show your heart the true path and establish your tongue. When two litigants sit before you, do not judge until you have heard the second in the same way as you heard the first, then you will understand what decision should be made. And I then always ruled the court in this way (or: and I never had doubts when making judgments)». №3582

884) It was narrated from Umm Salama, may Allah be pleased with her, that once the Messenger of Allah ﷺ said: «Verily, I am only a man, and you come to me with your lawsuits. And it may happen that one of you will be more convincing in his arguments than the other, and then I will rule in his favour based

on what I hear from him. And let the one to whom I award what rightfully belongs to his brother, take none of it, for I give him a particle of Fire!» №3583

885)   It was narrated from Abu Hurairah, may Allah be pleased with him, that he heard the Messenger of Allah ﷺ say: «A Bedouin cannot testify against a settled». №3602

886)   It is transmitted from Kasir ibn Qays: «I was sitting with Abu Ad-Darda in the mosque of Damascus, and a man came up to him and said: «O Abu Ad-Darda! I came to you from the city of the Messenger ﷺ for the sake of a hadith, which, as I was told, you transmit from the Messenger of Allah ﷺ - I have no other need. Abu ad-Darda said: «Indeed, I heard the Messenger of Allah ﷺ say: «Whoever sets off on a journey desiring to gain knowledge, Allah will make one of the paths leading to Paradise easy. Indeed, the angels will certainly spread their wings over the seeker of knowledge, expressing their satisfaction with what he does. And, verily, the inhabitants of heaven and earth, and even fish in the water column, will certainly ask for forgiveness for the one who knows! And the superiority of the possessor of knowledge over the mere worshiper is like the superiority of the moon on the night of the full moon over the other heavenly bodies, and indeed, those possessing knowledge are the heirs of the prophets, and the prophets leave neither dinars nor dirhams as a legacy. They leave knowledge as a legacy, and whoever has acquired it has acquired a great inheritance». №3641

887)   Narrated from 'Abdullah ibn 'Amr, may Allah be pleased with him and his father: «I wrote down everything that I heard from the Messenger of Allah ﷺ wanting to learn it by heart, and the Quraish forbade me to do this, saying:» You write down everything that you hear from Messenger of Allah ﷺ? But he is a man who speaks both in anger and in contentment. After that, I stopped recording. I told the Messenger of Allah ﷺ about everything and he pointed his hand to

his mouth and said: «Write, for, by the One in whose hand my soul is, nothing comes out of it but the truth». №3646

888) It was narrated from Abu Hurayrah, may Allah be pleased with him: «Having conquered Mecca, the Prophet ﷺ stood among the people and addressed them with a speech. After that, Abu Shah, a man from among the inhabitants of Yemen, stood up and said: «O Messenger of Allah! Write down these words for me,» and (the Messenger of Allah ﷺ) ordered: «Write down this (sermon) for Abu Shah». №3649

889) It was narrated from 'Abdullah ibn az-Zubayr, may Allah be pleased with him and his father: «I asked az-Zubair: «What prevents you from transmitting the hadith of the Messenger of Allah ﷺ like the rest of his companions?» He replied: «By Allah, I took a worthy place with him, however, I heard him say: «Whoever spreads lies against me, let him prepare to take his place in the Fire!» №3651

890) Narrated from 'Urwa: «Once Abu Hurairah sat down near the room of 'Aisha and repeated twice: «Listen, O mistress of the room,» while 'Aisha was praying at that time. When she finished praying, she said to 'Urva: «Does this man and his manner of speaking surprise you? If someone wanted to count the words of the Prophet ﷺ when he said something, he could do it». №3654

891) It was narrated from Abu Hurayrah, may Allah be pleased with him, that the Messenger of Allah ﷺ said: «Whoever is asked about something from knowledge (which the questioner needs) and he hides it, Allah will bridle him with a fiery bridle on the Day of Judgment». №3658

892) It was narrated from Zayd ibn Thabit, may Allah be pleased with him: «I heard the Messenger of Allah ﷺ say:« May Allah please the person who, having heard a hadith from us, remember it and pass it on to another. Perhaps the one to whom he conveys this knowledge

will understand and assimilate it better than himself. It happens that the bearer of knowledge does not understand it properly». №3660

893) It was narrated from Ibn 'Umar (may Allah be pleased with him and his father) that the Messenger of Allah ﷺ said: «Everything intoxicating is khamr, and everything intoxicating is forbidden, and whoever drank wine constantly until death (and did not repent), he will not drink heavenly wine in the eternal world». №3679

894) It is transmitted from Usama ibn Shariq, may Allah be pleased with him: «I came to the Prophet ﷺ, and his companions were sitting as if they had birds on their heads. I greeted those present and then sat down. And then the Arabs came from different directions and asked: «O Messenger of Allah! Should we be treated? He replied: «Be treated, for the Almighty and Great Allah, having created a disease, created a cure for it, except for one thing - old age». №3855

895) Abdullah ibn Buraida narrates from his father that the Prophet ﷺ did not consider anything a bad omen, however, when sending someone on business, he asked about his name, and if he liked it, he rejoiced and it was noticeable on his face, and if he did not like the name, it was also evident from his face. Entering the village, he also asked what it was called, and if he liked the name, he was happy and it was noticeable on his face, and if he didn't like the name, it was also noticeable on his face. №3920

896) The wife of the Prophet ﷺ Umm Salama, may Allah be pleased with her, reports: «The Prophet ﷺ recited the verse «Oh no! My signs appeared to you, but you considered them a lie, became proud and was one of the unbelievers »(Surah «al-Zumar», verse 59)». №3990

897) It was narrated from Abu al-Malih that once women from among the inhabitants of Sham came to 'Aisha, may Allah be pleased with her. She asked: «Where are you from?» They replied: «From among the people

of Sham.» 'Aisha asked, «You must be from a place where women go to (public) baths.» They said, «Yes, it is.» ('Aisha) said: «Indeed, I heard the Messenger of Allah ﷺ say: «Any woman who takes off her clothes outside of her house tears what is between her and Allah Almighty». №4010

898) It is transmitted from Ibn 'Umar, may Allah be pleased with him and his father, that the Messenger of Allah ﷺ said: «Whoever imitates some people (like them in clothes, behaviour, actions, lifestyle, etc.), he». №4031

899) Narrated from 'Abdur-Rahman ibn Ganma al-Ash'ari: «Abu 'Amir or Abu Malik informed me and I swear by Allah that he did not lie to me that he heard the Messenger of Allah ﷺ say: «They will appear in my community, people who will consider silk and hazz to be lawful.» Then he said something else and added: «And the others will be turned into monkeys and pigs and will remain so until the Day of Judgment.» Abu Dawud said that more than twenty people from among the companions of the Messenger of Allah ﷺ wore hazz clothes and among them were Anas and al-Bara ibn 'Azeeb. №4039

900) Abu al-Ahwas narrates from his father: «I came to the Prophet ﷺ in shabby clothes, and he asked: «Do you have property?» He replied: «Yes.» He asked: «And what kind of property?» He replied: «Allah has given me camels, sheep, horses and slaves.» (The Messenger of Allah ﷺ) said: «If Allah has given you property, let the traces of His mercy towards you and His honour be visible on you». №4063

901) Hilal ibn 'Amir reports from his father: «I saw how the Messenger of Allah ﷺ addressed people with a sermon in Mina, sitting on his mule. He was wearing a red cloak, and 'Ali, may Allah be pleased with him, stood in front of him, repeating his words in a loud voice». №4073

902) Salim ibn 'Abdullah narrates from his father that the Messenger of Allah ﷺ said: «Whoever drags the hem

of his clothes on the ground out of arrogance, Allah will not look at him on the Day of Judgment.» Then Abu Bakr said: «My izar moves down on one side (because I am thin) if I do not correct it in time.» The Messenger of Allah said: «Raise your izar to the middle of the lower leg, and if you do not want it, then to the ankles. And do not lower the izar even lower for anything, because this is a sign of arrogance, and, verily, Allah does not like manifestations of arrogance». №4085

903) It was narrated from Abu Hurairah, may Allah be pleased with him, that one day a beautiful man came to the Prophet ﷺ and said: «O Messenger of Allah, I am a person who loves beauty, and what you see from her was granted to me. And I don't like it when someone surpasses me even with the strap of their sandals. Is this arrogance? (The Prophet ﷺ) replied: «No. Arrogance is a refusal to accept the truth and a contemptuous attitude towards people». №4092

904) It was narrated from Khalid that al-Miqdam ibn Ma'diy Qarib, 'Amr ibn al-Aswad and another person from Bani Asad from among the inhabitants of Qynnasrin came to Mu'awiya ibn Abu Sufyan. Mu'awiya asked al-Miqdam, «Do you know that al-Hasan ibn 'Ali has passed away?» Al-Miqdam said: «Verily, to Allah we belong and to Him we return!» He asked him: «Does this seem like a disaster to you?» Al-Mikdam said in response: «Surely I don't think this is a disaster! After all, the Messenger of Allah ﷺ put him on his knees and said: «This one is from me, and Hussein is from 'Ali ?!» And a man from Bani Asad said: «This is the coal that Almighty and Great Allah extinguished!» (having said this, wanting to ingratiate himself with Mu'awiya and please him.) Al-Miqdam said: «As for me, today I will not leave my place until I make you angry and until you hear something from me that you do not like !» Then he said: «O Muawiya! If I tell the truth, prove me right, and if I lie, say that I lied! Mu'awiya said: «Good.» Then he asked: «I conjure

you by Allah, do you know that the Messenger of Allah ﷺ forbade (men) to wear gold?» He replied: «Yes.»
Then he asked: «I conjure you by Allah, have you
heard that the Messenger of Allah ﷺ forbade (men)
to wear silk?» He replied: «Yes.» Then he asked: «I
conjure you with Allah, do you know that the Messenger of Allah ﷺ forbade wearing the skins of pred-
atory animals and riding them?» He replied: «Yes.»
Then he said: «By Allah, I saw all this in your house,
O Muawiyah!» Mu'awiya said: «I knew that I could
not escape from you, O Mikdam (because your words
are the true truth).» Khalid said: «And he ordered to
give him what he did not give to the others and as-
signed his son an allowance (from the treasury) of two
hundred, and al-Miqdam divided this money among
his comrades. As for the man from the tribe of Asad,
he did not give anyone anything of what he received.
Muawiyah, learning about this, said: «Al-Miqdam is
a generous person who gives to others, and a person
from the tribe of Asad clings tightly to what belongs
to him». №4131

905) Abdullah (ibn Mas'ud), may Allah be pleased with
him, said: «Allah cursed the one who tattoos and the
one who asks her to do it, as well as tying (other hair)
hair, (or: plucking her eyebrows) and filing her teeth
for the sake of beauty and thereby changing the creation of the Almighty and Great Allah. A woman from
Bani Asad found out about this. She was called Umm
Ya'qub and she read the Quran. She came to 'Abdullah
and said: «It came to me that you cursed the one who
tattoos and the one who asks her to do it, as well as tying (other hair) hair, plucking her eyebrows and filing
her teeth for the sake of beauty and thereby changing
the creation of the Almighty Allah!» He said: «Why
should I not curse them if the Messenger of Allah ﷺ
cursed them and this is mentioned in the Book of Allah Almighty?» She retorted, «I read the Quran from
cover to cover, but I didn't find any mention of it!»
He said: «By Allah, if you read, you would find it!»
Then he read: «What the Messenger brought you, then

accept, and what he forbade you, avoid it» (surah al-Hashr, verse 7). She said, «But I saw some of that on your wife.» He said, «Come and see.» She entered and then she left. He asked, «What did you see?» She replied, «I didn't see anything like that.» He said, «If any of that was on her, she wouldn't be among us». №4169

906) Narrated from Anas (ibn Malik), may Allah be pleased with him, that the Messenger of Allah ﷺ forbade people to use saffron. №4179

907) It is narrated from ('Abdullah) ibn 'Umar, may Allah be pleased with him and his father, that the Prophet ﷺ saw a child, part of whose hair was shaved off and part left, forbade doing so and said: «Either shave off everything or leave everything». №4195

908) Hudhaifa (ibn al-Yaman), may Allah be pleased with him and his father, reports: «Once the Messenger of Allah ﷺ turned to us with a speech and told us, without leaving the place, about everything that will happen until the Day of Judgment. Whoever remembered what he said, he remembered, and whoever forgot, he forgot. These of his associates know this (in general). And, truly, seeing something of what he predicted, I remember the prediction itself, just as a person remembers the face of a familiar person whom he met after a long separation». №4240

909) 'Abdullah ibn 'Umar, may Allah be pleased with him, reports: «We sat with the Messenger of Allah ﷺ talking about the coming troubles and trials. And he mentioned many of them, and when he came to the «disturbance of blankets», one person asked: «O Messenger of Allah, what is the «disturbance of blankets»? He replied: «This is flight and death. And after it, there will be a ‹distemper of prosperity›. It will come out from under the feet of a person from my family like smoke. He will claim that he is from me, but in fact, he has nothing to do with me, because my relatives are only God-fearing. Then the people will reconcile and

jointly elect (as a ruler) a person who in fact will be as unsuitable for them as a hip does not fit a rib. Then there will be a «black turmoil», and it will not bypass anyone from this community (this turmoil will touch everyone and harm everyone), and when they say that it has stopped, it will continue. And during it, a person will wake up as a believer, and fall asleep as an unbeliever. And people will be divided into two camps - a camp in which there are only believers and no hypocrites, and a camp in which there are only hypocrites and no believers. And when this happens, expect the Dajjal to appear today or tomorrow». №4243

910) Nasr ibn 'Asim al-Laysi narrates: «We came to al-Yashkuri accompanied by several people from the Banu Layth. He asked, «Who is this?» We replied: Banu leys. We have come to ask you about Hudhaifah's hadith.» And he narrated the hadith and (among other things he mentioned that Hudhayfah) said: «I asked:« O Messenger of Allah, will there be evil after this good? He said: «Trouble and evil.» I asked: «O Messenger of Allah, will there be good after this evil?» He said, «O Hudhayfa! Study the Book of Allah and follow what is in it.» He repeated these words three times. I asked: «O Messenger of Allah, will there be good after this evil?» He said: «A truce with hidden malice and unity, but with corruption in their hearts.» I asked: «O Messenger of Allah, what is a truce with hidden malice?» He said: «The hearts of the people after him will not be the same as before.» I asked: «O Messenger of Allah, will there be evil after this good?» (The Messenger of Allah 🕮) said: «Trouble, blind and deaf, its initiators are heralds at the gates of Hell, inviting there. And if you, O Hudhaifah, die clinging to a tree trunk, it will be better for you than to follow one of them. - 'Abdullah ibn 'Amr ibn al-'As, may Allah be pleased with him and his father, reports that the Messenger of Allah 🕮 said: «What will you be like when the time comes (or: The time is coming) when people will be sifted through a sieve and a husk will remain - people are unreliable and do not fulfill their

promises and obligations. And there will be divisions among them, and they will behave like this.» With these words (the Messenger of Allah ﷺ) intertwined his fingers. The people asked: «What should we do, O Messenger of Allah?» He replied: «You should accept what you know (and this is true), and reject what you don't know, and take care of yourself, ceasing to pay attention to the (religious) majority». №4246

911) It was narrated from Sauban, may Allah be pleased with him, that the Messenger of Allah ﷺ said: «Indeed, Allah (or: my Lord) showed me the land, and I saw its east and west. And, verily, everything that was shown to me from it will belong to my community, and two treasures were given to me - red and white, and I asked my Lord not to destroy my community entirely through drought and not to give power over its members to the enemy from among them who would destroy them without exception, and verily my Lord said: «O Muhammad, if I make a decision, it is not cancelled. Verily, I will not destroy them all with a drought, and I will not give power over them to an enemy not from among them, who would destroy them without exception, even if people gather against them from all ends (or: from all ends) of the earth, until they begin to destroy each other and capture each other. And, verily, I fear for my community leaders who mislead (calling for innovations, impiety and sins). And when the sword (or weapons in general) is lowered into my community, it will no longer be raised until the Day of Judgment. And the Hour will not come until the tribes from my community join the polytheists and until the tribes from my community begin to worship idols. And verily, thirty liars will appear in my community, each of whom will claim that he is a prophet, but I am the seal of the prophets, and there will be no prophets after me. And a part of my community will not cease to adhere to the truth (having superiority over opponents), and the one who begins to contradict them will not harm them until the predestined by Allah Almighty comes». №4252

912) It was narrated from 'Abdullah (ibn Mas'ud), may Allah be pleased with him, that the Prophet ﷺ said: «If there were only one day left for the world to exist, Allah would extend this day to send a person from my offspring (or from people my house). His name will be the same as my name, and his father's name will be the same as my father's name (that is, he will be called Muhammad ibn 'Abdullah). He will fill the earth with justice after it has been filled with oppression and injustice.» And in the version of Sufyan (al-Sauri), says: «This world will not disappear until a person from my family becomes the leader of the Arabs, whose name will coincide with mine». №4282

913) Umm Salama (may Allah be pleased with her) narrates: «I heard the Messenger of Allah ﷺ say: «Mahdi is from my family, from the offspring of Fatima». №4284

914) It was narrated from 'Ali (ibn Abu Talib), may Allah be pleased with him, that the Prophet ﷺ said: «A man from Maverannahr named al-Harith ibn Harras will come out. His vanguard will be commanded by a man named Mansour. He will help the family of Muhammad to establish itself on earth (supporting them with property and strength), just as the Quraish helped the Messenger of Allah ﷺ to establish itself and every believer is obliged to help him (or: heed his call)». №4290

915) It was narrated from Sauban, may Allah be pleased with him, that the Messenger of Allah ﷺ said: «The time is approaching when other communities will call each other (to oppose) against you (and get your property) like people who invite each other to eat gathered around the dish (with food and nothing prevents them from taking this food). Someone asked, «Is it because there won't be many of us in those days?» He replied: «No, on the contrary, you will be many, but you will be like rubbish carried by a stream. Allah will take away the fear of you from the breasts of your enemies, and will place weakness in your hearts. Someone asked:

«O Messenger of Allah, what kind of weakness would that be?» He replied: «Love of this world and aversion to death». №4297

916) It is narrated from 'Ikrimah that 'Ali burned several apostates, and Ibn 'Abbas (at that time he was the governor of Basra), learning about this, said: «I would not burn them, because the Messenger of Allah ﷺ said:» Do not punish Allah's punishment» (not to kill with fire). However, I would execute them, because the Messenger of Allah ﷺ said: «Whoever changes his religion, execute him.» When 'Ali found out about this, he said: «Woe to Ibn 'Abbas!» №4351

917) It was narrated from 'Abdullah that the Messenger of Allah ﷺ said: «It is not allowed to shed blood (execute) a Muslim (whether it be a man or a woman) who testifies that there is no god [worthy of worship] except Allah and that I am the Messenger of Allah except in three cases. This is a married adulterer, soul for the soul (execution as a recompense for murder) and who renounced his religion and broke away from the community (apostate)». №4352

918) It is transmitted from Ibn 'Abbas, may Allah be pleased with him and his father: «A crazy woman who committed adultery was brought to 'Umar, and after consulting with his companions, he ordered to stone her. When she was led past 'Ali ibn Abu Talib, may Allah be pleased with him, he asked: «What is the matter with this woman?» They told him: «This is a madwoman from such and such a tribe. She committed adultery and 'Umar ordered her to be stoned.» ('Ali) said: «Take her back.» Then he came to 'Umar and said: «O Commander of the Believers! Don't you know that feathers are lifted from three: from a madman until he is healed, from a sleeper until he wakes up, and from a child until he becomes sane (i.e. adult)?» ('Umar) replied: «Yes, I know that.» ('Ali) asked: «So why is this one being stoned?» ('Umar) replied: «Indeed, there is no reason.» ('Ali) said: «Then let her go.» And he told me to let her go.» He said:

«And he began to exclaim:« Allah is great!» №4399

919) 'Amr ibn Shu'ayb narrates from his father the story of his grandfather that the Messenger of Allah ﷺ said: «Whoever heals, not being known as a healer, he compensates (damage caused)». №4586

920) Mu'awiya ibn Abu Sufyan, may Allah be pleased with him and his father, one day got up and said: «Indeed, the Messenger of Allah ﷺ once got up and addressed us with a speech, saying: «Indeed, the people of the Book who lived before you were divided into seventy-two groups, and verily, this community will be divided into seventy-three groups, seventy-two of which will be in the Fire, and one will enter Paradise - this is the (true) community. Ibn Yahya and 'Amr narrate the addition: «And people will appear in my community who will follow their whims, just as rabies follows its carrier.» And 'Amr added: «Rabies always follows the sick, penetrating his every vessel, into every joint». №4597

921) It was narrated from 'Aisha, may Allah be pleased with her, that the camel of Safiya bint Huyayy fell ill, and Zeinab had an extra one. The Messenger of Allah ﷺ said to her: «Give her a camel.» Zeinab said: «Should I give (a camel) to this Jewess?» The Messenger of Allah ﷺ became angry and did not communicate with her throughout Dhul-Hijjah, Muharram and part of Safar. №4602

922) 'Ubaydullah ibn Abu Rafi' narrates from his father that the Prophet ﷺ said: «Let it not happen to any of you (in such a position): he reclines on his bed, and when he is informed of some of my decrees from the fact that I commanded, or from what I forbade, he says: «We know nothing... We follow what we found in the Book of Allah!» №4605

923) Yazid ibn 'Umaira from among the comrades of Mu'az ibn Jabal narrates that whenever he sat, remembering Allah, he always said: «Allah is a fair and impartial Judge, so the doubters perished!» And one day he said:

«Verily, temptations await you. Wealth will increase in those times, and the Quran will be accessible to everyone, and the believer and hypocrite, male and female, young and old, slave and free will teach it. The time is coming when a person will say: «Why do people not follow me, because I read the Quran?! Indeed, they will not follow me until I invent something else for them!» Do not dare to follow what they invent, for innovation is an error. And I warn you against the possessor of knowledge who has deviated from the true path. Indeed, Shaitan can speak the word of error in the language of the possessor of knowledge, and at the same time, it happens that the hypocrite speaks the word of truth. (Yazid) narrates: «I asked Mu'adh: «May Allah have mercy on you, how can I distinguish the word of error spoken by the possessor of knowledge? And how can I know the word of truth in the words of a hypocrite? Mu'adh replied: «It is possible. Avoid accepting from the words of the possessor of knowledge those (the falsity of which) are known and which make people exclaim: «What is he saying ?!» However, this should not make you feel hostile towards the possessor of knowledge himself, for he may correct his mistake. And accept the truth you hear, it's like light». №4611

924) It is transmitted from Humaid: «Al-Hasan came to Mecca, and the faqihs of Mecca asked me to ask him to give them a day and give them instructions. He said: «Good.» They gathered, and he addressed them with a sermon, and I have never seen a man who would give more instructive and penetrating sermons. One person asked: «O Abu Sa'id! Who created Satan? He exclaimed: «Glory be to Allah! Is there any other creator besides Allah? Allah created Satan, and He created good and evil.» The man said: «May Allah destroy them! How can they build lies on this Sheikh?!» №4618

925) Ayyub said: «Two categories of people are erecting a lie on al-Hasan: those who want to raise their author-

ity, and people in whose hearts there is anger and hatred, and they say: «Didn't he say something? Didn't he say something?» №4622

926) Sufyan said: «Whoever thinks that 'Ali was more worthy to rule (after the death of the Messenger of Allah ﷺ), he accuses Abu Bakr, 'Umar, Muhajirs and Ansar of sin, and I do not think that in this case, his deeds will rise to heaven!» №4630

927) It was narrated from Abu Bakra that once the Prophet ﷺ asked: «Which of you had a dream?» One person said, «I. I dreamed that scales descended from the sky and you and Abu Bakr were weighed - and you outweighed, then Abu Bakr and 'Umar were weighed - and Abu Bakr outweighed. Then 'Umar and 'Uthman were weighed, and 'Umar outweighed, and then the scales were lifted back. And the Companions saw from the face of the Messenger of Allah ﷺ that it was unpleasant for him to hear this. №4634

928) 'Aseem said: «I heard al-Hajjaj say, standing on the minbar:» You must fear Allah to the best of your ability, and there can be no exceptions, and you must listen and obey the ruler of the believers, 'Abdulmalik, and can be no exception here. Indeed, if I commanded people to leave one gate of the mosques, and they left the other, their blood and property would cease to be inviolable for me, and if I would exact from (the tribe) rabi' for (the harm caused in due time to the tribe) Mudar, it would be permissible for me before Allah. And is there anyone who will justify me, (if I harm or kill) 'Abd Hudhail, who claims that his recitation is from Allah, for this is only the rajaz of the Bedouins and Allah did not reveal it to His Prophet ﷺ? And is there anyone who will justify me (if I harm or kill) this non-Arab mavalis, among whom is the one who claims that if he throws a stone, then even before it falls to the ground there will be (another turmoil)? Verily, I will destroy them so (that they will disappear) like yesterday!» №4643

929) It is narrated from Safina that the Messenger of Allah ﷺ said: «The successors of the Prophet ﷺ will rule for thirty years, and then Allah will grant power to whom He wills.» Sa'id narrates: «Safina said to me: 'Count: Abu Bakr is two years, 'Umar is ten, 'Uthman is twelve and 'Ali is so many.» I said to him: «Yes, but these claim that 'Ali, peace be upon him, was not a caliph.» He said: «Banu al-Zarqa's backsides are lying!» – referring to Bani Marwan». №4646

930) It is transmitted from 'Abdullah ibn Zam'a: «When the condition of the Messenger of Allah ﷺ (during his illness) worsened, I was just with him along with a small group of Muslims and Bilal called him to prayer. He said, «Tell someone to pray with the people.» 'Abdullah ibn Zam'a went out and saw 'Umar, who was surrounded by people, and Abu Bakr was absent at that time. ('Abdullah says): «I said:« O 'Umar! Get up and pray with the people.» And he stepped forward and said the Takbir. Hearing his voice (and he was loud at 'Umar), the Messenger of Allah ﷺ asked: «Where is Abu Bakr? And Allah does not want this and Muslims! And Allah does not want this, and the Muslims!» After that, he sent for Abu Bakr, and he came and performed prayer with the people, which 'Umar had previously performed. №4660

931) It was narrated from Jabir, may Allah be pleased with him and his father, that the Messenger of Allah ﷺ said: «Between the servant of Allah and disbelief is the abandonment of prayer». №4678

932) Az-Zuhri said about the words of the Almighty «Say:» You did not believe, so say: «We submitted /aslamna /»: «We believed that Islam is words, and faith is deeded». №4685

933) It is narrated from Ibn 'Umar, may Allah be pleased with him and his father, that the Prophet ﷺ said: «The Qadarites (fatalists) are the fire worshipers of this community. If they get sick, don't visit them, and if they die, don't accompany their funeral litter». №4691

934) Narrated Abu Dharr: «The Messenger of Allah ﷺ said: «How will you behave when the rulers after me will appropriate this property /fai/?» I said, «O Messenger of Allah, I will put my sword on my shoulder and cut with it until I meet you.» He said, «I'll point you to something better. Be patient until you meet me». №4759

935) It was narrated from Zayd ibn Wahb al-Juhani that he was part of the army of 'Ali, who went to the Kharijites, and 'Ali said: «O people, verily, I heard the Messenger of Allah ﷺ say: «A group of people will leave my community who will recite the Quran in such a way that your reading is nothing compared to their reading. And your prayer is nothing compared to theirs. And your post is nothing compared to their post. They will read the Quran, thinking that this is an argument in their favour, although it is against them, and their prayer will not rise above their collarbones. They come out of religion the way an arrow pierces a game and comes out the other side. If the army that would kill them knew what was promised to them by the mouth of their Prophet, they would have abandoned all other affairs. Among them, there is a man with a shoulder, but without a forearm, and on his shoulder is a kind of nipple, on which there are white hairs. So will you go to Muawiyah and the people of Sham and leave behind your families and property? I swear by Allah, I think that they are, for they shed forbidden blood and attacked people. So go forth in the name of Allah!» (The narrator of this hadith) Salama ibn Kuhayl says: «And Zayd ibn Wahb led me to all places. When we were at the bridge, he said: «We met, and the Kharijites were then commanded by 'Abdullah ibn Wahb ar-Rasibi. He said to them: «Throw your spears and draw your swords from their scabbards, for verily I fear that they will admonish you, as on the day of Harura!» And they threw down their spears and drew their swords. They were met with spears, and they began to die, falling on each other. And the Muslims lost only two people killed that day. Then 'Ali said: «Look for a man with

a mutilated hand.» They began to search but found no one. Then 'Ali went himself and approached the dead, who was lying on top of each other. He ordered them to be taken apart. And he found this person at the very bottom. 'Ali exclaimed: «Allah is great!» - and then he said: «Allah spoke the truth and His Messenger brought it to us!» Then 'Abidah as-Salmani got up and said: «O commander of the believers, swear by Allah, besides Whom there is no other deity, did you hear this from the Messenger of Allah ﷺ?» 'Ali replied: «Yes, by Allah, besides Whom there is no other deity.» And he asked him three times, and he swore three times». №4768

936) It is narrated from Hammam (bin al-Harith) that (once one) a man began to praise 'Uthman in the presence of al-Miqdad, and then al-Miqdad took the earth and began to throw it in the face (of the praiser), saying: «Verily, the Messenger Allah ﷺ said: «If you see those who praise others, throw earth on their faces!». №4804

937) It was narrated from 'Abdullah ibn Mughaffal, may Allah be pleased with him, that the Messenger of Allah ﷺ said: «Verily, Allah is kind, He loves kindness and bestows for it what He does not bestow for severity». №4807

938) It is narrated from the words of Hudhaifah, may Allah be pleased with him, that he said: «Your Prophet ﷺ said: «(Committing) every deed approved (by the Shariah) is a sadaka». №4947

939) It is narrated from the words of the mother of the faithful, Umm Salama, may Allah be pleased with her, that when the Prophet ﷺ left her house, he always said, raising his gaze to the sky: «O Allah, verily, I resort to You to fall into error or to be led astray, from committing a mistake myself, and from being made to err, from committing an injustice myself, and from being treated unfairly, from being in ignorance, and from to be kept in ignorance.» / Allahumma, inni a'uzu bi-kya

an adylla au udalla, au azilla au uzalla au azlima au
uzlima, au ajhala au yujhala 'alayya /. №5094

940) It was narrated from the words of Abu Hurairah, may
Allah be pleased with him, that the Messenger of Allah ﷺ said: «When one of you comes to the assembly,
let him salam (those present), and when he wants to
leave, let him (also) salam them, for the first is no more
necessary than the second». №5208

941) It is reported that the mother of the faithful 'Aisha,
may Allah be pleased with her, said: «I have not seen
anyone more like the Messenger of Allah ﷺ in appearance, in lifestyle, in virtues and speech than Fatimah,
may Allah exalt her! When she came to him, he stood
up to meet her, took her by the hand, kissed her and
seated her in his place. And when he came to her, she
stood up to meet him, took him by the hand, kissed
him and seated him in her place». №5217

«Sunah» an Nasai

His name was Ahmad ibn Shuayb ibn 'Ali al-Nasai, and his kunya was Abu 'Abdu-r-Rahman. An-Nasai was born in the now non-existent city of Nisa (his nisba is given by the name of this city), which was located to the west (only 18 km) of the city of Ashgabat, the once shining capital of the Parthian kingdom. Nisa is an ancient settlement with dwellings of the local aristocracy, surrounded by huge hectares of flowering gardens. In 651, Nisa became part of the Arab Caliphate. In 1220, Nisa, like other major cities of Central Asia, suffered a general catastrophe: the siege and destruction by the Mongols. As has been noted more than once, a very large number of early Muslim scholars were from Central Asia. An-Nasai spent the second half of his life in Egypt, and shortly before his death, he went to Palestine, where he died. His reason for leaving Egypt was the envy of other people of his vast knowledge. After arriving in Palestine, he was attacked by a group of Kharijites and died from his wounds. Al-Hakim wrote about him: «In addition to all his virtues, Abu Abdur-Rahman was also martyred.» Muslim biographers were unanimous on the cause of his death.

Sunan an-Nasai, as-Sunan as-Sughra or al-Mujta-ba (Arabic ننس النساسئي, السنن الصغرى, المجتبى) is a collection of hadith authored by Abu Abdurrahman an-Nasai. «Al-Mujtaba» means «selected, chosen», because the hadiths contained in it are selected from another collection of hadith an-Nasai - «as-Sunan al-Kubra». The collection is transmitted by the only way from the student of an-Nasai Ibn al-Sunni, from whose students it spread. The collection contains 5758 hadiths, however, if repeated hadiths are removed, their number will be halved, because one of the features of «Sunan» an-Nasa'i is to bring the same hadith in several sections. Sunan al-Nasa'i is the largest of the four Sunan of the Six Books.

Even though al-Nasa'i made stricter requirements for hadith than other authors of the Sunan, his work did not receive such attention from interpreters and commentators. The same is the case with the translations of Sunan al-Nasai, which, unlike the Sahihs of al-Bukhari and Muslim and the Sunan of Abu Dawud and at-Tirmidhi, have never been published in full translation into other languages.

942) It is reported that Anas (may Allah be pleased with him) said: «The period that the Messenger of Allah ﷺ determined for us to cut our moustaches, cut our nails, remove hair from the pubis and the armpits, was no more than forty days. And another time he said: «Forty nights». №14

943) It is reported that 'Aisha said: «(Some people) say: «Verily, the Prophet ﷺ bequeathed to 'Ali.» (At that moment) he asked me to bring him a basin to urinate in it, but his soul was tired, and I did not feel (that he had already died). So to whom did he bequeath (something)?!» №33

944) It is reported that Tariq al-Muharibi said: «Arriving in Medina, we saw the Messenger of Allah ﷺ standing on the minbar and addressing people with a sermon, saying: «The hand of the giver is exalted, start with those whom you support: from your mother, from your father, from your sister, from your brother, and then fur-

ther in order of distance (family relationship)». №2532

945) It is reported that Anas said: «When the Prophet ﷺ
entered Mecca, compensating for a small pilgrimage
(«umrat-ul-qada»), 'Abdullah ibn Rawaha walked
ahead and proclaimed: «O descendants of the unbelievers! Make way for him! Today we will beat you according to his revelation! (Inflicting) blows that shatter
heads, And make the lover forget the beloved! Hearing these verses, 'Umar said to him (as if reproaching
him): «O Ibn Rawaha! Are you reciting a poem in the
territory that Allah has made reserved, in front of the
Messenger of Allah?!» However, the Prophet ﷺ said,
«Leave him alone! For I swear by the One in Whose
Hand my soul is, his words hurt them more than arrows». №2893

946) It is reported from Anas that the Messenger of Allah ﷺ
said: «Out of everything worldly, I was inspired with
love for women and incense, and prayer was made the
delight of my eyes». №3939

947) It is reported that Ibn 'Abbas said: «Once one of the
Ansar converted to Islam, and then apostatized and
joined the (adherents) of polytheism, and then began
to greatly regret (about what had happened). He sent to
his tribesmen (a message, saying): «Ask the Messenger of Allah ﷺ about me: do I have (the opportunity)
to repent ?!» His tribesmen came to the Messenger of
Allah ﷺ and said: «So-and-so regrets (what happened).
He commanded us to ask you: does he (possibility) repent?!» And then (verses) were sent down, in which
it is said: «How will Allah guide people who have
become unbelievers after faith ...» (sura «Ali Imran»,
verse 86), and before the words (of Allah): «Forgiving,
Merciful ...». (Sura Al-Baqarah, verse 173). (People)
sent him (an answer to his question) and he entered
Islam (again)». №4068

948) It is reported that Tariq ibn Shihab said: «Once when
the Prophet ﷺ put his foot in a (leather) stirrup, a certain person asked (him): «Which jihad is the best?»

(The Prophet ﷺ) replied: «The word of truth (spoken) by an unjust ruler!». №4209

949) It is reported that Tariq al-Muharibi said: «Once a man said: «O Messenger of Allah! In pre-Islamic times, these (people from the clan) Bani Sa'laba killed such and such. Take from their compensation in our favour! (The Messenger of Allah ﷺ) raised his hands (so high) that I saw the whiteness of his armpits, and then said twice: «A child is not responsible for the crime of his mother!». №4839

950) Anas ibn Malik, may Allah be pleased with him, said that one day a Bedouin came to the door of the Messenger of Allah ﷺ and put his eye to the hole in the door [and began to look in]. The Prophet ﷺ saw him and went towards him with [something] a metal or wooden stick to gouge out his eye, seeing this [Bedouin] departed. Then the Prophet ﷺ said to him: «If you were late, then I would gouge out your eye». №4858

951) It is narrated from Anas that the Prophet ﷺ said: «There are three things by which a person will know the sweetness of Islam: When Allah and the Prophet ﷺ become closer to him than anyone else; when he fell in love with another person only for the pleasure of Allah; and when it is even more hateful for him to return to disbelief than to be thrown into the fire» №4989

952) It is narrated from Anas that the Prophet ﷺ said: «I ordered to fight people until they recognize that there is no one worthy of worship besides Allah and that I am the Prophet of Allah. If they recognize this, they will pray with us towards the same Qibla, eat our sacrificial animals, and pray as we pray; then their blood and their property will be forbidden for us, and they will have all the rights and obligations that all Muslims have» №5003

953) ALi, may Allah be pleased with him, said that the Prophet ﷺ swore to me that only a true believer would love Ali, and only a hypocrite would hate Ali. №5022

954) Abu Suhayl narrated from his father: That he heard Talha bin Ubaydullah say: «A man from Najd with dishevelled hair approached the Messenger of Allah; he spoke loudly, but his speech could not be understood until he came closer. He asked about Islam. The Messenger of Allah ﷺ said: «Five prayers every day and night.» He said, «Should I do something else? He said, «No, unless you do it voluntarily.» The Messenger of Allah ﷺ said: «Fasting in the month of Ramadan.» He said, «Should I do something else?» He said, «Not unless you do it voluntarily.» Then the Messenger of Allah ﷺ told him about the zakat. He said, «Should I do something else?» He said, «Not unless you do it voluntarily.» The man left saying, «I will do no more, no less.» The Messenger of Allah ﷺ said: «He will succeed if he speaks the truth». №5028

955) It was narrated that Abu Hurayrah said: «The Messenger of Allah ﷺ said: «Verily, this religion is easy, and no one ever overloads himself with religion unless it overcomes him. So try and get as close as possible and calm down and gain strength by worshipping in the morning, afternoon and the last hours of the night». №5034

956) It was narrated from Ibn ‹Umar that: The Messenger of Allah ﷺ said: «The parable of the hypocrite is a parable of a sheep that oscillates between two flocks, now one, then the other, not knowing whom to follow». №5037

«Sunah» ibn Majah

Sunah Ibn Maja (Arab. ‎سنن ابن ماجه‎) is a collection of hadiths written by Ibn Maja and one of the six most authoritative Sunni collections of hadiths. The collection contains more than 4000 hadiths, divided into 32 books (kutub) and 1500 chapters (abwab). His full name is Abu Abdullah Muhammad ibn Yazid ibn Maja al-Rabi al-Qazwini. Born in Qazvin in 824 according to the Christian chronology.

Ibn Maja visited Iraq, Hijaz, Sham and Egypt to collect hadith. Among the teachers of Ibn Maji were such well-known theologians of their time as Abu Bakr ibn Abu Shayba, Muhammad ibn Abdullah ibn Numair, Jubar ibn al-Mughalis, Ibrahim ibn al-Munzir al-Hizami, Abdullah ibn Muawiyah, Hisham ibn Ammar, Muhammad ibn Rumkh, Dawood ibn Rashid and others. And about Imam Ibn Maja himself, and his books, many laudatory statements of scientists have been preserved. Abu Yala al-Halimi said: «People believe Imam Ibn Maja and rely on his knowledge in matters of the science of hadith.» Muhammad ibn Jafar al-Kattani in his book «Risalatil mustatrafa» writes the following: «Convinced that the book «Sunahn» by Imam Ibn Maj is reliable, weighty and very useful in the field of fiqh, scholars recognized it as the sixth sahih collection».

Ibn Tahir said: «Looking through the collections of hadiths of Imam Ibn Maj, one can see that they consist of a large number of chapters, there are no repetitions of hadiths, the hadiths are written in an elegant order, and one can be sure that he used the best methods in collecting hadiths and writing a book. «. Although this book is not as famous, it has corresponding recognition and significance.

957) Abu Hurayrah reported that the Messenger of Allah ﷺ said: «Whoever obeys me obeys Allah, whoever disobeys me disobeys Allah». №3

958) It is narrated from the words of Abu Hurairah that the Messenger of Allah ﷺ said: «A group from my ummah will not stop adhering to the command of Allah all the time and whoever opposes it will not harm it». №7

959) It is reported from al-Mikdam ibn Ma'dikarib (may Allah be pleased with him) that the Messenger of Allah ﷺ said: «Soon the time will come when a person will sit leaning on his sofa, and when my hadith is transmitted to him, he will say: «Between us and you is the Book of the Great and Almighty Allah. What we find in it is lawful/halal / we consider lawful, and what we find forbidden / haram / we consider forbidden. Whereas, verily, what the Messenger of Allah ﷺ forbade is the same as what Allah Himself forbade». №12

960) It is reported from the words of Ibn 'Umar, may Allah be pleased with both of them, that the Messenger of Allah ﷺ said: «Do not forbid the slave women of Allah to pray in the mosque.» His son said to him, «But we will certainly forbid it.» And he, very angry, said: «I tell you (hadith) of the Messenger of Allah ﷺ, and you say we will certainly forbid them (this)?» №16

961) It is reported that Ishaq ibn Kabis, according to his father, said that 'Ubada ibn as-Samit al-Ansari, one of those who took an oath under a tree and was a companion of the Messenger of Allah ﷺ, took part in a military campaign with Mu'awiya on lands of the Byzantines. When he looked at the people who were selling pieces of gold for dinars and pieces of silver for dirhams, he said: «O people, you are engaged in usury /riba/! I heard the Messenger of Allah ﷺ say: «Do not sell gold for gold, except like for like, do not add anything to it and do not delay (on payment).» Then Muawiyah said to him: «O Abul-Walid, I do not see usury in this if someone does not delay the payment!» 'Ubadah said: «I tell you from the Messenger of Allah, and you tell me your opinion? If Allah takes me (from here), then I will no longer live with you on the same land where you rule over me! Having finished his business there, he soon reached Medina, where 'Umar ibn al-Khattab asked him: «What brought you about Abul-Walid?» And he told him about this story and what he said about his housing. (Then 'Umar) said: «O Abul-Walid, return to your land, and may Allah disfigure the land where there are no you and those like you!» He then wrote to Mu'awiya: «From now on, you cannot command this man. Lead the people to what he said, for verily, such as the command (of the Prophet ﷺ)». №18

962) It is reported by 'Abdurrahman ibn Abi Layl, who said: «We asked Zayd ibn Arkam: «Tell us a hadith from the Prophet ﷺ.» To which Zeid ibn Arkam replied: «We have grown old and forgotten. And the hadith from the Messenger of Allah ﷺ is a serious matter!». №25

963) We were informed by Muhammad ibn 'Abdullah ibn Numeyr, who narrated from Abu al-Nadr, narrated from Shu'ba, narrated from 'Abdullah ibn Abu as-Safar, who said: «I heard Sha'bi say:» I was with Ibn 'Umar for a year and did not hear him transmit (tell hadith) anything from the Messenger of Allah ﷺ». №26

964) It is reported that Karaza ibn Kaab said: «Sending us to Kufa, 'Umar ibn al-Khattab (may Allah be pleased with him) began to see us off, walking to a place called Syrar. He asked, «Do you know why I went with you?» We replied: «By the right that the companions of the Messenger of Allah ﷺ and the rights of the Ansar deserve.» 'Umar said: «I walked with you because of the words that I wanted to say to you so that you remember them while I accompany you. Verily, you will come to a people whose hearts boil towards the Quran, just as the contents of a cauldron boil. When they see you, they will stretch their necks in your direction and say: «(Arrived) companions of Muhammad.» Transmit less hadith from the Messenger of Allah ﷺ, and I will become your partner (in receiving a reward for calling)». №28

965) It is reported that Jundub ibn 'Abdullah, may Allah be pleased with him, said: «We were young and frisky people, being with the Prophet ﷺ and we studied faith/ iman / before starting to study the Quran. Then, by studying the Quran, we increased our faith in it.». №61

966) Narrated from 'Ali ibn Abu Talib, (who) said: «The Messenger of Allah ﷺ said: «Faith/iman / is knowledge with the heart, pronouncing with the tongue and doing deeds with parts (of the body)». №65

967) It is narrated from the words of 'Abdullah ibn Mas'ud, may Allah be pleased with him, that the Prophet ﷺ said: «Reviling (scoldling) a Muslim is a sin, fighting with him in disbelief». №69

968) It is reported that Suraqa ibn Ju'shum said: «(Once) I asked:« O Messenger of Allah! Will all things happen, as written and predetermined (as written and the ink is dry), or is everything ahead (that is, will happen in the future, without predestination)? The Prophet ﷺ said: «Certainly, as it is written and ordained. And everyone will be relieved of what he is destined for». №91

969) It is reported that Bara bin Azib said: «We were returning with the Messenger of Allah from his Hajj, which he had performed, and stopped at some place on the road. He commanded a common prayer, then took Ali by the hand and said: Am I not dearer to the believers than they? They said, «Yes, indeed.» He said, «Am I not dearer to every believer than he?» They said, «Yes, indeed.» He said, «This man is the patron of those whose master I am.» O Allah, accept as friends those who consider him a friend, and accept as enemies those who consider him an enemy». №116

970) It was narrated that Ibn Umar said: «The Messenger of Allah said:» Hasan and Husayn will be the leaders of the youth of Paradise, and their father is better than them». №118

971) Khubshi bin Junadah is reported to have said: «I heard the Messenger of Allah say: 'Ali is a part of me and I am a part of him and no one will represent me except Ali». №119

972) It is reported from the words of 'Abdurrahman ibn Thabit that Sa'd ibn Abu Waqqas said: «When Mu'awiya arrived on one of his hajj's, Sa'd came to him. They mentioned 'Ali (ibn Abu Talib) and he (Muawiyah) began to revile him. Then Sa'd got angry and said: «You are talking about a person about whom I heard the Messenger of Allah ﷺ say:» The one whom I am the protector, is the protector and Ali? I also heard him say: «You are in the same position before me as Harun was under Musa, except that there will be no (another) Prophet after me.» I also heard him say: «Today I will certainly hand over this banner to a person who loves Allah and His Messenger!» №121

973) It was narrated from Abdullah that: The Messenger of Allah said to Abu Ubaydah bin Jarrah: «He is a trustworthy person of this ummah». №136

974) It was narrated that Ali said: «The Messenger of Allah said:» If I appointed someone as my successor without consulting anyone, I would appoint Ibn Umm Abd

(Abdullah ibn Masud)». №137

975) It was narrated from Abu Hurayrah that the Messenger of Allah ﷺ said: «Whoever loves Hassan and Hussain loves me, and whoever hates them hates me too.». №143

976) It was narrated from Saeed bin Abu Rashid that Yala bin Murrah told them that: They went with the Prophet to a dinner to which they were invited and Husayn played there in the street. The Prophet went to the people and extended his hands, and the child began to run back and forth. The Prophet made him laugh until he caught him, then he put one hand under his chin and the other on his head, kissed him and said, «Hussein is part of me and I am part of him. May Allah love those who love Hussein. Hussein is a tribe among tribes». №144

977) Zayd bin Arkam is reported to have said: «The Messenger of Allah said to Ali, Fatimah, Hasan and Hussain: 'I am peace to those with whom you make peace and I am war to those with whom you are at war». №145

978) It is reported that 'Aisha, may Allah be pleased with her, said: «The Messenger of Allah ﷺ said: «Whenever 'Ammar (ibn Yasir) was not given a choice between two, he always chose the most correct of them». №148

979) Ibn Buraidah narrated that his father said, «The Messenger of Allah said: 'Allah commanded me to love four people and He told me that He also loves them.' He was asked: «O Messenger of Allah, who are they?» He said: «Ali is one of them,» and he said this three times, «as well as Abu Dharr, Salman and Miqdad». №149

980) It is reported that 'Abdullah ibn 'Amr said: «I heard the Messenger of Allah ﷺ say: «Neither the earth wore, nor the sky did not overshadow a person with a more truthful language than Abu Dharr!» №156

981) 'Abidah (as-Salmani) narrated that (once) 'Ali

(ibn Abu Talib) mentioned the Kharijites and said: «Among them, there is a man with a hand defect (or: with a small hand), and if you did not begin to show cruelty, then I would tell you what Allah promised in the language of Muhammad ﷺ to those who would kill them. ('Abidah said): «I asked: «Did you hear this from (himself) Muhammad ﷺ!?» He replied: «Yes, I swear by the Lord of the Kaaba!», repeating (these words) three times». №167

982) It is reported that Ibn Abu 'Awfa said: «The Messenger of Allah ﷺ said: «Kharijites are dogs of Fire!». №173

983) It is reported that Jabir ibn 'Abdullah (may Allah be pleased with him) said: «In the season (of the Hajj in Mecca), the Messenger of Allah ﷺ introduced himself to people and said:« Is there (among you) a person who will take me to his people, for these Quraish prevented me from conveying to the people the speech of my Lord!?» №201

984) Kathir ibn 'Abdullah ibn 'Amr ibn 'Awf al-Muzani said: «My father told me from my grandfather that the Messenger of Allah ﷺ said:» Whoever resurrects any sunnah from my sunnah and people begin to follow it, then he there will be a reward equal to the reward of all those who follow her (this Sunnah). And for those who follow (this sunnah), the reward will not decrease at all. And whoever makes an innovation /bida'a/ and people begin to follow this (innovation), then on him will be the sin of all those who will make this bida'a, although they (those who follow this bida'a) there will be no less sin». №209

985) Narrated Abu Dharr, may Allah be pleased with him: «(One day) the Messenger of Allah ﷺ said to me: «Oh Abu Dharr so that you leave your house in the morning and learn one verse from the Book of Allah, it is better for you than praying in one hundred rak'ats. And so that you leave the house in the morning and learn one section of knowledge, by which (people) act or do not act, it is better (for you) than praying a

thousand rak'ats». №219

986) It was narrated from Abu Hurairah that the Messenger of Allah ﷺ said: «Allah leads to an understanding of the religion of the one whom He wishes good». №220

987) From the words of Abu Hurairah (may Allah be pleased with him) it is reported that the Messenger of Allah ﷺ said: «Verily, from among the deeds that will benefit the believer after his death, this is the knowledge that he learned and spread; the righteous son he left behind; the Quran which he left as a legacy; the mosque he built; the house he built for travellers; the bed of the river which he made, and the alms which he gave out of his property while alive and well, and which will benefit him after his death». №242

988) It is narrated from the words of Jabir ibn 'Abdullah that the Prophet ﷺ said: «Do not acquire knowledge to be proud of them in front of scholars, argue with fools or give preference to one assembly over another, and if anyone does so, then Fire, Fire (will become his abode)». №254

989) It is reported that 'Ali said: «The Messenger of Allah ﷺ said:« A barrier (or cover, veil) between the jinn and the shameful places of a person will be when he enters a latrine and says: «Bismillah». №297

990) It is reported that 'Aisha, may Allah be pleased with her, said: «I never saw the Messenger of Allah ﷺ so that he, leaving for a long time, would not then wash with water». №354

991) It is reported that Shaqiq ibn Salama said: «I saw Uthman and 'Ali who performed ablution, washing each part of the body three times, and they said that this was the ablution of the Messenger of Allah ﷺ». №413

992) It is reported from the words of Suleiman ibn Bureida, who transmitted from his father that one day a man came to the Prophet ﷺ and asked him about the times of prayer. And the Prophet ﷺ said to him: «Pray with

us these two days.» When the sun passed its zenith, he ordered Bilal to say the adhan and then ordered the noon prayer to be performed. Then he ordered to perform the afternoon prayer when the sun was high above, and at the same time, it was white and shining. Then he ordered the sunset prayer to be performed when the sun had set, and then he ordered the evening prayer to be performed when twilight had (only) disappeared. Then, when the dawn began (to appear), he ordered the morning prayer to be performed. On the second day, he ordered to make a call for the midday prayer and delayed it so that the heat (a little) subsided, and (only) after that he performed the midday prayer. Then he performed the afternoon prayer when the sun was high, however (at the same time) he delayed it (performing) longer than on the previous day. Then he performed the sunset prayer before twilight disappeared, and performed the evening prayer (already) after the third part of the night had passed. Then he performed the morning prayer when (already) it was beginning to get light (i.e., when the dawn had already turned yellow), after which he said: «Where is the (man) who asked about prayer times?» And the man replied: «I am (here), O Messenger of Allah.» And then he said: «The time of your prayers between those (intervals) that you saw». №667

993) It is reported that Ibn 'Abbas (may Allah be pleased with them both) said: «There was a woman who prayed for the Prophet ﷺ, (and she was) the most beautiful of people. Some people went forward and stood in the front row so as not to see her, while others stepped back so that they stood in the last row, and when they bowed from the waist, they looked (at her) from under the armpits, (pulling their hands away from the sides). And then Allah Almighty sent down because of her (the verse in which it is said): «Verily, we recognized those who move forward from you and move back». №1046

994) It is reported that 'Abdullah ibn Abi Awfa said: «When

Mu'az arrived from Sham, he bowed to the ground in front of the Prophet ﷺ who said: «What is this, O Mu'az ?!» He said: «I arrived in Sham and saw how (Christians) bow to the ground before their bishops and patriarchs, and wished in my soul that we (should) do this before you.» The Messenger of Allah ﷺ said: «Do not do this! Indeed, if (I had to) command someone (of the people) to bow before another in prostration besides Allah, then I would, of course, command the woman to bow before her husband! I swear by the One in whose hand is the soul of Muhammad, no woman will fulfil her duties towards Allah until she fulfils her duties towards her husband. And if he asks her (for intimacy), even if she is on the saddle (of her camel), she should not refuse». №1853

995) 'Abdurrahman ibn Salim ibn 'Utba ibn 'Uwaym ibn Sa'eed al-Ansari reported from his father, who transmitted from his grandfather, who said: «The Messenger of Allah ﷺ said:» You should marry virgins, for verily their lips are sweeter (than others), their wombs are purer and they are more (other) content with little». №1861

996) Abu Hurayrah reported that the Messenger of Allah ﷺ said: «A woman does not marry a woman and a woman does not marry herself. Verily, she is an adulteress who marries herself». №1882

997) Narrated from Anas bin Malik: that the Prophet ﷺ passed by some part of Al-Medina and saw some girls playing duff (drums) and sang a song, saying: «We are girls from Banu Najjar, what a great neighbour Muhammad.» The Prophet said: «Allah knows that you are also dear to me!». №1899

998) It was narrated that Ibn Abbas said: «Aisha arranged a wedding for her relative among the Ansar. The Messenger of Allah ﷺ came and said: «Have you already brought the girl (to her husband's house)?» They said yes. He said, «Did you send someone to sing songs with her?» She said no.» The Messenger

of Allah ﷺ said: «The Ansar are people with romantic feelings. Why don't you send someone with her to sing along: «We have come to you, we have come to you, may Allah bless you and us?» №1900

999) It is reported from Jabir ibn 'Abdullah that the Messenger of Allah ﷺ said: «The best remembrance (of Allah) is the words «La ilaha illa-Allah / there is no deity worthy of worship except Allah /», and the best prayer is the words «al-hamdu li -Llah / all praise be to Allah /». №3800

1000) It is reported that 'Amr ibn Aws narrated that his father Aws said: «Once we were sitting near the Prophet ﷺ who told and reminded us when suddenly a certain person came to him and secretly reported (about one of the hypocrites). The Prophet ﷺ said: «Go and take his life!» When (this) man turned and began to leave, the Messenger of Allah ﷺ called him and said: «(Ask this hypocrite):« Do you testify that there is no deity worthy of worship except Allah? (This man) replied: «Yes, (he bears witness to it).» (The Prophet ﷺ) said: «Then let him go! I was ordered to fight people until they say that there is no deity worthy of worship except Allah, and when they do, their lives and property will become forbidden to me.». №3929

1001) It is reported that Anas ibn Malik said: «Once someone asked:« O Messenger of Allah! When will we stop commanding what is right and forbidding what is wrong?» (The Prophet ﷺ) replied: «When that which appeared among the communities that lived before you appears among you.» Then we asked: «O Messenger of Allah! And what appeared among the communities that lived before us? He replied: «When power (passes) to the younger of you, abominations (spread) among the older of you, and knowledge (passes) to the lowest of you!». Zayd said: «The words of the Prophet ﷺ» ... and knowledge (passes) to the lowest of you» means: when knowledge passes to the wicked».№4015

Dear reader!

I'm glad that you met my book.
I wish you could share your feedback on amazon.
Other people feel much more comfortable seeing that the book is readable. It gives them confidence that they will receive the support they need.
Please help us to get the hadiths to as many people as possible.

Made in the USA
Las Vegas, NV
06 November 2023

80348681R00173